HOW TO DESIGN, BUILD & EQUIP
Your Automotive Workshop ON A BUDGET

Jeffrey Zurschmeide

CarTech®

CarTech®, Inc.
39966 Grand Avenue
North Branch, MN 55056
Phone: 651-277-1200 or 800-551-4754
Fax: 651-277-1203
www.cartechbooks.com

© 2011 by Jeffrey Zurschmeide

All rights reserved. No part of this publication may be reproduced or utilized in any form or by any means, electronic or mechanical, including photocopying, recording, or by any information storage and retrieval system, without prior permission from the Author. All text, photographs, and artwork are the property of the Author unless otherwise noted or credited.

The information in this work is true and complete to the best of our knowledge. However, all information is presented without any guarantee on the part of the Author or Publisher, who also disclaim any liability incurred in connection with the use of the information.

All trademarks, trade names, model names and numbers, and other product designations referred to herein are the property of their respective owners and are used solely for identification purposes. This work is a publication of CarTech, Inc., and has not been licensed, approved, sponsored, or endorsed by any other person or entity.

Edit by Josh Brown
Layout by Monica Seiberlich

ISBN 978-1-61325-247-5
Item No. SA207P

Library of Congress Cataloging-in-Publication Data

Zurschmeide, Jeff.
　How to design, build & equip your automotive workshop on a budget / by Jeffrey Zurschmeide.
　　p. cm.
　ISBN 978-1-934709-51-1
　1. Automobile repair shops. 2. Workshops--Equipment and supplies. I. Title. II. Title: How to design, build and equip your automotive workshop on a budget.

TL153.Z87 2011
629.28'72--dc22

2011010614

Printed in USA

On the Cover

Main Image: *Even if you just use pencil on graph paper, make a basic scale drawing of your shop and think through where everything goes. Make sure you leave room to open car doors.*

Left Inset: *The classic two-post lift is the toy that every hobbyist would like to have in a workshop. However, there are substantial differences in design and quality among two-post lifts.*

Middle Inset: *Insulation is critical for a comfortable shop. It keeps the shop cooler in summer, warmer in winter, quieter at all times, and generally dryer and less prone to condensation.*

Right Inset: *The first step in an inspected electrical installation is the rough-in—this is where you run wires and place boxes, but leave them open so the inspector can see that you used the right supplies.*

Title Page: *An organized and tidy garage is a much more relaxing and pleasant place to work. The key is to make a system that works for you and that you will be motivated to maintain. It doesn't have to be expensive to be functional.*

Back Cover Photos

Top Left: *These benches and tables look far more expensive than they are. They're based on ordinary Gorilla Racks, cut in half. A benchtop of plywood and 1x1 lumber fits over the top of the Gorilla Racks, and then the owner had a sheet-metal company make stainless skins for the assembly.*

Top Right: *This heavy-duty cherry picker has side bracing and long legs for support. This kind of shop crane can pick up just about anything you want.*

Middle Left: *Be sure to leave as much elbow room as possible in your shop design. No one ever complained about having too much available space in the shop.*

Middle Right: *This shop is not as expensive as it looks; everything in this workshop has been done with forethought and without waste.*

Bottom Left: *Here's a different take on metal shelves. These are 12-inch-deep metal shelf frames without the shelves on them, and they work great for tires. Because you can adjust the height of the supports, you can fit any size tires in these.*

Bottom Right: *This finished workshop includes rain gutters, stubs for electrical power and plumbing, and a nice garage door. It's ready for the projects described throughout this book.*

CONTENTS

Acknowledgments 4
Introduction 5

Chapter 1: Planning your Workspace 7
Playing it Safe 7
Necessary Tools to Get Started 9
Take Stock of Your Space 11
Develop a Floor Plan 12
Plan for Features 14
Develop a Scheduled Budget 21
Build a Whole New Workshop 22

Chapter 2: Walls and Floors 24
Wall Covering 24
Floor Covering 27
Windows and Skylights 30

Chapter 3: Electricity and Lights 31
Installing Electricity 31
Electrical Permits and Inspections 32
How Much Power Do You Need? 32
Installing a New Meter and Main Breaker Panel 33
Installing a Subpanel 33
Selecting Wire, Breakers and Outlets 35
Project: Install a 120 Using Hard Metal Conduit ... 38
Project: Install a 120 Using Romex
  Non-Metallic Cable 41
Project: Install a 240 Using Flexible
  Metal-Clad Cable 43
Lighting Your Workshop 45
Project: Install Fluorescent Lights 48
Garage Door Opener 49

Chapter 4: Water and Heat 50
Installing Plumbing 50
Project: Install a Fresh Water Supply 53
Project: Install a Wash Basin 56
Project: Install a Water Heater 57
Project: Install a Dishwasher 58
Heating Your Workshop 60
Providing Ventilation 62

Chapter 5: Compressed Air and Welding 64
Installing Compressed Air 64
Project: Install, Wire and Plumb a Compressor 70

Building a Paint Booth 73
Project: Create a Full-Size Paint Booth 74
Project: Create a Benchtop Spray-Painting Box 76
Setting Up Your Shop for Welding 77
Welding Safety 79
Welding Supplies 81
Preparing to Weld 82
Welding Accessories 83
Project: Build a Welding Table 85

Chapter 6: Create and Organize Storage Space ... 87
Installing Cabinets and Shelves 88
Project: Build Heavy-Duty Wood Shelves 93
Project: Build Lightweight Wood Shelves 97
Storing Wheels and Tires 98
Project: Build a Low-Cost Tire Rack 99
Workbenches 100
Project: Build a Low-Cost Heavy-Duty Workbench ... 101
Using Attic and Rafter Space 104

Chapter 7: Automotive Tools 106
A Word about Renting 107
Safety Gear 107
Toolboxes 109
Hand Tools 111
Free-Standing and Bench-Mounted Tools 114
Automotive Bodyworking Tools 119
Engine Tools 121
Automotive Electrical Tools 122
Miscellaneous Automotive Tools 124

Chapter 8: Hoists, Cranes and Lifts 126
Ceiling-Mounted Hoists 126
Portable Cranes 127
Portable Lifts 128
Fixed Lifts 131

Chapter 9: Human Amenities 136
Do You Need a Bathroom? 136
Keeping Mice Away 136
Shop Furniture 137
Fun Stuff 139
Project: Outfit Your Workshop 143

Resources 144

ACKNOWLEDGMENTS

I believe a variety of opinions and experiences make a better book. In the course of my work on this book, I've talked with several professionals in critical fields for workshop builders and dozens of amateur mechanics who have built their own workspaces and produced excellent restorations, race cars, and street cars. This book is the result of extensive consultation with a great many people. The project would have been impossible without them.

Specifically, I need to thank John Smith as the builder of the example workshop for his excellent management and building expertise. Dave Rice donated his time and expertise to help me swing hammers and design the shelves and workbench. Paul Eklund at Primitive Racing Enterprises allowed me to witness the process of moving his rally car fabrication and installation business into a bare shop space. I spent time with George Mehallick of Mini Madness, Mark Scholz at PortlandHomesforCars.com, Teresa Nicola at Collected Spaces, Eddie Nakato at AR Auto Service, Jim Havlinek at Shop Equipment Company, and Chris Watkins at Garage Themes. Eric Emerson at Whirly Jig gave me the inside information on rotisseries, Dorian Libal was my electrical guru, and Ed Slavin of Northern Illumination enlightened me about lighting. Andy Banta, Chris Kantarjiev, Miq Millman, Russ Nyberg, Jeremy Wilson, Larry LeFebvre, Gordon Ledbetter, Jeff Boerio, Scott Goodrich, Greg Swanson, Richard Ullian, Philip Weaver, and many others generously let me invade their workspaces and shamelessly steal their ideas.

INTRODUCTION

This book is designed to help the practical hobbyist mechanic make the most of any available space, while staying within almost any budget. Many of the ideas presented for workbenches and storage can be implemented at low cost, or even for free if you're extra resourceful.

What is surprising is how nice your shop can look and how well your shop can function after a very small investment. In the balance of looking good and functioning smoothly, it's more important that your shop works for you. It's great if your shop looks like a million bucks, but first and foremost your workshop should be a convenient place to pursue your hobby, and a place where you enjoy working. In the end, it doesn't matter if your workbench doesn't match your toolbox—you'll be the envy of every amateur mechanic if your shop is comfortable, well-organized, and outfitted to produce good results.

This book is designed to give you necessary information as you consider various tools, designs, installations, and products available for your automotive workspace. It includes some practical tips for common situations that hobbyist mechanics encounter in a standard garage. I've generally avoided endorsing any particular brand of equipment or furniture, but I say what works and what doesn't work. Most items mentioned are representative products that show what's widely available on the market. All products mentioned by name in this book are high-quality products that I would (and probably do) use in my own workshop.

In researching this book, I looked at a variety of successful hobbyist workshops, built for a wide range of purposes, and I also checked out some professional shops. Professionals cannot afford to waste any time getting basic work done, so their shops tend to be extremely well-organized, with important tools and features close at hand.

This book includes step-by-step procedures to help you create the basic electrical wiring sufficient to connect a bank of lights, a compressor, and a welder circuit. There is also a procedure for routing power from your household electrical service panel to

The key to a successful automotive workshop is organization. If you have things set up in a compact and efficient manner, you have more room to work.

INTRODUCTION

a subpanel. If you plan to install a new service meter with its own panel, I recommend you read more detailed books about wiring and electrical service, or call a professional.

Plumbing basic shop fixtures is also covered with step-by-step instructions. But since making a mistake with your plumbing is less likely to kill you than a mistake on your electrical wiring, this is an area that more people are likely to undertake successfully on their own.

Here's a tip that has helped many novices: Find a club or a group of compatible people in your area who can help you keep your shop busy and fun. The internet and books like this one are nice tools for learning and discussion, but folks on the other side of the country can't help you put up more lights or show up in a truck to help you go pick up building supplies. A local club is also a good way to get access to specialty tools. If one member has an engine hoist, then maybe everyone has the use of that engine hoist, and you can spend your budget on a tool that no one else has yet. Treat your club right, and you'll always have help when you need it.

If you're lucky enough to have a larger workshop, there's no limit to what you can achieve. With a little planning you can have a professional-quality workshop.

Electrical infrastructure, plumbing, heat, compressed air, and ventilation can all be yours without breaking your wallet, if you're willing to invest a little bit of work and research.

If you're starting with a brand-new garage, spend some time thinking through exactly what you want to achieve and what you need to have on hand to achieve it.

CHAPTER 1

PLANNING YOUR WORKSPACE

Just about everyone involved in the car hobby has a project car, or two, or more. Lots of hobbies involve in-depth projects but, unlike crocheting and stamp collecting, you really can't dive into a car project while sitting at your kitchen table. Of course there's plenty of automotive work you *can* do at the kitchen table, including carburetor rebuilds (talk to your spouse before you do that), but the really big wrench work requires its own dedicated space.

Most of us have a limited amount of car space and an even more limited budget, so we have to make good use of the space and money we have. Magazines, books, and TV shows that feature garage profiles tend to gravitate towards high-end workshops that most of us can only dream of owning. After all, who wouldn't like to park the Ferrari on hand-quarried Italian marble and pick brand-new tools out of a $2,000 state-of-the-art tool cabinet? Sadly, most of us have to work with a much thinner wallet.

Playing it Safe

Your first plan and your first budget should be for your safety in your shop. That means more than just buying a fire extinguisher and sticking it under the workbench. You need to think through a number of less pleasant scenarios, especially if you expect to spend a lot of time alone in your shop.

People die in their workshops every year—usually because a car falls on them, they electrocute themselves, or have a tool accident. Many more people suffer preventable injuries in their garages and workshops. Don't let that happen to you.

Fire safety kits are essential. That means a 5- or 10-pound A-B-C Fire extinguisher (or two of them) and a smoke detector. Many fires happen after you leave your shop, and

Here's what most of us have to work with—a basic two-car garage. This can be anywhere from 18 to 24 square feet. But that's enough space to restore an old car and perform your own maintenance and repairs.

HOW TO DESIGN, BUILD & EQUIP YOUR AUTOMOTIVE WORKSHOP ON A BUDGET

CHAPTER 1

A smoke detector is cheap insurance when you're working in your shop, especially if you've been welding or painting.

The best smoke detector is a hard-wired unit; there are no batteries to replace and you can connect it to a burglar alarm system if you have one.

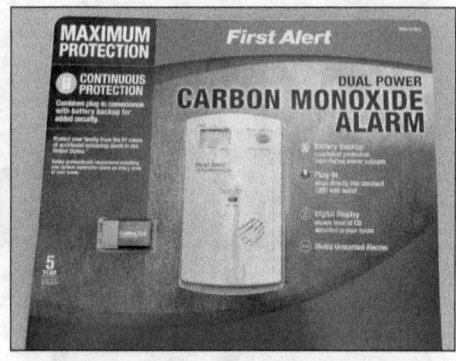

A carbon monoxide detector is perhaps more important than a smoke detector. If you run your car inside the garage at all, you're at risk for monoxide poisoning. And don't fool yourself, everyone runs cars in the garage when they need to.

a smoke detector can help you guard against a big loss. A basic battery-operated smoke detector is sufficient, but a hard-wired detector is even better because you don't have to tend the batteries.

When you're buying extinguishers and smoke detectors, also pick up a carbon monoxide (CO) detector at the same time. CO is an odorless gas that can kill you in a confined space. It's not just car exhaust that creates it in your shop—if you have any kind of flame-based heater, that's a source of CO. A monoxide detector is cheap insurance.

To go along with all the fire suppression and the smoke and carbon monoxide detectors, you should plan for adequate ventilation for your workshop. Spilled or dripped gasoline, oil smoke, paint fumes, cleansing agents, and many other sources emit toxic fumes. You should get the fumes out of your shop as quickly as possible. A good ventilation system also helps keep your shop smelling good (especially if it's attached to your home) and safe to work in. In the summer, venting hot air helps to keep your shop comfortable, especially if you can pull air in from a crawl space or other cool air source.

If you want to install top-grade fire protection, you need an automatic fire suppression system. These are more expensive, starting at about $500, but they offer the best protection, especially if you're performing fire-hazardous work such as painting in your shop.

It's good to have a first-aid kit in your shop, in addition to a couple dry-chemical fire extinguishers. Make sure you get fire extinguishers designed for the types of fires you're likely to have in an automotive workshop—that is, electrical and oil/gasoline fires. If you have a gasoline fire,

A good ventilation fan is essential if you plan to paint, weld, or run engines a lot in your workshop. It doesn't have to be this elaborate for most of us; a big, industrial fan gets the job done.

Professional shops often have automatic fire-suppression systems, especially paint and body shops that use flammable chemicals daily.

 **Air Circulation**

Keep your air circulating by mounting a fan as high as possible in your shop, pointed toward the drive-through doors. In the winter, you can shut the doors and run the fan to circulate the warm air from your heater. Especially if you have a high ceiling, keeping the warm air moving makes your shop more comfortable faster, conserves energy, and thereby saves you money. ■

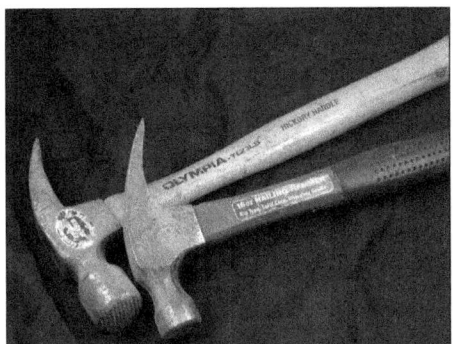
The most basic carpenter's tool is a good hammer. Treated properly, a framing hammer and a nailing hammer last a lifetime.

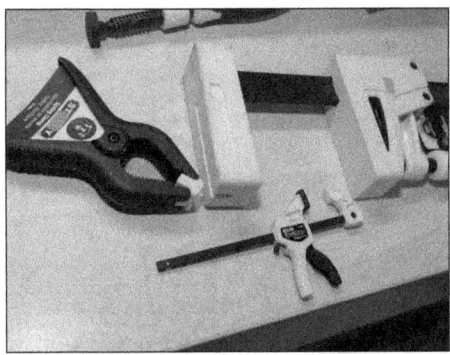
You want carpenter's clamps for building out your workshop, and then you can keep them around for use in welding, gluing, painting, and uncountable other uses.

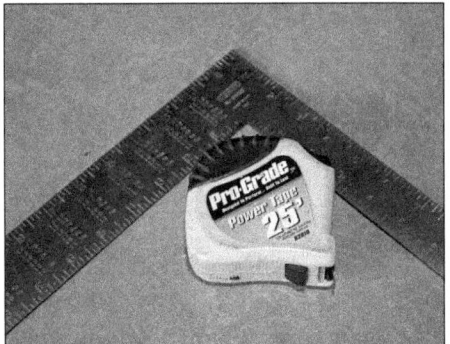
The carpenter's square has been around since the Egyptians were building the pyramids. It works admirably as a straightedge and for making sure your corners are square.

don't ever pour a bucket of water on it, or you'll just create a fireball and spread the fire.

Necessary Tools to Get Started

The skills involved in building out an automotive workspace have more to do with carpentry, wiring, and plumbing than with turning a wrench on a car. Most of us have the necessary experience, however, and need only be careful while we work to improve our skills. The old adage of "measure twice and cut once" works especially well for amateurs.

There are two sets of tools you need in your garage or workshop. The first set is the woodworking tools to build your basic workshop structures. The second set is the tools you use frequently in the course of automotive projects. It's a good idea to get started with your carpentry tools right away because they are fewer and, on the whole, less expensive. You can build your collection of automotive tools over time. (Specialty tools used in automotive projects are covered in Chapter 7.)

For most of the projects described in this book, you need just a basic set of household carpentry tools to complete the work. Electrical and plumbing (either water or air) projects take some specialized tools, and the ones you need are described at the beginning of each project. But here is the basic set of tools you need to get started with your auto shop construction:

Hammer

You need a good claw hammer. A mid-size (16-ounce) smooth-faced nailing hammer does the trick. If you have a nice knobby-faced, 24-ounce framing hammer, that's even better for building workbenches and other structures out of framing lumber (2x4, 2x6, and 4x4).

Look for a good hammer with a handle made of fiberglass or quality wood. Estwing hammers with metal necks are also very good, especially if you tend to miss your swing and bash the neck of the hammer against your work. In general, heavier hammers are harder to control if you don't use them all the time, so don't get too ambitious if you're not an expert hammer swinger. You can drive the same nails with a lighter hammer—it just takes a little longer.

Clamp

Carpenter's clamps are indispensable for holding things together while you get them nailed, bolted, or screwed together. Later, they come in handy for clamping parts to your bench while you're working; so get several of these in various sizes.

Tape Measure and Carpenter's Square

The old carpenter's motto of "measure twice and cut once" is true. You absolutely need a good tape measure and a carpenter's square to do good work. Your tape measure should extend at least 25 feet.

A carpenter's square is a precision tool and has ruler marks inscribed on all its edges. You can use it to measure an inside or outside angle and, of course, to be sure of your 90-degree angles. New carpenter's squares can be surprisingly expensive, but the good news is that they are widely available at garage and estate sales for just a couple dollars each.

Angle Finder/Protractor

A carpenter's angle finder is a basic tool with an adjustable (and clampable) pivot. Simply place it against any arbitrary angle and

CHAPTER 1

An angle finder (left) helps you build accurately when things aren't exactly square. A laser level (right) is great for projecting straight lines when building, or when leveling a car's suspension.

A carpenter's bubble level is a great tool, but note that there's a free app for your iPod Touch or iPhone that does the same thing.

You can build every wooden project in this book with a basic circular saw. Check out garage sales and you're sure to find one at low cost.

clamp it down. Then you can take the finder and use it as an angle template to repeat the exact angle or its complementary angle. A protractor may be fixed or adjustable, but is graduated with degrees and allows you to measure any angle.

These angle finders are handy when you need to make a clean 45-degree cut to create a leg support for your workbenches, tables, or a tire rack. And if you need to make a support at an arbitrary angle because there's not room to fit a 45-degree support, an angle finder is indispensable if you want good results.

Carpenter's Level

A good level is essential for shelves, workbenches, and many other projects. Ideally, you have a few levels around in various sizes and styles. A 4-foot-long carpenter's level is also great for drawing straight lines.

Circular Saw

If you plan to build your own shelves, workbenches, working tables, and tire rack, you need a good circular saw. And because building these items yourself is a source of custom results, good quality, personal satisfaction, and great cash savings, you should be planning to build them yourself. Any well-known name brand of circular saw that uses a standard 7¼-inch blade works just fine.

If you decide to buy your saw at a garage sale, make sure that all the safety guards are in place and that the power cord isn't cut or frayed. It's a good idea to test it before you buy, if the seller allows you to.

Read the owner's manual for your saw to get specific instructions. One of the nice things about these saws is that you can adjust the blade depth for the lumber or plywood you're working with. You want the blade just barely deeper than the wood. To cut a 4x4 post, you probably need to make two cuts.

Cordless Driver Drill

Another tool that saves you countless hours is a good cordless driver drill. These are used to drill pilot holes with standard bits and bolt holes with wood-boring bits. With a driver drill, you can also use it to shoot construction screws into your work. You want a good drill of at least 12 volts, with a clutch in it so you can set a maximum torque for delicate work. Also, a good driver drill comes in handy again and again when you're working on cars.

Sawhorses

While not strictly necessary, you may want to buy a set of sawhorses, or build them very early in your project schedule. You can use the tailgate of a pickup truck or a folding table as a work surface, but the first time you saw through your folding table, you'll wish you were using sawhorses. Later on, these are useful for supporting larger parts while you work or paint. If you plan to do your own hammer and dolly bodywork, sawhorses are especially essential.

You may also want to consider a small multi-utility table like a Black & Decker Workmate. These little folding stands incorporate clamps and an adjustable opening. They fold up to a convenient storage size and have many uses in an auto shop.

A cordless driver drill allows you to construct your projects with screws instead of nails. Screws are easier to put in and easier to take out if you need to undo your work later.

10 HOW TO DESIGN, BUILD & EQUIP YOUR AUTOMOTIVE WORKSHOP ON A BUDGET

PLANNING YOUR WORKSPACE

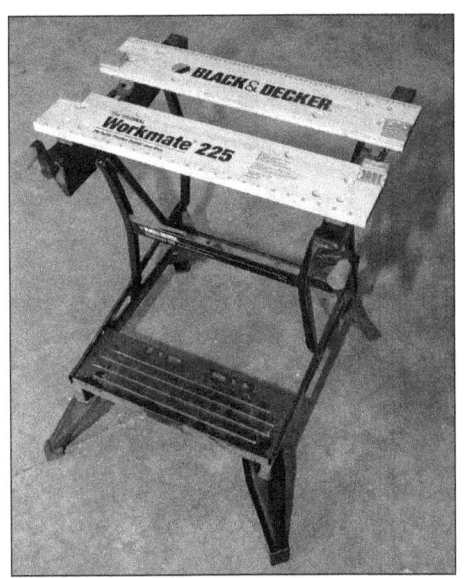

A Black & Decker Workmate is a great tool for an auto shop because it can grab and hold parts, and it folds up when not in use.

Take Stock of Your Space

Every automotive workspace is unique. There are standards, of course, such as the one- and two-car garage. But the placement of doors, lights, and household appliances still makes each garage a little different. And of course, every car collection and every mechanic is unique, so even two identical garages on the same street end up different because of the varying needs and preferences of the owners.

What Do You Want to Achieve?

The best way to start your plan is by sitting down and going over what you want to do in your garage and what you want your garage to do for you. Are you looking for a space in which to polish your already-perfect collector car, or do you plan to start with a junker and completely restore it? Will you need to perform messy work, or even paint a car in your workshop?

It's rare that someone can have a completely dedicated automotive workshop space. Usually the space must be shared with laundry, household storage, lawnmowers, and other necessary possessions. This means you must balance the purpose of your space between your automotive needs and whatever else needs to stay dry.

If possible, you want to keep your automotive area as separate as possible from the other household

The Importance of Elbow Room

There are very few people in this world who have all the space they need in their workshop. It doesn't matter how big your shop may be, if you're like most people, you fill it up sooner than you expect.

But it's important to keep your shop from becoming a gigantic storage area, packed to the rafters with stuff you "might need someday." Of course, Murphy's Law says that from time to time you find a need for some car part or old box about a month after you get rid of it. But generally, the benefits of maintaining a spacious and orderly shop far outweigh the benefits of keeping an immense stock of used spark plugs and old carpet.

If your shop is overcrowded, junk ends up stacked on your cars, or stacked to the ceiling in an unstable pile. It's harder to find what you're looking for, and you spend too much time hunting through boxes rather than getting tasks done. In the worst case, you can end up with items falling and denting your car (or your head) as you search for parts.

If you have to, consider buying a garden shed or renting a storage unit to keep your workspace suitable for work. If you're paying rent to store all that junk, it's more likely that you'll develop a more critical philosophy about what you keep and what you sell or throw away.

The guideline is easy: Design your shop to be spacious and orderly, and then work to keep it that way.

Be sure to leave as much elbow room as possible in your shop design. No one ever complained about having too much available space in the shop.

CHAPTER 1

Keeping your shop neat and tidy is critical. This workbench was built by a professional cabinet maker, so you know it's nice.

cues, and facilities for storing and serving cold beverages fall into this category. A good shop makes your house a magnet for all of your car enthusiast friends, and everyone likes to be proud of a great workshop, so be sure to ask yourself if you plan to entertain or just work in your space.

Develop a Floor Plan

You need to read and learn before you pound a nail or whip out your checkbook. It pays to do your homework. You want to learn what's available for your workshop today and what fits your space. To do that, you start with a measuring tape.

Do you really know how big your garage or workshop is? Chances are good that you don't. Even if you just

utilities. Nothing breeds family discontent faster than having car parts stacked on the washer and dryer.

Luckily, good planning and organization is tremendously helpful in keeping things from attempting to occupy the same space at the same time.

Try to find a balance between all the things you might want to do in your shop and what you know you need to do in the next six months to a year. Sometimes the truth of the matter is that you really just need a clean, dry space to store your car and parts. Others need bench space for fabrication tools and table space to assemble an entire car from component parts.

Be sure to learn from what others have done before you. If you're planning to restore a vintage pickup truck, the other members of the vintage pickup truck club in your area (and online) should have some good ideas about the kind of space and accommodations for equipment that you are likely to need.

Some workshops have earned the name "Man Cave" because they function not only as a place to get work done, but also as a den or clubhouse. Workshops that feature sofas and comfortable chairs, TVs, barbe-

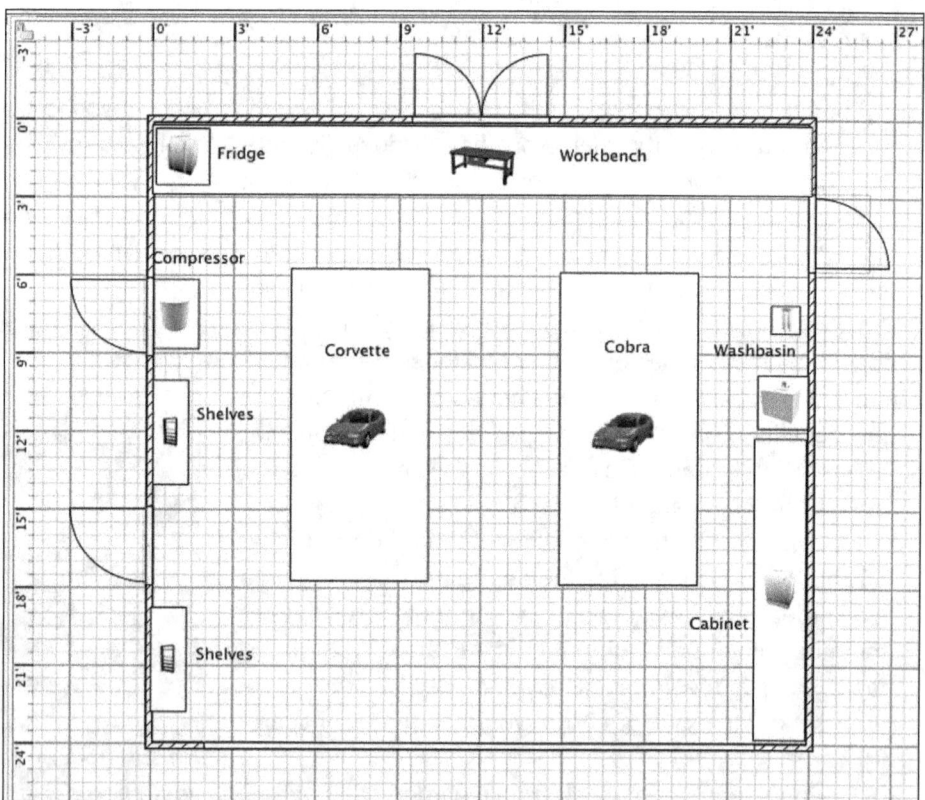

Even if you just use pencil on graph paper, make a basic scale drawing of your shop and think through where everything goes. Make sure you leave room to open car doors.

HOW TO DESIGN, BUILD & EQUIP YOUR AUTOMOTIVE WORKSHOP ON A BUDGET

PLANNING YOUR WORKSPACE

had a 20- by 40-foot shop built for you, it could really be more like 18 by 38, or 20 by 42 when it's finished. That may or may not be critically important, but it's more important after you've used some of that space for shelves and workbenches and you still need to park two cars in it.

A standard two-car garage built in America today is generally considered to be 24 feet by 24 feet. But if you look at older homes, that used to be an oversized garage. The current minimum width is about 18 feet and anywhere from 18 to 24 feet deep. If your two-car garage is 24 feet square, that's 576 square feet, and people have built cars for the Indianapolis 500 in smaller spaces than that (though not so much lately). Many single-car garages are 12 feet wide by 18 to 24 feet deep.

Don't forget to measure the distance from the floor to the ceiling. If you hope to install a lift or use a shop crane, overhead space is critical. The ceiling and roof also affects lighting decisions and insulation and heating plans. If you have a lot of space overhead, you may want to create some long-term storage up there too.

Before you design your workbench or shelving system, you need to make sure you can really fit all the big items you want into your workspace. For example, if you're planning to put a lift in a two-car garage, remember that any lift space must be at least 10 feet wide. You need to accommodate your car with some wiggle room on either side of the lift.

If you have two cars, make sure they'll fit into the space after you install the lift and any shelves or benches along the side walls. Similarly, plan early for your worktables and for installation of major appliances like a media blasting cabinet and a compressor. If you don't get the big items in first, you'll never get them in at all.

Eventually you have to figure out how to fit all your stuff into the space you have, and you need to have an accurate idea of where you plan to put everything. The best way to do this is to simply draw it out. If you don't have basic graph paper, you can print sheets of several styles of blank graph paper from the internet (see Resources).

I like to make layout drawings of several possible floor plans. I use plain 1/4-inch graph paper and I make each square on the paper equal to a square foot of shop space. I mark in doors and windows, and I make several copies of the basic shape and use different sheets to plan electrical, plumbing, air, and physical layout of benches, equipment, and storage.

With accurate measurements of cars and other large objects, you can create several possible plans and quickly see how things will fit. As a general rule, you need 2 or 3 feet to walk comfortably between cars or between cars and benches. Cars that are being stored long-term still need at least 12 inches between them just to slide by, and good luck getting the doors open!

Floor-Plan Software

If you like to get a little more high-tech than graph paper and a carpenter's pencil, consider downloading some floor-plan software. One good free software package is called SweetHome 3D, and it is available on the Windows, Macintosh, and Linux operating systems in 16 different languages.

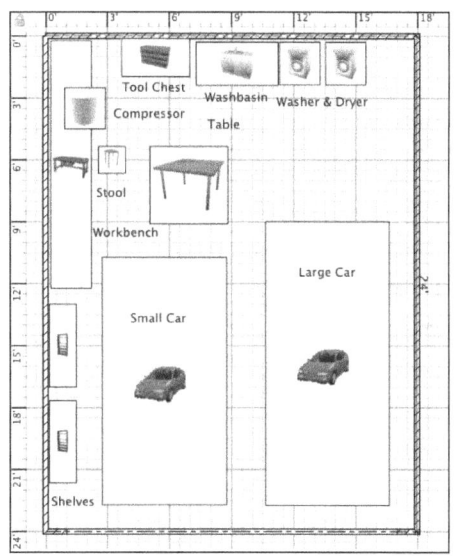

When you make scale drawings, make sure you have accurate measurements of the cars you plan to put in the space; some of the old iron is surprisingly big.

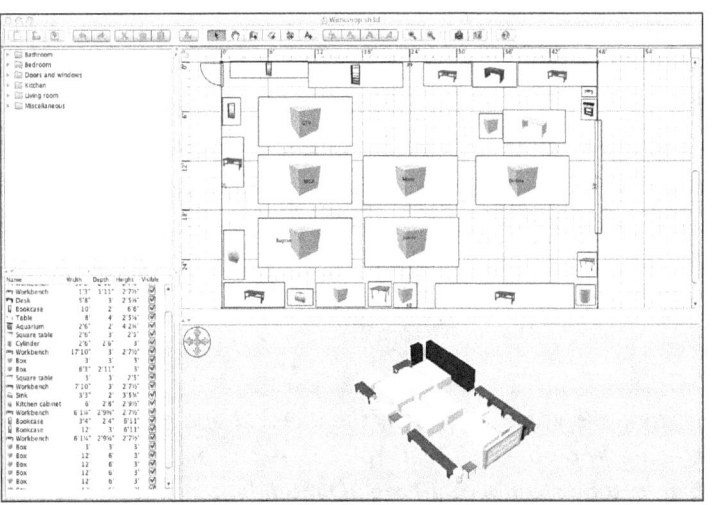

For a larger workshop, you can scale down the drawing and figure out how many cars you can effectively stuff into the space.

CHAPTER 1

Using this software, you can specify the exact dimensions of your available space, even if it's not a basic rectangle. Once the working space is outlined, you can add windows and doors, and then place pre-drawn objects in the space. As you place each object, you specify its dimensions and location in the floor plan. You can move any object as you choose while you work. You can set the basic grid of the picture to any scale you choose, and the grid lets you see exactly how much space is left between objects.

The SweetHome 3D software is optimized for household rooms rather than workshop or garage space, but you can download additional automotive graphic objects such as cars and tools from the SweetHome 3D site. The basic SweetHome 3D software image library already includes tables, shelves, and workbenches. The software also includes basic object shapes such as cylinders and cubes that you can label as needed.

With a little creativity, you can produce a functional layout and specify the exact size and location of each object in your workspace.

SweetHome 3D also generates a three-dimensional image of your design that you can rotate to visualize from all angles. You can also take a "virtual tour" to see what your layout looks like from any vantage point within the space. When you're happy with your work, the software can generate a high-resolution artist's rendering of your finished design.

The SweetHome 3D software is free to download and use, but the creator accepts donations from satisfied customers. Let your conscience be your guide.

Plan for Features

As you thought through your workshop project, you identified the

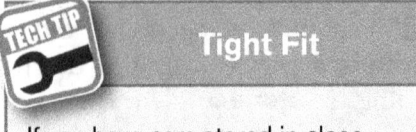
Tight Fit
If you have cars stored in close quarters, leave the windows rolled down so you can reach in and get to the steering wheel to push them out of their storage slots. ■

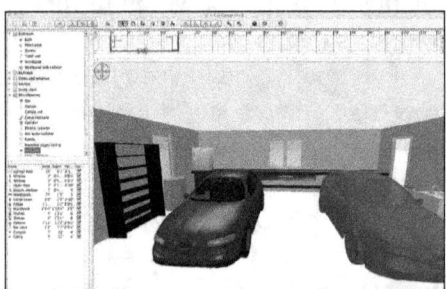

When you have designed your workshop in SweetHome, you can take a virtual walk-through to see what it will look like when it's done, then make changes based on any problems you perceive.

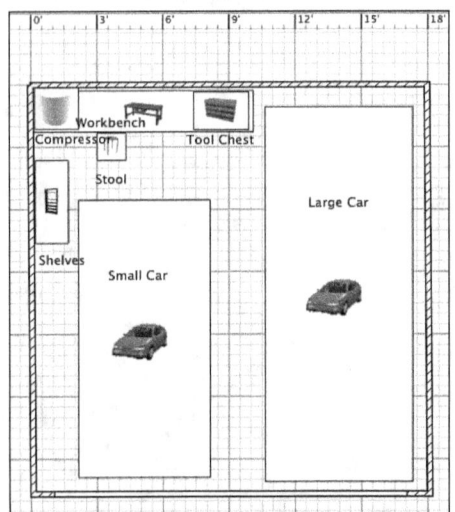

This layout plans for an 18-foot car on the right and a 14-foot car on the left. It still leaves room for shelves, toolbox, compressor, and a 10-foot workbench in a two-car garage.

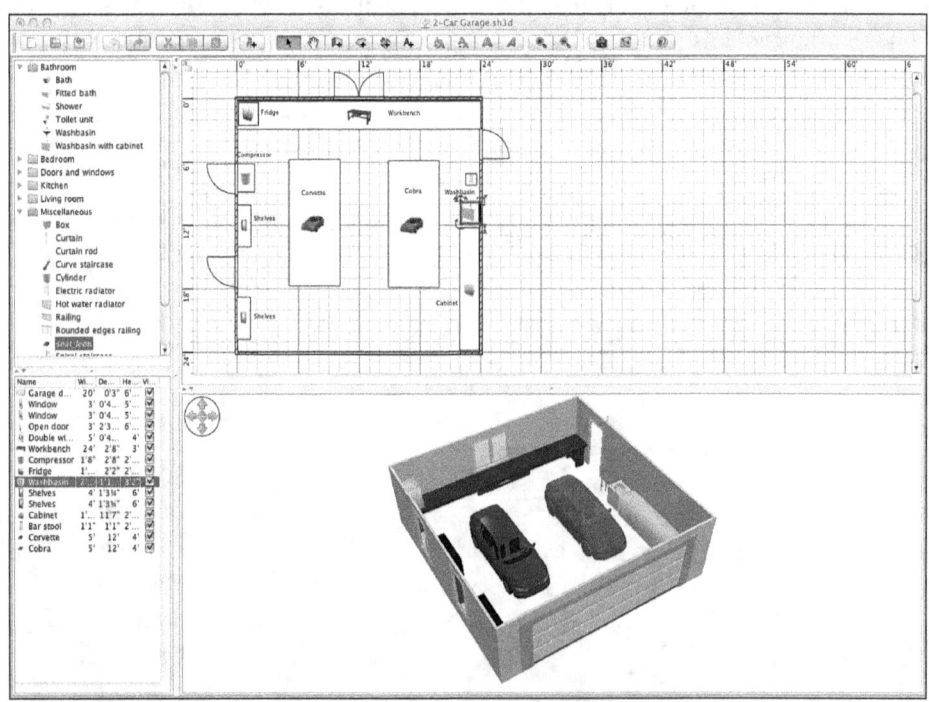

The SweetHome software allows you to specify the exact shape and size of a space and then drag and drop objects into it. You can resize the objects and label them. The software shows you a real-time 3D model too.

features you want in your shop space. Now you need to think through each of the systems that will provide services and amenities in your workshop.

The Structure

Most people start with a shop or garage that already has a concrete floor, but it's not too rare to find older shops with wood floors. And in some cases people are starting with a pole building or metal-frame structure with a dirt or gravel floor. Obviously, it's just about impossible to work on cars without a hard floor. Jacks and jackstands sink into dirt, and moisture is a constant threat. You can live with wood floors, but they have to be kept in good condition and they're still not the best answer.

If you have a choice, you want a brand-new concrete floor at least 5 inches thick and reinforced with metal bars. This allows you to install any kind of automotive lift and bear any size vehicle you can manage, up to a bulldozer. The other advantage of new concrete is that it's clean, and you can paint it with sealing epoxy paint after it has cured for 30 days.

Similarly, if you have a choice about building your shop or garage, a metal-framed building works well. Metal minimizes fire dangers and is relatively inexpensive to build. However, wood-framed buildings are also nice, and wood makes it easier when the time comes to attach insulation and finish the interior surfaces.

Whatever structure you're using, make sure the roof is watertight. If you are starting with an old barn or pole building, consider having the roof redone with a new vapor-and-moisture barrier. This is a job for professionals unless you're very experienced, but the results will be fantastic.

If you get the chance to build from scratch, get as many features built in at the start as you possibly can. Even if you don't plan to have plumbing or a lift, build your shop so that you can put them in later.

SweetHome has one of several software products on the market for designing and visualizing your workshop (and your whole house) space. Others provide tools for plumbing or electrical layout overlays, but the SweetHome software is available freely on the Internet.

This garage was well-planned from the start, with an alcove for TV, stereo, bathroom, sitting area, roll-up and walk-through doors, and a finished ceiling with recessed lighting. Of course, it's not a budget installation, but planning doesn't cost you a dime.

CHAPTER 1

If you have a choice of doors, get a roll-up drive-through door. These are secure and easy to operate and can be motorized. For walk-through doors, get a metal door for security and fire safety.

Finally, if you are building new construction or substantially remodeling an existing space, plan for windows and skylights. With modern window and skylight designs, letting in natural light does not mean letting out heat in winter.

Electricity

Electricity is the first system you want to plan out. Even if your garage is already wired with outlets, chances are you'll want more circuits. You probably need individual 240-volt circuits for a large compressor, welder, or lift. You need 120-volt circuits for any additional lighting, outlets, and other equipment you want to install. You may also want a separate circuit for the workbench outlets or for hanging-spool work lights and extension cords.

The best way to plan the electrical services is to get out your pad of graph paper and make another map of your workspace. You can ultimately overlay this map with your floor plan to make sure you have everything located properly.

First, locate the circuit panel on the map, or if the main circuit panel is not in the workspace, decide where to place a subpanel. If the workspace is not directly connected to your home, consider whether a separate power drop with its own meter is the best solution. This gives you a separate accounting of the power used in the shop, and any popped circuit breakers or other electrical issues won't affect your household service. You can usually get the power company to bill both meters on one statement.

Before you get too far into your plans, check with your local government and power provider about codes and inspection requirements. Your homeowner insurance may also have requirements for professional inspection before it'll cover your workshop for fires. You can usually do the work yourself, but an expert inspection is always a good idea.

When you've covered all the fundamentals, you can map out your circuits. I like to keep circuits short and intuitively placed. For example, if you want three walls supplied with outlets, it's nice to put each wall on a separate circuit, or two circuits for the right and left sides.

When you can overlay your electrical plan and find all your major equipment is covered, you'll know what you need to budget for conduit, junction boxes, wire, outlets, and breakers. Be sure to leave some electrical room to grow!

Plumbing

Plumbing is the next system you want to plan, because you want to get your plumbing installed before you move all your stuff into the shop. Generally a plumbing system is much simpler than an electrical plan. The concept of having one "wet wall" is a good one, and you should try to keep all your water-based equipment in one area if at all possible.

If your household hot-water heater is close by, you won't need a separate heater for the shop. However, it's not a bad idea to get a small apartment-size water heater or a new

Plan for as large a breaker panel as you could possibly ever need, and you'll still fill it up with circuits eventually.

> **TECH TIP — Breaker Homework**
>
> Don't forget to take a look at the circuit panel and count the available number of breaker slots. You need one breaker slot for every 120-volt circuit and two slots for each 240-volt circuit. You should also find out whether your house has 50-amp, 100-amp, or some other level of service if you plan to run a lot of current in the shop. If your house has an electric furnace, electric kitchen appliances, and electric clothes dryer, and you're trying to run a 5-hp compressor, a lift, and a bunch of lights, you could overload the main breaker. ■

> **TECH TIP — Plan Ahead**
>
> If your plan calls for installing an electric lift but you know that the actual installation is several years away, it doesn't hurt to install the conduit and wires and simply coil the loose ends at either end of the circuit. Just don't connect the wires to the circuit panel until you're ready to use them. ■

tankless water heater for dedicated shop use. If you choose this route, be sure that a circuit on your electrical plan is dedicated to the water heater.

As with your electrical plan, make a copy of your shop space drawing and pencil in your water plans. The general rule of leaving room to grow also applies to your water supply. Put in a couple of tee fittings with the open end plugged in case you want to add more water outlets later. You should also plan for an easily accessible master water shutoff for the shop.

Be sure to plan for drains to take water out of the shop and pipes to bring water in. If you are putting up new construction and you want to wash cars, or you expect to bring a lot of water into the shop in the form of snow, you may want to plan for an extensive drain system and slope the concrete slightly to make drainage easy and effective. Similarly, if you think you may eventually install a bathroom in the shop, stub out plumbing for the toilet and shower now, even if it doesn't connect to the rest of the sewer system.

Plumbing adds a great deal of convenience and utility to a workshop. Hot water is one of the hallmarks of civilization and you should plan to have it in your garage.

Heat Options

One key to a successful garage build is to make sure the place is comfortable from the first day. That usually means heat and light. Even if you're just using a propane bottle with a small burner for localized heat, make sure that you're comfortable where you're working, or your shop will not be a place of peace and refuge for you.

If your garage is not attached to your home or not served by your central heating system, you want to plan for auxiliary heat if you live where winter temperatures average below 40 degrees Fahrenheit. The easiest way for most people to implement a heating system is by using electricity or bottles of liquid propane.

The advantage to electrical heat is that you can usually set a thermostat and safely keep the shop above freezing when you're not around. You can't do that easily with propane bottles and burners. If you have natural gas service to your garage or shop, you can install an automatic heater, but these are a large investment. Tool catalogs sell 110-volt electric heaters that are designed to be ceiling-mounted and to heat and circulate air. Pay careful attention to the British Thermal Unit (BTU) ratings and the size of the area that a heater is designed to serve.

When you make your plan for shop heat, take into account the energy sources available to you, the climate in your area, and, most importantly, fire and carbon monoxide safety.

Compressed Air

Compressed air is one of the most useful features you can put in

If you live where temperatures drop to uncomfortable levels in the winter, plan to have some kind of heat in your shop. Even a small space heater takes the edge off the chill in the morning or late at night.

Pipe Protection

If your climate drops below freezing in the winter, be sure you plan to protect your pipes from freezing. You should also decide if you want to run the shop pipes behind drywall or out where they are visible. In freezing climates, running pipes on the surface minimizes damage in the event the pipes freeze and crack—having them visible makes finding leaks easier. ■

Even if you aren't connected to water and sewer from the outside, put in stubs if you're having a workshop or garage built for you. A little planning now makes your future much easier.

HOW TO DESIGN, BUILD & EQUIP YOUR AUTOMOTIVE WORKSHOP ON A BUDGET

your shop—a good air system is second only to light and heat in making your shop a more useful place. The best news is that compressed air is not expensive or difficult to install, so you should absolutely plan to install a compressor and air tank. However, installing a compressor requires electrical and at least minimal plumbing connections to route the air. It's good practice for both electrical and plumbing skills.

You should plan to purchase and install the largest and most capable compressor you can find. You never hear someone complain about having too much compressed air, but you can hear people complain all the time that their compressors are too small and the tanks don't hold enough air to keep the motors from cycling constantly while they're working.

Compressors are large, so work your air routing into the layout from the beginning. In addition to the location of the compressor and its proximity to 120- or 240-volt power, you also need to think through how you're going to get the air from the compressor to the various sites (blast cabinet, paint booth, working bay, workbench, etc.) where it will be used. The plan can be as simple as a spool with a long hose or as complex as a full plumbing system with multiple pressure outlets around the shop.

If you plan for compressed air from the beginning, you are able to minimize the amount of shop space you have to give up for the equipment. Many mechanics prefer to place the compressor outside the shop, in a special shed or closet that further limits the noise problem when the compressor is running. You just need to extend the wiring to the shed and route the air back into the shop.

Heavy Lifting

If you're like most amateur mechanics, you'll do about 90 percent of your work alone. That poses a problem when it is time to lift heavy objects like engines and sometimes even car bodies off the chassis. If possible, you want to get a lift to bring the whole car up to eye level. But no matter what, you need to use technology to help boost your muscle power (and avoid injury.)

The thing to remember is that you can buy, store, and use portable lifting devices more or less as you need them, but a full automobile lift requires planning and preparation, often before you even start building your shop or garage. Depending on the style of lift you choose, you need different grades of concrete floor. To get the ultimate in convenience and utility—a two-post lift—you need to have at least 4 to 5 inches of reinforced concrete to bear the weight of the lift plus the weight of the car on two small pedestals.

Thinner concrete floors can support a four-post lift, where you drive the car up onto ramps and lift it. But then you lose the ability to have the car's wheels dangling free, so suspension, steering, and brake work is less convenient. Four-post lifts also take up substantially more space than two-post lifts.

Two-post lifts are the best but, in addition to the floor requirements, they also cost about twice the price of a four-post lift. Either style of lift requires a dedicated 240-volt (occasionally 120-volt) circuit to operate.

Of all the services you can put in your shop, compressed air really helps projects go quickly; it's necessary for painting as well as air tools.

Cold Freeze

Don't leave a propane-powered heater burning in your shop when you're not there. It's too easy for those heaters to cause a fire. If temperatures are not too far below freezing, simply leave some halogen or incandescent lights on to keep things from freezing up.

Don't break your back or use precariously perched plywood on a jack to lift heavy items. Get a good hoist or crane to do the job.

PLANNING YOUR WORKSPACE

If you would like to install a lift at any point in the future, you should begin planning for it right away.

Chapter 8 has installation details for all kinds of automotive lifts and heavy lifting tools and equipment.

Storage

Perhaps the most important plan you make at the beginning of your garage project is the plan for storage. The automotive hobby generates a tremendous amount of extremely useful and valuable junk that you want to store. If you can store your supplies neatly and in such a manner that you can quickly find the pieces you need when you need them, you will be happier than if you have to spend an hour rooting through piles of stuff stashed in decaying cardboard boxes every time you need a part.

Clutter also affects your mental state while you work. Have you ever tried to work on a carburetor, for example, using a tiny corner of your workbench because the whole thing is covered in the detritus of your last 10 projects? Your tools start falling off the edge and you can't find the tiny screw you just set down a moment ago, and suddenly your recreational puttering in the shop is looking like a nightmare.

How much space do you think you need for the stuff you have? You should at least double that estimate, because automotive stuff expands to fill all available space. Also consider the size, weight, and shape of the stuff you're storing. You need to tailor your storage plan to fit the various sizes and weights you will be moving.

You also need to plan an inventory strategy from the beginning. Having a part doesn't mean much if you can't find it when you need it. With a good storage system and inventory system, you'll be on track to work efficiently and have more peace of mind while you work.

Chapter 6 has details and advice for implementing storage and inventory strategies in any size garage with any amount of stuff to store.

Amenities

Storage may be the most important factor in your plans, but amenities are the most fun. This is how you make your workspace a home. And luckily, most amenities don't take much in the way of infrastructure.

You want to think through a plan for furniture, because you will certainly have guests in your workspace sooner or later. Most people also enjoy a radio or other music player to keep them company, or a TV and video player of some kind.

Planning for refreshment is also a good idea. Refreshment arrangements can be as basic as a cooler under the workbench or a garage-sale refrigerator, or as elaborate as a custom tap set up for dispensing cold draft beverages. Whatever you choose, you don't want to neglect the fuel that keeps the mechanic running. Don't forget about a way to warm up your lunch, especially if your household kitchen is more than a few steps away.

The one human amenity that requires some advanced infrastructure planning is a bathroom or wash basin. If you have space for a bathroom, even a simple one, you need to make sure that the plumbing is in place to bring water in and carry wastes away. If you're having a shop or garage built, it's a good idea to have the contractor stub out the plumbing

Even simple storage like old filing cabinets and some plywood shelves help keep stuff organized and out of the way. Invest in some plastic totes just a few at a time and thank yourself later.

Don't neglect the human side of your shop. You don't necessarily need a state-of-the-art sound system, but some tunes, a cold drink, and a place to sit down make for a nice shop.

CHAPTER 1

Workshop Profile: Porsche Palace

The best-planned workshop in the world couldn't be much better than this pro-quality space. Every aspect of this garage shows excellent planning and preparation. While the budget to build this shop is certainly beyond most people's means, the principles work for any shop space.

The workshop is large enough to accommodate every activity and vehicle that it needs to house. If your available space is limited, you may have to limit the number and size of projects you take on. But if you want a comfortable and effective space, don't overload it.

This shop creates a functional working layout by placing a lift and working bay directly in front of the drive-through garage door, with additional parking off to one side. Storage is placed against the wall near the parking space, with workbenches and necessary tools surrounding the lift and working bay. The washbasin is located near the walk-through door for easy cleanup on the mechanic's way out.

For the floor, this owner opted for a polished and sealed concrete surface rather than a painted coating. This surface resists spills and reflects light well. The walls are painted white to reflect light, and generous windows let in natural light. Fluorescent and incandescent fixtures provide excellent light levels throughout the workshop, with extra light over working areas.

The air compressor is located in its own closet to minimize noise, and the shop's working areas are plumbed with surface-mounted PVC pipe and air couplings for convenience. Electrical lines and water pipes are hidden behind the finished walls.

Workbenches are light-duty metal-skinned wood, mounted to the walls. From a budget perspective, they are home-built and certainly far less expensive than pre-made units. Shelves are variously light- and heavy-duty; all inexpensive metal freestanding units. Finally, human amenities include a simple working desk and some basic cabinets to hold books and a stereo for entertainment. This owner spent money on the building and on the critical tools such as the lift and professional-quality air compressor. The combined effect is a comfortable, efficient space where the mechanic can do good work in a relaxed and functional environment.

This shop is not as expensive as it looks; everything has been done with forethought and without waste.

The compressor lives in its own little closet to minimize noise, and the plumbing throughout the shop is done in PVC.

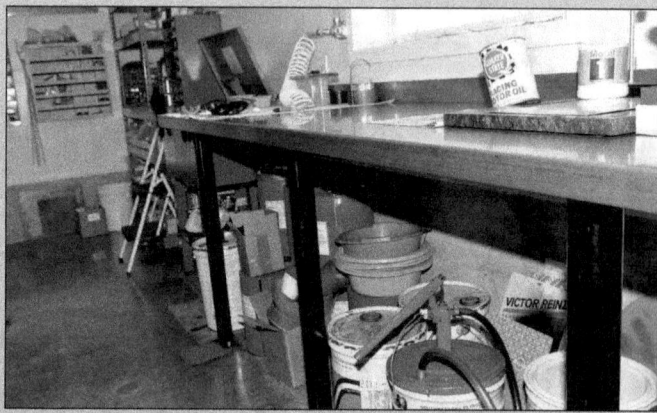

A basic workbench made of steel legs and a sheet-steel-covered benchtop. This bench is attached to the wall studs at the back. You wouldn't want to drop a V-8 engine on it, but it is great for parts assembly.

fixtures even if you don't plan to connect them right away, or ever. If you install them at the beginning, they'll be there if you ever need them.

Develop a Scheduled Budget

Many home improvement books and TV shows seem to assume that their audience has an unlimited (or at least very large) budget. Real-world experience says that this is rarely the case. And in any event, we would all rather spend our money on our vehicles than on unnecessary workshop expenses. The principle of frugality is foremost in the projects described in this book, but you will still be spending a significant sum to get your workshop set up the way you want it. Simply buying the basic tools, such as a compressor, toolbox, heavy-duty jack and stands, washbasin, parts cleaner, and so on, will cost you plenty.

What you need to do very early in your planning process is to create a detailed and prioritized budget for your workshop improvements and features. The order of tasks is also a factor in your budget planning. If you can avoid it, for example, you don't want to build your workbenches before you've sealed and painted the floor. Therefore, you need a scheduled budget to most efficiently get your shop into the shape you want.

You need to be realistic about what you can afford and what you plan to do. Any big project always costs more than you expect. Double your estimate and it'll still cost more than you expected. So make an accurate budget and realize that Rome wasn't built in a day, and your workshop won't be a showpiece next weekend or even next month.

You need to figure out what to do first and what can wait. The nice thing about developing your garage is that you can use some of the free or low-cost ideas in this book, and then replace or upgrade those installations later as you are able.

Some spaces simply do not accommodate the kind of shop equipment we'd all like to have. You have to take an honest look at your space and remember that you also have to work in the available area, so if you have an old-fashioned single car-garage and a large car, your elbow room may be extremely limited.

My suggestion is that you start by writing things down. Some people like a pad of paper and a pencil, and others prefer a spreadsheet or a blog—use whatever works for you. The point is to get it all down in a big list so you can really see how much (or how little) you need to do. Make a master list with your planned major projects and then a sublist for each project with detailed costs for supplies and equipment and a time estimate for completion. Don't forget labor costs if you decide to hire out some of this work. If you're doing the work yourself, be sure to account for the cost of tools and supplies you need to buy. Prioritize this list both in terms of what's important to you and what you need to get done first.

With your itemized and prioritized list of modifications, you should be able to make a scheduled budget for work that fits your finances and your calendar. Don't sweat it too much if you get behind on the schedule—everyone does. Right now the trick is to enjoy the journey as much as the destination.

Most budgets place large expenditures first, but in a scheduled budget, you'll list your items in the order you intend to purchase and/or implement them. Scheduled items often fall around weekends when you have time to work in the shop and around paydays, when you have the cash to make your purchases.

The following is an example of a scheduled budget for basic improvements to an existing two-car garage. You can see that the projected dates and costs are all filled in, but the actual costs and finished dates should be filled in as you purchase and complete each item, so you can revise your plan as you go.

Begin Date	Item	Projected Cost	Actual Cost	Finish Date
January 15	Drywall	$445	$404	January 20
January 22	Wiring	$750	$723	January 25
January 30	Floor paint	$2,000	$2,000	January 30
February 10	Workbench	$300	$348	February 28
February 15	Compressor	$500	$499	March 10
February 20	Washbasin	$250	$250	
February 28	Shelves	$400		
March 1	Move-in	$0		
March 31	Fridge	$100		
Totals		$4,745	$4,224	

CHAPTER 1

Item	Projected Cost	Actual Cost
24 sheets of drywall	$200	$168
Joint tape	$30	$31
Joint compound	$35	$36
Drywall screws	$20	$20
Drywall hand tools	$40	$40
5-gallon exterior paint	$100	$90
Paint rollers	$20	$20
Totals	$445	$405

Above is an example of a scheduled budget for a basic drywall job.

Develop your budget with projected costs, and then keep track of how much you actually spent to help you budget more accurately in the future. Also place a planned finish date on your budget, and note when you actually finished the improvement. It's not important if you fall behind, but it helps to understand how long these jobs actually take. When you restore a car or build a hot rod, you can use the same process to estimate, schedule, and track your work.

Build a Whole New Workshop

Most of the procedures and examples in this book were developed from the actual build-out of a new workshop. This building is a 24x36 metal-skinned pole structure built in the back yard of a standard suburban house. While building a new structure cannot be called a budget alternative, the building was designed to be as inexpensive as possible at about $30,000 total cost, including plumbing, electricity, and interior structures and finishing. It's possible and even typical to pay a lot more than that for a comparable building.

To undertake a building project like this, you start by checking your local building codes and restrictions. In the case of this suburban neighborhood, the limitations on extra buildings included property line and sewer easement setbacks, a limitation that the building could not be taller than the existing house, and a rule that the building could not cover more square feet than the existing house. There were also aesthetic requirements that the building include modern rain gutters and downspouts, and the color of the building must be an approximate match to the existing house. Permit costs were about $250.

A metal-skinned pole building with a wooden structure is a good, low-cost way to build a workshop. Comparable stick-built buildings with wood or other siding cost substantially more, as do steel-frame buildings.

The project begins with scraping and leveling the site and digging trenches to accommodate plumbing and electrical connections. Be sure to accurately locate all sewer, water, gas, and other lines that may pass under the site. There are strict codes about building over such lines, and you may be liable for relocating expenses if you build over buried utility lines. During this project, the sewer pipe from the house had to be relocated

First the site is leveled and the post holes dug. All the poles are set and leveled. This workshop measures 24 feet wide and 36 feet deep—enough to comfortably fit workbenches, shelves, appliances, and four cars.

After the posts are set in concrete, the trusses are brought in and raised using winches at the top of each pole. Then the side studs are nailed in place.

PLANNING YOUR WORKSPACE

The entire shop is wrapped in R7 insulation with a plastic vapor barrier on the inside. Then the roof plates are put on and the doors and windows framed in.

Once the skin is on the building, the concrete contractor comes back to pour the heavy-duty 4-inch slab for the interior of the building, along with a driveway apron and standing pads outside the two walk-through doors.

when a post hole was mistakenly drilled through the pipe! This added an unexpected $1,800 cost to the project, but made the attachment of sewer and water lines to the building easier and less expensive.

The basic structure of a pole building is a set of vertical 6x6 posts set in concrete 4 feet in the ground in 3-foot-diameter holes. For wall attachments, 2x6 boards are screwed horizontally to the outside of the poles. Triangular roofing trusses are then lifted into place and rafters are attached to the roof trusses to support the metal roof skin. Any planned doors and windows are framed into the structure at this time.

Before the surface metal goes on, a thin layer of fiberglass insulation (R7) with a thick vinyl vapor barrier is installed. Finally, sheet-metal siding and roofing is screwed to the structure and the doors and windows are installed.

When the structure is fundamentally complete, some extra rock is placed on the floor of the building and the concrete slab is poured. This 4-inch-thick slab is of 35,000-psi compression-strength concrete. This accommodates some two-post and all four-post lifts, and virtually any wheeled vehicle that fits through the garage door. Before the concrete was poured, buried connections for a toilet, sewer drain, water-line inlet, and electrical conduit were placed. The concrete project also included a drive-up apron into the garage door and two small standing pads outside the two walk-through doors.

The garage door is a standard 16-foot modular design, and the two walk-through doors are standard steel-skinned fire doors with locking residential doorknobs.

The finished building measures 24 feet wide by 36 feet deep. The distance from the concrete floor to the bottom of the roof trusses is about 8½ feet, with another 4 feet to the peak of the roof. The walls offer the wide side of 2x6 lumber for attaching interior finishing, and the entire structure features enough insulation to keep the building comfortable at most temperatures experienced in the local climate. It's a blank canvas for building an automotive workshop, which is an excellent way to start.

This finished workshop includes rain gutters, stubs for electrical power and plumbing, and a garage door. It's ready for the projects described throughout this book.

HOW TO DESIGN, BUILD & EQUIP YOUR AUTOMOTIVE WORKSHOP ON A BUDGET

CHAPTER 2

WALLS AND FLOORS

It's quite possible to work on your car in your driveway. Thousands of "shade tree" mechanics do it every day. They string an extension cord from the house and get to work. For the most part, they get results that are just about as good as they'd produce if they had a proper garage. The difference is that working on your car projects in your driveway is generally a far less pleasant and safe experience than working in a well-equipped garage or shop space.

A warm, dry, clean, and pleasant space to work in and house your toys requires some inside finish work. The extent of that finishing is up to you, and there are several good options to consider. You may even decide to mix and match based on the area you're covering. You can finish a garage or workshop to indoor home standards, or any other finish down to bare studs with a metal skin to block the wind. In this chapter I look at some of the upsides, downsides, and expenses of different kinds of interior finish.

Wall Covering

Nothing says "unfinished" like a bare stud wall. You're going to want to put some kind of finish work over your walls if they don't already have some kind of covering. Plus, if you plan to run electrical services with Romex cable, you need to cover it to meet code. You have a lot of good options for wall covering, and some are substantially less expensive than others.

Ordinary household sheetrock (also called drywall) and fire-code sheetrock are both good choices for interior wall coverings. This material is made of compressed dried gypsum powder, with a heavy paper covering on both sides. It comes in 4x8-foot or 4x10-foot sheets and costs about $7 to $10 per sheet for 1/2-inch boards.

The upsides of sheetrock are that it effectively hides insulation, plumbing, and wiring; adds some insulation value of its own; and looks perfectly acceptable, especially if you finish the job with mud and tape and then paint the walls. Sheetrock almost always has white paper on one side, so it's already nicely reflective when you install it. You need a sheetrock saw, a box-cutter razor, and a good straightedge to cut this material. And once you get the hang of it, sheetrock isn't difficult work with.

The downsides of sheetrock begin with the fact that it's heavy and often

A finished shop interior doesn't have to be up to residential standards. But you do want the walls smooth and painted because it helps reflect light around the shop, and it just looks more cheerful that way.

24 HOW TO DESIGN, BUILD & EQUIP YOUR AUTOMOTIVE WORKSHOP ON A BUDGET

difficult to hang if you're working by yourself. You can rent a sheetrock lift, and you really need this if you plan to put in a ceiling using this material. Sheetrock is also easy to break, especially if you're trying to work with it overhead, and it comes apart if it's exposed to water. But from the perspective of the automotive workshop builder, the biggest downside of sheetrock is that it lacks the structure necessary to allow you to put in nails and hooks and hang heavy items on the wall. You have to get hooks and nails into the studs behind the sheetrock or they pull right out with just a few pounds of weight.

You can see the difference between one coat of paint on the top half and two coats of paint on the bottom half of this OSB wall. OSB drinks up a lot of paint, so put on a light first coat. Let that coat dry for an hour or two to seal the wood, then paint a heavier second coat that won't soak in.

You don't have to spend a fortune to paint your shop walls. Used building materials stores like the Habitat for Humanity ReStore often stock sealed full cans of unused paint. You might have to mix and match your paint, but if you stick with basic white the differences won't be too noticeable.

One of the downsides of sheetrock is that it's easy to knock a hole in it with just about anything, including your foot.

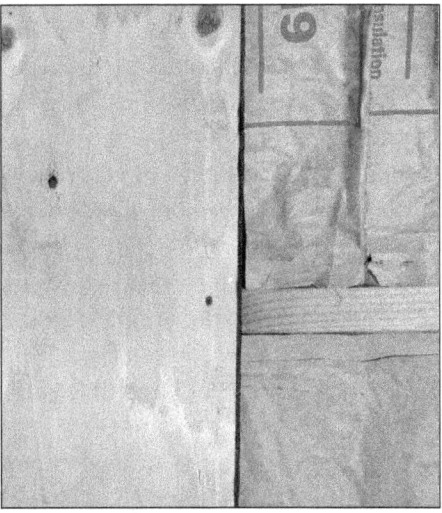

You don't want to leave paper-backed insulation uncovered. Plywood or OSB is a good choice for wall coverings, but you need to paint it.

TECH TIP — Maximize Your Light

Make the most of your investments in light by painting your walls a light color. This reflects light all over the shop and makes your work easier on your eyes. ■

You can be as meticulous as you like with your paint, or just get it onto the walls, because they will be covered by shelves and posters.

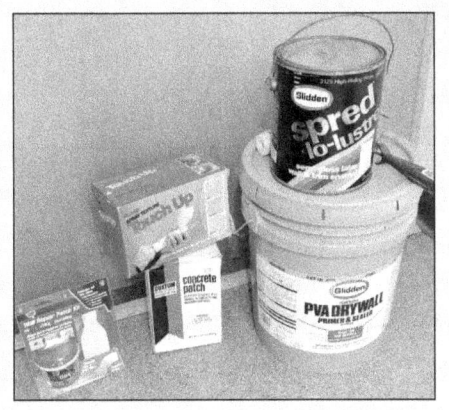

For the ultimate in nice looks plus utility, put sheetrock over the plywood over the insulation. As an added bonus, fire-code sheetrock doesn't cost much more than the basic product and helps your workshop resist fires.

A better option is to use some form of plywood as your wall covering. With 1/2-inch sheets, you can screw in hooks, hang cabinets, and put just about anything you want on the wall. Real structural plywood costs quite a bit, but if you get the oriented strand board (OSB) sheets in 4x8-foot sizes, they cost about the same or less than sheetrock. This material is easy to cut with a circular saw or table saw, and it weighs less (but not a lot less) than sheetrock. Big box and recycled building-supply stores often have new OSB or plywood at bargain prices.

The downside of OSB or plywood is simply that you absolutely have to paint it once it's up. But that's easy and well worth the extra time and expense.

Plywood versus Oriented Strand Board

Oriented strand board, or OSB, is a budget alternative to conventional plywood. Plywood is made up of thin sheets of wood shaved and peeled off the log. The sheets are laid out alternating crossways to each other in three, five, seven, or nine layers, with glue and sealants bonding the layers together. This gives plywood its strength. You can get plywood in grades from A to D, with the most common construction plywood being C or CDX. CDX plywood has a smoother C-grade side and a rougher D-grade side, but almost all plywood has a smoother side and a rougher side. The X stands for exterior use, which means that the wood uses water-resistant glues. The best plywood is marine grade, which is made of hardwoods, is highly water resistant, and very expensive.

In contrast, OSB is made from small strands of shredded wood that has been mixed with glue and sealants and pressed into a sheet. OSB has some advantages over plywood, with the main one being that, in 1/2-inch thickness, it's about half the cost of CDX plywood. OSB is easy to work with and is generally just as strong as plywood for wall coverings. Howerver, it's easier for screws to pull through OSB so you can't hang as much weight unless your screws go through to the studs behind.

The big downside to OSB is that it's more susceptible to water than CDX plywood. OSB absorbs water and swells up. For this reason, you should always leave a space at the bottom of the wall so your OSB (or drywall) isn't in direct contact with the floor, so you can hose down the shop floor without damaging the walls. Do not use OSB at all if you're likely to need to hose off the walls or ceiling.

Oriented strand board in 1/2-inch thickness is about half the cost of comparable plywood and a bit less than sheetrock. It's a great bargain alternative. Be sure to place a 2x4 under the sheet so it doesn't reach the floor, where it may soak up moisture.

When you put a good coat of paint on it, OSB is a perfectly nice-looking wall material that holds screws and plenty of hanging weight.

WALLS AND FLOORS

Wonder Wall

If you're looking for a fun and effective wall covering, consider buying some "bathboard" at your local big-box home-supply store. This is also called "melamine" and it's the exact same material used to make whiteboards. You can get this material in 4x8-foot sheets for about $20 per sheet, and your walls can become the world's largest white board for notes and diagrams! Screw a clean soup can to the wall every 10 feet or so to hold some dry-erase markers to use on your boards. Don't ever use a Sharpie-type marker though; you will have those notes on the board forever! ■

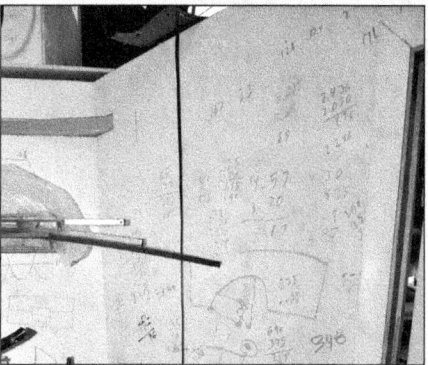

This adaptation is brilliant. Melamine bath board is an expensive wall board, but it turns your walls into a giant whiteboard for about $20 a sheet. This is perfect for workbenches where you want to make notes frequently.

Prayer Mat

Experienced mechanics often have a "prayer mat" around the shop. These are simply small rectangles of discarded carpet about 2 by 4 feet in size. When you need to get down on the ground to work, toss a prayer mat on the floor and you'll stay cleaner (and warmer if the floor is cold). A prayer mat also works great if you have to fix a car at the side of the road. ■

Floor Covering

Most garages and workshops have plain concrete floors. These are great for most purposes, but you can upgrade your floor with a variety of floor coverings.

Floor paint in an automotive workspace is always a good idea. The paint not only looks great, but it provides an impermeable barrier between ground moisture and your cars. It also protects the concrete floor from soaking up oil, gasoline, and other spills.

Most floor paints use some kind of epoxy or cyanoacrylate-based (Krazy Glue) formulation to make them hard and suitable for cars. If you painted the floor with ordinary house paint, the paint would stick to the tires and come right up the first time you drove a car with warm tires onto the surface. As it is, you need to carefully prepare the concrete floor to hold onto the epoxy paint. If you have a brand-new slab, that's the time to paint it—before you ever park a car on the surface. Oil, dirt, and gasoline trapped in the concrete prevent the paint from adhering to the surface. You need to use an acid etch and other cleaners to prepare an older concrete floor for paint.

This garage was painted with inexpensive two-part Rustoleum epoxy floor paint and the results are fantastic for $100. Just follow the instructions carefully.

A concrete floor can be polished and sealed rather than painted. It looks great and doesn't soak up oil.

CHAPTER 2

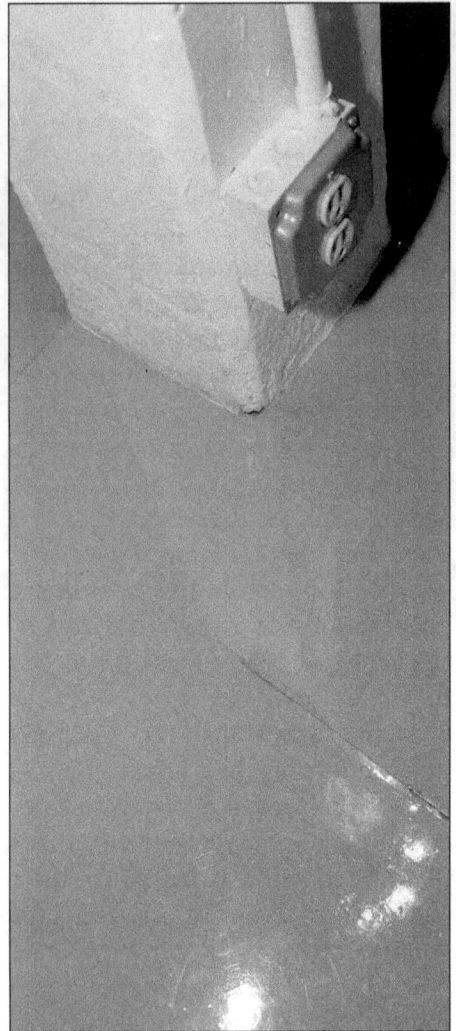

This high-gloss floor was painted with cyanoacrylate floor paint. The result is museum quality.

Polyaspartic floor paint is extremely high-end material. It's expensive but there's nothing better on the market.

These interlocking floor tiles look great, but they're on the expensive side, and they swallow small nuts and screws instantly.

Standing Pads

Standing pads are thick, soft rubber pads designed for people who work on concrete floors and who have to stand in one palce for extended periods of time. This is just a chunk of rubber foam that gives you a soft place to stand. Your feet will thank you! ■

A standing pad is a nice touch to save your feet. If you have firm pads like this one, you can also put them under free-standing tools and your air compressor to reduce noise and vibration.

Avoid Floor Tiles

Avoid stick-on floor tiles. "They're horrible. They just do not work," says Eddie Nakato of AR Auto Service in Lake Oswego, Oregon. The adhesive on these tiles cannot stand up to the pull of a hot, sticky tire, and they get dirt and oil in the cracks between the tiles. Before you know it, your new tiles are coming loose, and they look terrible. ■

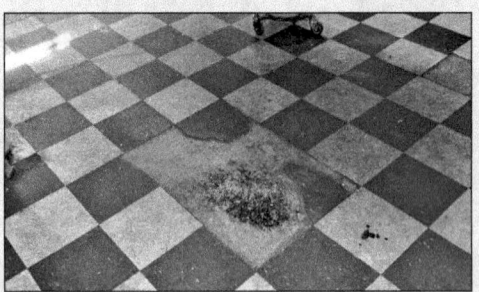

Stick-on floor tiles are an invitation to disaster—they're just not made for the rigors of a working auto shop.

WALLS AND FLOORS

A newer and more expensive material is a polyaspartic floor coating, based on polyurea. This material goes on quickly and hardens wonderfully. It is used on bridges and other concrete structures that have to be protected from water; it completely seals against moisture. If you have problems with moisture wicking up through your concrete, polyaspartic finishes are likely the right choice for you. The other benefit of polyaspartic coatings is that you can paint them on the floor at any time of year—they are not subject to cold temperature restrictions.

When you're applying the floor coating, you can often mix in some sand (of course, there is special sand for this purpose, but you can use any clean sand from the hardware store) or other abrasive to provide better traction on the painted surface. This is nice if you expect the floor to be wet frequently (as in a body or detail shop). But the abrasive also turns the floor into a big sheet of sandpaper if you rub against it, so weigh the tradeoffs. It's entirely possible and appropriate to sand the part of the painted floor where people walk and to not sand other areas.

Expert Interview: Garage Themes

Chris Watkins makes his living finishing garage and workshop spaces, so he's worked with every kind of space and budget. He owns Garage Themes (www.garagethemes.com).

Q: How do you design garages for your clients?

A: I use a computer program designed for cabinet makers. This software allows me to drop in objects like appliances, doors, electrical, electronics, and other garage objects. So, for example, if someone wants to put a large flat-screen TV over the workbench, I can show what it will look like.

Q: How do you start a project with your clients?

A: I ask them how they want to use the garage. You get a number of different stories: from people who just want to spend some time out in the garage with the car, and that takes you down one track; or they just want to be clean and organized, and that takes you down another track. Most of my business has traditionally been with storage and organization, but definitely also making it look good.

For example, I have a client who wants a nice home for his Mustang and at least part of the garage to be tricked out for it. I start with cabinets and some kind of automotive theme. I have a three-toned paint concept to use as a starting point, to go with a steel-wrapped workbench. The space I'm talking about is the size of a one-car garage. He has a three-car garage, but he doesn't want to do the whole thing.

Q: We're standing on some of your work right now. What can you tell me about this floor covering? It has a lot of surface and nooks and crannies; how is it to keep clean?

A: In general it's pretty easy to keep it clean. There's sand on the stairs and steps where we are, but not on the main floor. With this particular floor, there was a layer of epoxy paint under it. I abraded it with 36-grit sanding discs and now it has two layers of epoxy finish with a polyaspartic topcoat. I did the job with one assistant, and it was a pretty manageable job with two guys.

Q: What's the big difference between epoxy and polyaspartic coverings?

A: Temperature sensitivity and water sensitivity. With epoxy, an air temperature of 50 degrees F or more is best. If you get below 50 degrees, you're adding cure time to it. You can run the stuff colder than that, but if it's less than 40 degrees, I'd be concerned and I'd want more cure time, especially if you're going to go over it with a polyaspartic top coating. I've done some floors all in polyaspartic, with a primer and then a topcoat, and you can lay down that stuff at 20 below zero. But you need to make sure that it's dry when you use polyaspartic coatings. That's because the epoxy I use is water-based, but the polyaspartic coating is not water-based and it doesn't like water at all. So if you have a high-moisture-content floor, it can be problematic for any coating system because you have cold and water that permeates and causes delamination on the floor.

Windows let in light, and modern windows have vinyl sashes and low-emittance glass, so you don't lose much insulation value by having them in your shop.

Skylights are a great way to take advantage of natural light. For a more expensive but very innovative option, consider solar tube skylights.

Windows and Skylights

Windows and skylights are great to have in your shop, because they let in natural light, which helps reduce the energy bill and gives the shop a cheery aspect. But old single-glazed windows and skylights also leak heat in the winter. Fortunately, if you replace old windows now, low-emittance (Low-E) double-glazed windows with vinyl sashes are the modern standard and they are the cheapest solution around. You can also get Low-E skylights or even use solar tubes, which are small insulated skylights with lenses and reflectors designed to carry natural light down the tube and disperse it into the room.

When you install windows, be sure to include shades or some form of curtains so you can get some extra insulation, dim the shop to eliminate glare, or just keep the contents of your shop private.

A better option than stick-on tiles, but not as durable as epoxy or polyaspartic floor paint, is an interlocking floor covering. This solution looks great, and it keeps your stuff off the floor, but small parts like nuts and washers can fall down into the flooring and you may not be able to roll heavy tools like engine hoists over the material conveniently. This material is also on the expensive side if you have a large area to cover. Interlocking floor covering is great for spaces at your workbench where you might be standing for extended periods of time.

Wall Bumpers

You can go online and order pads that install on your walls to absorb impacts from your car doors. If you have a small parking space and you need to park close to the walls, these can save your paintjob and your walls from scuffs and dings.

These wall guard bumpers are a great idea to finish the interior of a small garage. They prevent car doors from taking a chunk out of the wall and the walls from scratching car doors. This type of item is available from several suppliers online.

CHAPTER 3

ELECTRICITY AND LIGHTS

A garage or shop provides shelter from heat, cold, and moisture, and it provides you the chance to take advantage of basic services like electric-powered tools, effective lighting, and a garage door opener. Basic electrical service makes your work go smoother and turn out better, but most of all it makes the working process more enjoyable. Electrical infrastructure is what turns a basic shed into a workshop.

If you understand how electricity works and if you have the basic skills required to use a hammer, screwdriver, and a pair of pliers, you can complete the projects described in this chapter. The key with these projects is to take your time and make sure everything is neat and correct before you throw the switch. You want your basic infrastructure to work right the first time and keep working for a long time to come.

These projects involve some fairly large investments of time and money, so budget plenty of both to get where you want to be. Of course, the most workable plan is often to build out your infrastructure over time to spread out the effort and expense. A few necessary circuits and some basic lights are enough to get you going, and then you can add more fancy services later.

Installing Electricity

Electricity powers your lights, air compressor, power tools, stereo, and refrigerator. Whatever the size of your workspace, you need electricity.

CAUTION: Electricity is the most useful service available to you, but it is also the most dangerous to install and work with. You can be killed if you're not careful with your wiring, or you can set your garage full of cars on fire. Always use proper work methods, adhere to the building and wiring codes, and, most of all, use your common sense when working on the wiring.

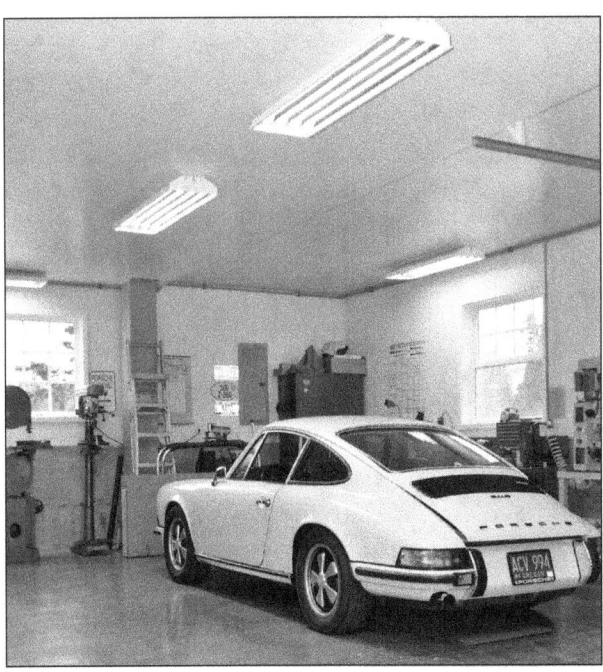

The difference between a storage unit and a workshop is often that a workshop has access to light and electricity. Make sure that your garage has plenty of both for maximum usefulness.

HOW TO DESIGN, BUILD & EQUIP YOUR AUTOMOTIVE WORKSHOP ON A BUDGET

Keep to the Code

Electricity, heat, ventilation, and water plumbing all have associated building codes that vary somewhat from place to place. You should always build to the code in your area, or build to better than code, primarily because it is not safe to have substandard work in your shop or garage.

Also, if you have work that is not built to code in your shop, garage, or home, you can have a hard time selling the property later when the home inspection is done. You may also be subject to fines or worse if building inspectors notice violations.

So get a copy of your local code and follow it.

Electrical Permits and Inspections

Before you start running wire and installing circuit breakers, you need to learn if the project you have in mind requires any building permits and inspections. Generally speaking, you are required to obtain permits and inspections even if you're simply running a new circuit from an existing house panel, as is likely in an attached garage.

You almost certainly need permits and inspections if you are running a new subpanel from your main service to a detached garage. You absolutely must obtain permits and inspections if you are setting up a new meter and main circuit panel for your shop, regardless of whether it is attached or detached. Utility companies will not install a meter and connect to your main circuit panel without a permit and official inspection.

Depending on your municipal rules, you may be legally required to obtain a permit just to install a garage door opener. After speed limits, this is probably the most widely ignored law in the country, but check with your local planning department to be sure.

Obtaining a Permit

If your project requires permits and inspections, here's how: Go to the offices for the municipality (city, county, etc.) that governs your site and fill out the permit paperwork. It's usually a formality, and some municipalities now let you submit permit requests online. You pay the fee and they issue the permit, which you post on the building. You must get this part done before you begin work. Note that the permit process may be slightly different for you, as a homeowner doing your own work, than if you engage a contractor.

How Much Power Do You Need?

When your permit is in hand, contact the utility company. If you request a new service drop from the power lines in your neighborhood, they need to know things such as your location, or whether there are trees or obstacles between the shop and the nearest power pole. They may send an inspector to see the location and advise you. There may be a connection fee to install the service. They need to approve the location of the meter because their staff has to come and read it.

The utility people will also ask you what level of service you need. Older homes often have just 50 or 100 amps of service, while newer homes may have up to 200 amps or more. If you're working in an attached garage and your home has an electric furnace, electric stove, and other major electric appliances, you may already be close to or at the service level. You may need to upgrade your home's service, which means different wire sizes, different main breakers, and, potentially, a different circuit panel. Or you may choose to install a new meter main with separate service for your shop. The other reason the utility asks about service levels is that they may be close to capacity in your neighborhood.

The best option for a workshop is a separate 60- or 100-amp service with its own meter. This way if you blow the breakers running your welder and compressor at the same time, the crisis is limited to your workshop, and it doesn't affect your family's home. And with at least 100 amps, you're unlikely to overload the shop panel under normal use. With a separate meter, you can also keep track of the amount of power you use in your workshop separately from your home.

ELECTRICITY AND LIGHTS

Installing a New Meter and Main Breaker Panel

The utility company tells you what they need to connect the wires. Typically, the utility wants you to have all the work done to the weatherhead, which is the domed pipe that comes out of the roof of your building and is where the wiring meets the utility's wiring. In some cases the wiring runs underground, and the utility then tells you what is needed in that case. Be prepared to rent a trencher (such as a Ditch Witch) if underground wiring is the standard in your community.

Next, you need to purchase the main panel, meter housing, all the necessary conduit, wires, and plugs, and perhaps a service mast and weatherhead if you're installing a new service drop. When you have the circuit panel installed, all of the conduit connected, the junction, switch, and plug boxes installed, and all the wires run for your circuits, (including the grounding electrode conductor, sized appropriately to your main breaker size), you can arrange for the "rough-in" inspection. Don't install any receptacles, switches, or fixtures yet, and you don't cover the conduit, Romex, or other wires in any way. This is so the inspector can verify that you used the right kind of wire in the right size for the circuits you're creating.

Next, install the meter housing, service mast, and all of your switches, receptacles, and fixtures, but don't put covers on the plugs or switches yet. This is when you have an inspector perform the "service inspection." He approves your installation so the utility company can connect and turn on the power for you. Most utilities do not connect your service until this inspection is complete.

Finally, put on the covers and label your circuits on the panel and complete your project. When it's all done and everything is working properly, the inspector comes out one more time to sign off on the project.

The first step in an inspected electrical installation is the rough-in—this is where you run wires and place boxes, but leave them open so the inspector can see that you used the right supplies.

It's often tempting to shortcut this process, but don't do it. If you have a fire traced to unpermitted and uninspected wiring, your homeowner or auto insurance could decline to cover your loss. Also, you or someone else could be electrocuted. If this all sounds like too much for you, hiring an electrical contractor may be the way to go. A professional can handle all the permits and inspections for you.

Installing a Subpanel

If you have enough capacity and space on your household electrical service panel, you may be able to run a subpanel for your garage or shop. This is generally done when there's plenty of power available and the distance to the workshop is not too far. This is usually a less-expensive solution than a separate power drop, but you do run the risk of tripping the main circuit breaker in your home.

Much of the expense of a subpanel is the same as if you installed a new meter and main panel. You need to purchase a circuit panel and all the necessary conduit and wires to make the connection to the main panel.

For this project, a professional electrician installed a 100-amp subpanel in a separate workshop building located approximately 40 feet

Voltage Terms: Is it 110/220 or 120/240?

Most people talk about 110-volt or 220-volt appliances and tools, but most manuals and books talk about 120- and 240-volt circuits. In the past, electrical service came in 110 and 220 volts, and sometimes you see references to 208 or 230 volts, but modern residential electrical service in North America now comes in 120 and 240 volts, and the older 110/220 volt terminology is just a matter of habit. In this book, I use 120/240 terms, but there's really no practical difference when it comes to plugging in your appliances and having them work.

CHAPTER 3

When you first install a subpanel, it's completely bare. You pull wire and install breakers next.

The equipment required for this subpanel was:

- 100-amp main breaker panel
- 100-amp breaker for the subpanel
- 100-amp breaker for the main panel
- 1½-inch PVC conduit, plus pre-made bends, primer, and glue
- 100 feet of number-2-gauge aluminum wire
- Ground rod, ground wire, and ground clamps

The total cost of the equipment was about $350, and the panel includes six 20-amp 120-volt breakers for shop circuits, which just about handles all the 120-volt circuits in the shop. It's important to note that the aluminum wire is a larger gauge than copper wire rated for the same amperage, but aluminum wire is softer and easier to pull through conduit, weighs less than copper, and costs about 15 percent of the price of comparable copper wire.

When this shop building was constructed, the contractor wisely put a 24-foot length of re-bar called a "Ufer Ground" into the concrete floor with a short length protruding under the location for the panel,

If you have to run electricity between buildings, you need to use heavy-duty PVC conduit, which is at least 18 inches underground.

and also cast the electrical conduit down through the floor and out into the ground, so the workshop end of the connection was easy. You might have to chisel some concrete and pound in an 8-foot ground rod if those parts are not available to you. An easier solution would be to bring the conduit up out of the ground and then pierce the building wall.

I used heavy-duty Schedule 40 PVC conduit, and I used plenty of PVC primer and glue on it to make a perfect seal to keep water out of the pipe. The end at the workshop was already in place for me, and I ran the other end up the outside wall of the house to the main panel.

The electrician brought a fish tape, which is a long piece of springy steel with a hook on the end. The steel winds onto a spool for easy use. You extend the fish tape through the conduit, and when it comes out

from the main house. Since the main panel was in the garage of this house, it was easy to dig a trench and pull wire through a PVC conduit. Note that trenches for electrical conduit must be at least 18 inches deep and preferably 24 inches if you plan to drive over the site with cars.

Aluminum wire is a good choice if you have to pull a long distance to the subpanel. It's lighter, softer, and far less expensive than copper wire of comparable carrying capacity.

 **Trencher Rental**

Renting a walk-behind trencher for half a day costs about $130, but I used the trencher to dig the channel for the water connection to the house supply at the same time, saving some money. If you have to rent a trencher for a day, see if any of your friends might be able to share the expense in exchange for some trenching. ■

 **Slippery Wire**

When pulling wire through a long or bent conduit, liberally lubricate the leading end with dishwashing soap so it pulls around the bends easier. ■

ELECTRICITY AND LIGHTS

Assemble the PVC conduit with smooth bends for easy wire pulling, and use plenty of primer and PVC glue for a good seal.

Push-Pull

It's really helpful to have a friend push wires from one end while you pull from the other end.

the other end, attach the wires to the hook and pull the wires back through the conduit while winding the fish tape back onto its spool. If you are working with a straight length of conduit, or it is only slightly bent, you can generally just push the wires through, but if you have more than about 90 degrees of total bend, you want the fish. A fish tape is available at any home supply store for about $10 to $25.

As with a new service drop, once you have the wires pulled and ready to connect, leave everything open so the inspector can verify that you used the right kind of wire in the right size for the power of the breakers in the main panel and subpanel. Do not attempt to use the subpanel until this inspection is complete.

From this point the finishing and inspection process is the same as for new service.

With the help of a comprehensive electrical manual, you can safely wire a subpanel yourself, but it doesn't cost much to hire an electrician to assist you, and the professional's knowledge of code standards and practices gives you confidence that you've done it right. At a minimum, do your research and plan out your project with the wire, breakers, and conduit you want to use and have a professional review your plans to make sure it's all conforming to code. Inspectors do not hesitate to make you rip everything out to start over if you didn't get it right!

Selecting Wire, Breakers and Outlets

When your basic service is established, you can plan out your circuits. As you do, consider how much current each circuit requires. Single-use

An electrician's fish tape makes it possible to pull heavy wires over a long distance. You feed in the tape and pull the wires from one end while a friend pushes from the other end.

A circuit breaker at the main breaker panel feeds the new subpanel. My new breaker is second from the top, on the left.

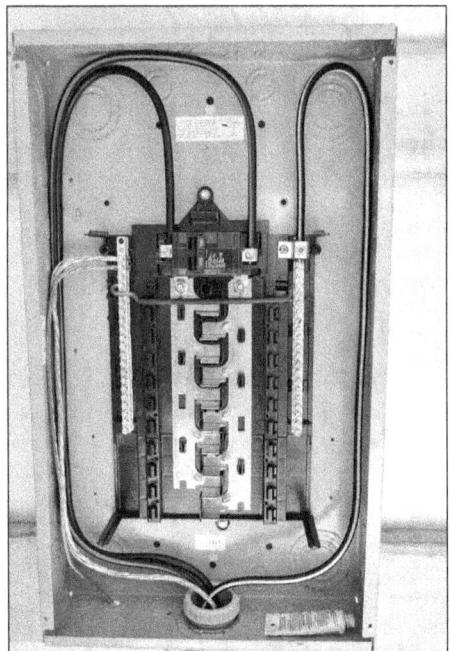

The wires come through the subpanel and run up around the sides of the box to a main breaker. With this setup I can cut power to the shop from the main panel or at the top of this panel.

circuits such as the hard-wired water heater, air compressor, or welder are easy—you can look up how much current the device needs and plan your circuit accordingly. But a row of outlets is a little different—you don't necessarily know how much current is needed for a fridge, stereo, drill press, and anything else you may have plugged in. So it's best to build with a margin of safety.

According to standard wiring practices, a circuit of 120-volt outlets generally uses a 15-amp breaker and 14-gauge wire. For an automotive workshop, it's better to use a 20-amp breaker and 12-gauge wire at all times. There's almost no downside to this, except that it's slightly more expensive. The 20-amp 120-volt outlets look a little different from a standard 15-amp outlet, but accept standard plugs and 20-amp plugs. You can use standard 15-amp outlets on a 20-amp circuit, but you cannot insert a 20-amp plug into a 15-amp outlet.

When it comes to dedicated circuits, and especially 240-volt circuits, read the owner's manual or the sticker on the side of the appliance to determine the current requirements and plan accordingly. For example, a modern, stationary 7.5-hp, two-stage, 240-volt, 80-gallon air compressor requires a 30-amp 240-volt circuit. That circuit requires a minimum of 10-gauge copper wire, but you may also use 8-gauge copper wire for an additional safety margin.

Another decision to make when wiring 240-volt circuits is whether to run three or four wires. Older 240-volt circuits used two 120-volt hot wires and a ground wire, while newer standards specify an additional neutral wire for these circuits. It's always best to run four wires, so plan to do that for every circuit.

If you're building new walls, you have the option of running the circuit wires in the walls using non-metallic sheath cable (commonly known by the trade name Romex). Romex is much easier and less expensive to run than pulling wires through conduit, and the junction boxes are plastic and can be nailed right to the studs. If you are running circuits on the surface of an existing wall, you need to use hard metal (EMT) or PVC conduit with individual wires or metal-clad flexible cable to meet codes.

NOTE: If you are retrofitting or upgrading an existing garage, you may have old wiring already in place. Depending on the age of the installation, this could be ungrounded "knob and tube" wiring, or early cloth-covered non-metallic cable. You can work with this kind of wiring, but you'll need a book or

You can see the difference between the 20-amp outlet on the left and the 15-amp outlet on the right. The 20-amp outlets cost a little more.

Copper Wires

With the exception of extremely large wires for a new service drop, you should not need to use aluminum wires in your shop. Aluminum wires are subject to corrosion and heat expansion, plus they have different gauge standards than copper. Use copper wires throughout your workshop. ∎

Extra Protection

Always place a ground fault circuit interrupter (GFCI) outlet in the first position (closest to the service panel) on all your outlet circuits. This is another breaker that trips if there's a short anywhere in the system. A GFCI costs about $15 to $20 and protects all the outlets farther down the line. And it also adds an extra level of protection for your circuits and building. ∎

A GFCI should go in the first outlet position on every circuit of outlets. This protects all the outlets farther down the line.

ELECTRICITY AND LIGHTS

professional advice specifically dedicated to dealing with antique electrical service. To build a modern automotive workshop, you're better off removing all that old stuff and running new wire for all your needs.

You can buy Romex at a deep discount at used building supply stores. This brand-new roll was found at the Habitat for Humanity ReStore for $25.

Wire Gauges by Circuit Power

Circuit	Wire Gauge	Romex	Metal-Clad
120V 15A	14	14/2	14/2
120V 20A	12	12/2	12/2
240V 20A	12	12/3	12/3
240V 30A	10	10/3	10/3
240V 40A	8	8/3	8/3
240V 50A	6	6/3	6/3

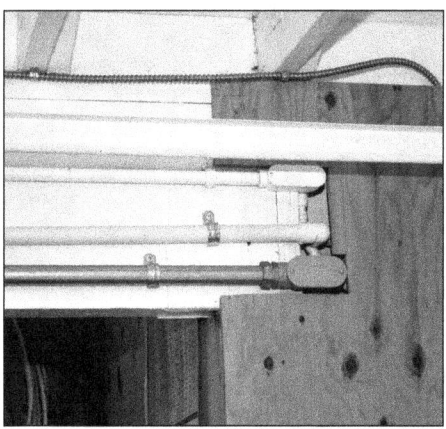

Shown here are metal-clad cable (top), two types of PVC conduit, and rigid-metal (EMT) conduit (bottom).

Using a Conduit Bender

You need a conduit bender to put usable bends in metal electrical conduit. There's just no way around it. In order to push or pull wires through the tube, all bends must be smooth. If you try to bend the conduit without a bender, it crimps and become useless. Luckily, a conduit bender is inexpensive (about $25 for the bending head, plus the cost of some 3/4-inch water pipe for leverage) and easy to use.

The conduit bender has a smooth, curved channel that prevents the bending metal from crimping and a tab that grabs the conduit to pull it around the channel. Some conduit benders have bubble levels built into the bending head, and all have graduated marks to let you know when you have reached 30, 45, 60, and 90 degrees in your bend.

Simply lay your conduit on the floor and measure to where you want your bend to start. Place the bender on the conduit, matching the starting mark on the bending head to the mark on the conduit, and pull the bender around to make your bends. It takes a little practice to get the bends just right, so don't get discouraged if your first bends are a little funky.

If you're using PVC conduit, you heat it with a heat gun and bend it, but be careful not to overheat and melt the material. (*Ugly's Electrical References* by George V. Hart and Sammie Hart is a handbook that covers pipe bending in detail.)

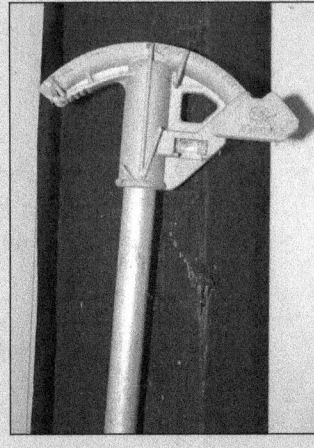

Use a conduit bender like this to make curves in EMT metal conduit. A little practice will have you bending like a pro.

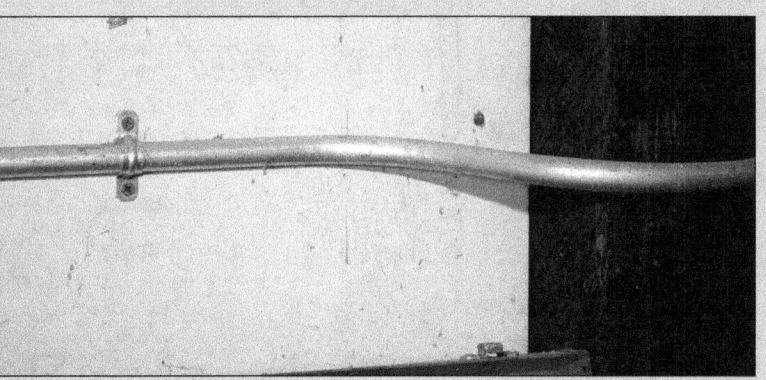

With EMT surface-mount conduit, you go around obstacles rather than through them.

HOW TO DESIGN, BUILD & EQUIP YOUR AUTOMOTIVE WORKSHOP ON A BUDGET

CHAPTER 3

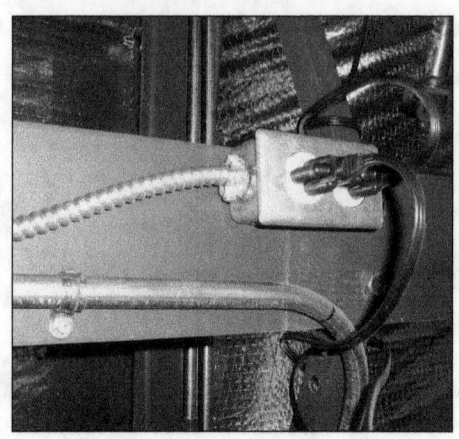

Metal-clad cable is nice because you can run it on the surface or through studs as needed. It's great for metal-framed buildings where drilling through beams is more difficult.

You can mix and match conduits and Romex to suit your needs. If you choose PVC conduit (or anything except unbroken EMT), you need to run a dedicated ground wire, which is a good idea no matter what.

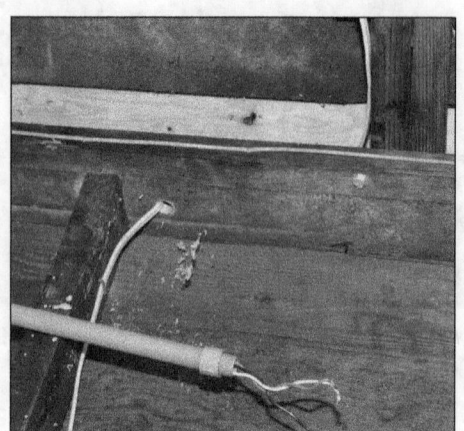

Project: Install a 120 Using Hard Metal Conduit

For the purposes of this project, I assume that you have a main circuit panel or subpanel in your workshop or garage and service is activated. If you are building a new shop or garage, wait to the point where you have a service panel in the shop before starting this project.

Because you're working in a garage or workshop, I also assume that you're running this circuit on the interior surface of the wall in hard metal conduit, with metal junction boxes. If you plan to run the circuit through the stud wall, as inside a house, you can use Romex-style (shielded wires in an outer sheath) wiring, and different codes apply. (See "Project: Install a 120 Using Romex Non-Metallic Cable" for instructions on using Romex on page 41.)

Tools needed:
- Flathead screwdriver
- Conduit bender
- Conduit cutter
- Carpenter's pencil or Sharpie-type marker
- Roll of twine or an electrician's fish tape tool
- Power screwdriver/drill
- Outlet polarity tester

Supplies needed:
- Lengths of conduit (1/2-inch or 3/4-inch) sufficient to span the distance you need
- Junction and receptacle boxes
- Pipe couplings, connectors, and conduit hangers
- 90-degree-bend junctions (if necessary)
- Plugs, switches, and fixtures (as necessary)
- Rolls of wire in white, black, and green insulation in the appropriate gauge for the circuit
- Box of wire nuts in the appropriate size
- Roll of electrical tape
- Circuit breaker of appropriate amperage for the wires and designed for your panel
- Box of screws to attach components to the wall

If you use a metal outlet box and EMT fittings in an unbroken chain, you can use the conduit as a ground path. It's better to run a dedicated ground wire, however, and it costs very little.

You need a conduit cutter for best effect; a hacksaw is a crude substitute that leaves a ragged edge.

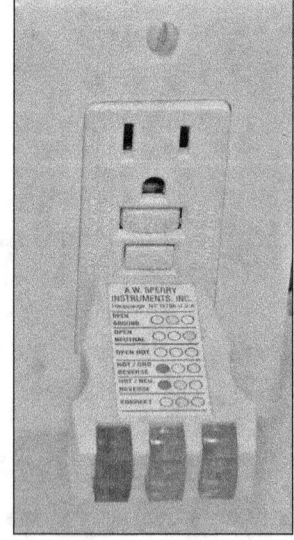

Everyone should have an outlet tester. These devices let you know if your outlets are wired correctly and cost just a few dollars.

ELECTRICITY AND LIGHTS

Follow these steps:

1 Carefully plan and measure your circuit from the panel to its end. Note where you plan to install your outlets and how many boxes and junctions of each type you need. Then use the pencil to mark the walls or ceiling where each component goes. Measure and note the distance between each fixture.

2 Determine the amperage of your circuit—this defines the gauge of wire you need according to your local code. Most circuits for 120-volt outlets are 15 or 20 amps. Choose 20 amps if you have a choice, and use 12-gauge wire.

3 Decide if you want to run a separate ground wire. If you do, then always run your ground wire in conduit and install ground pigtails in the outlet and junction boxes. It is necessary to ground EMT conduit to your ground wire so you can't accidentally energize the pipe in case a hot wire touches the metal and there is a break somewhere in the pipe. If you're using rigid metal conduit threaded together with metal fittings all the way back to the circuit panel, the conduit counts as a ground path and you can connect the ground wire on each outlet to the junction box. However, it costs almost nothing to run a dedicated green ground wire on each circuit, especially if you think you might decide to plug computers or other more delicate electronic devices into your outlets.

4 Lightly tack each fixture in its desired position, and lay out the fittings to connect the conduit to each junction box.

Put all your boxes in place and run your EMT conduit to the junction before you pull any wires.

5 Make any necessary bends in your conduit to go around corners or clear obstacles. If you have sharp corners to navigate, use 90-degree "LB" junctions. These have a removable side, because you cannot pull wires easily around the corner. The idea is that you pull the wires straight through and out the hole in the junction, then feed them through the next run of conduit and finally close the hole in the junction.

6 Push or pull your wires through each piece of conduit. You can use an electrician's fish tape to pull them if necessary.

7 With each section of conduit prepared, attach your fixtures and hang each piece of conduit. Put your junctions in place and leave the outlet boxes open with the wires hanging out. Outlets are usually wired in parallel—wires come into the outlet box from the last outlet, connect to the outlet, and then wires connect to the other side of the outlet and head to the next outlet in the chain.

Run both black wires (coming in and going out) to the same gold-screw side of the outlet, and run the white wires to the silver-screw terminals. The ground wire goes to the green terminal.

This is the end of a breaker that clips onto the copper bus bars of the circuit breaker panel. Most modern breakers just snap into place.

This is an LB junction, used to make sharp, 90-degree corners. You open the back, pull the wires through, and then feed them back in for the next run of conduit.

Recycled Deals

You can often find breakers, boxes, fixtures, and all the supplies you need at bargain prices at the recycled building-supply shop. You might not get every piece, but you'll save on the things you find there.

CHAPTER 3

The back of an outlet has a strip gauge that shows you how much to strip for a hook or press-fit connection. You can see the 14-gauge wire going into the press-fit on the back of the outlet.

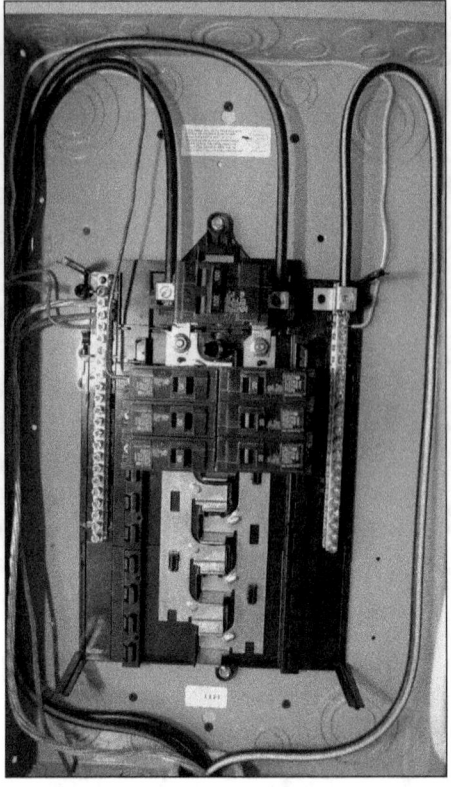

Circuit wires come into the box from the left side. The black wire goes over the top into the top-left breaker and the green ground wire goes to the ground bus on the left. The white neutral wire goes around the top of the box to the neutral bus on the right.

8 After your work is inspected and approved, connect your outlets or other fixtures. If you need to connect bare wires to each other at any point, use screw-on wire nuts and wrap the connection solidly with electrical tape. Most modern outlets have a wire strip gauge cast into their plastic body. Modern outlets may also have "push-in" connections for 14-gauge wire, where you simply strip a length of wire and push it into a hole on the back of the outlet body. These are generally considered a less-solid connection than using the screws on the back or sides of the outlet. Always remember that the gold-colored screws go with the black (hot) wire, and the silver-colored screws connect to the white (neutral) wire. The green screw connects to the green (ground) wire.

9 Finally, install the covers on the fixtures and then go to the circuit panel. Make sure the power is turned off at the main breaker. Install the new circuit breaker and label it on the panel. Attach the final piece of conduit to the side or back of the panel and route the wires to the circuit breaker and to the neutral and ground bus bars. Close the panel and reset the main breaker, then turn on the breaker for your new circuit.

If the circuit includes outlets, test each outlet with a polarity tester. This is a small device that plugs into the outlet. If everything is wired correctly, two green lights are displayed. If you have accidentally reversed the hot and neutral wires or the hot or neutral and ground wires, different lights are displayed. If you have miswired any outlet, correct the problem before using any part of the circuit.

CAUTION: Always stand to one side of the panel when turning on a breaker in case there is an unknown fault in the panel. If the breaker trips when you turn it on, you have a short somewhere in your work. Turn the whole panel off and disconnect the new circuit completely—hot, neutral, and ground—before you go looking for the problem.

Pigtail

When wiring a number of outlets in a series, it's quite difficult to get both green ground wires around the ground screw of the outlet. It's better and easier to "pigtail" the wire by stripping both ends and a short tail of scrap ground wire and then joining all three wires with a wire nut and wrapping the nut with electrical tape. You can then attach the pigtail to the outlet easily. ■

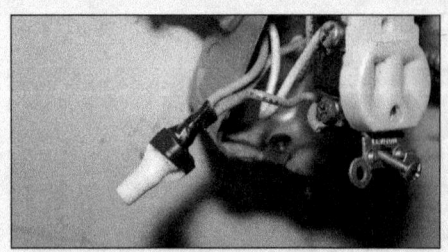

Always pigtail the ground wires so that only a single wire goes to the ground screw on an outlet. It's far more work to get two wires under the screw.

ELECTRICITY AND LIGHTS

Project: Install a 120 Using Romex Non-Metallic Cable

The main difference between this project and the surface-mount metal conduit project is that Romex is both wire and conduit, all in one neatly sheathed package.

Romex is a trade name for non-metallic sheathed cable, and the big advantage with this material is that you don't have to buy and connect conduit. Code allows you to simply drill holes through studs and route the Romex through the holes to your fixtures. Romex is flexible so there are no corner pieces or conduit bending. Plus the junction boxes and outlet boxes can be made of plastic because Romex includes its own ground wire.

When you buy supplies for a Romex project, you can generally get the ones labeled "for new construction" at your home supply store. These are designed to work with Romex and to be quickly and easily installed in an open stud wall. In fact, codes require that Romex be concealed for protection, because its plastic sheath doesn't provide much protection against puncture or abrasion. Romex and its boxes are designed to be installed behind sheetrock or OSB/plywood.

One nice thing about Romex is that the wire sizes are printed right on the sheath material every few feet. Generally, Romex comes in 12/2 or 14/2 configuration. That means two sheathed wires of either 12- or 14-gauge inside, plus an unsheathed bare copper ground wire. Yes, there are really three wires in a 12/2 Romex. For 240-volt circuits, you can also get 12/3 Romex, which has three sheathed wires and a bare ground, or 10/3 for your 30-amp circuits, 8/3 for 40-amps, and 6/3 for 50-amp circuits.

Romex also comes in several varieties of sheath, including a gray-sheath version called UF (or direct burial cable) for buried or outdoor installation, and a couple varieties of white-sheath, depending on whether your installation might be subject to moisture.

For the purposes of this project, I assume that you have a main circuit panel or subpanel in your workshop or garage, and that service is activated. If you are building a new shop or garage, wait until you have a service panel in the shop before starting this project.

Tools needed:
- Framing hammer
- Flathead screwdriver
- Carpenter's pencil or Sharpie-type marker
- Power screwdriver/drill with a wood-boring bit at least ¾ inch
- Outlet polarity tester

Supplies needed:
- Lengths of Romex (12/2 gauge) sufficient to span the distance you need
- Nail guards
- "New construction" junction and receptacle boxes
- Plugs, switches, and fixtures (as necessary)
- Box of wire nuts in the appropriate size
- Roll of electrical tape
- Circuit breaker of appropriate amperage for the wires and designed for your panel

Follow these steps:

1 Carefully plan and measure your circuit from the panel to its end. Note where you will install your outlets, with a maximum of 12 feet spacing between outlet boxes, and how many boxes of each type you need. Then use your pencil to mark the walls or ceiling where each component goes. Measure and note the distance between each fixture.

2 Determine the amperage of your circuit—this defines the gauge of wire you need according to your local code. Most circuits for 120-volt outlets are 15 or 20 amps. Choose 20 amps if you have a choice, and use 12/2 Romex.

3 Lightly tack each fixture in its desired position, and use your drill to make holes in the studs as needed to thread your Romex from box to box. Next run your lengths of Romex. Make sure the Romex is secured with cable staples no more than 12 inches from each box unless the hole in the stud is within that 12-inch run.

4 Attach your fixtures firmly and run the Romex into each box. Leave the outlet boxes open with the wires hanging out. Outlets are usually wired in parallel—wires come into

Wire Protection

When putting Romex through studs, get some nail guards to protect your wires. These are metal plates, or sometimes little cylinders that go through the studs to keep future workers from driving a nail through your Romex wires. Nail guards are generally required by code if your pass-through holes are less than 1¼ inches from the outside of the stud. ∎

HOW TO DESIGN, BUILD & EQUIP YOUR AUTOMOTIVE WORKSHOP ON A BUDGET

With more than two wires coming into this junction box, every connection is pig-tailed if you choose to put an outlet here.

6 Finally, install the covers on the fixtures and then go to the circuit panel. Make sure the power is turned off at the main breaker. Install the new circuit breaker and label it on the panel. Attach the final piece of Romex to the side or back of the panel with a Romex clamp, and strip the sheath off inside the panel. Route the wires to the circuit breaker and to the neutral and ground bus bars. Close the panel and reset the main breaker, and then turn on the breaker for your new circuit. If the circuit includes outlets, test each outlet with a polarity tester.

Consider a weather-tight covered outlet for any circuit that might encounter rain or water spray. They are a little more expensive, but are nice if you want to wash a car or use spray paint in the area.

CAUTION: Always stand to one side of the panel when turning on a breaker in case there is an unknown fault in the panel. If the breaker trips when you turn it on, you have a short somewhere in your work. Turn the whole panel off and disconnect the new circuit completely—hot, neutral, and ground—before you go looking for the problem.

the outlet box from the last outlet, connect to the outlet, and then wires connect to the other side of the outlet and head to the next outlet in the chain.

5 Once your work is inspected and approved, connect your outlets or other fixtures. If you need to connect bare wires to each other at any point, use screw-on wire nuts and wrap the connection solidly with electrical tape. Be sure to pigtail your ground wires as described in "Pigtail" on page 40.

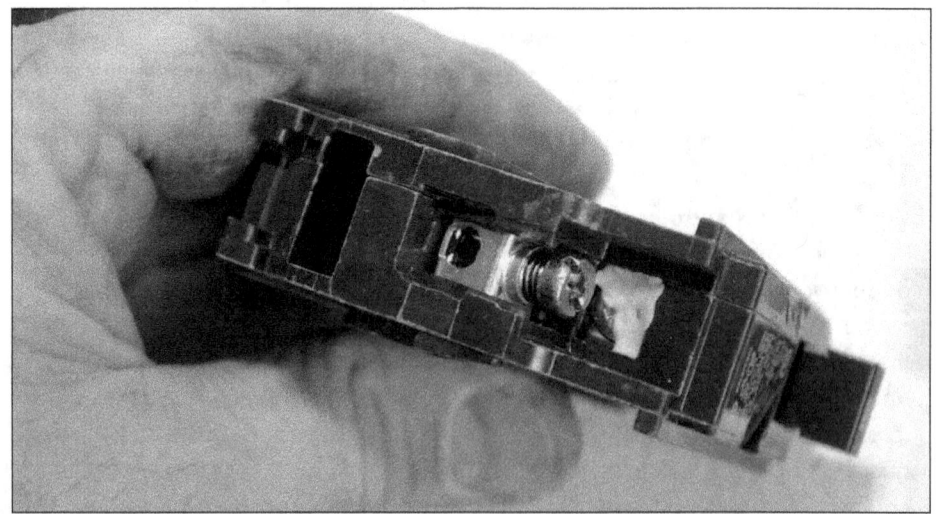

The hot wire side of a circuit breaker is shown here. After the breaker is installed in the panel, put the stripped black wire end in the hole and tighten the screw to make the connection.

Project: Install a 240 Using Flexible Metal-Clad Cable

This project is only slightly different from the "Install a 120 Using Hard Metal Conduit" project on page 38, so I'll focus on the differences. The main difference is that metal-clad cable is a spiral metal conduit with the wires inside all in one neatly sheathed and flexible package. This material is expensive, up to about $5 per foot depending on the number and size of wires in the cable, but it's very handy for getting around difficult spaces and protecting a 240-volt circuit.

Be sure you buy metal-clad (MC) cable, rather than armored (AC) cable. The two types have different purposes, and you want MC for your shop because it has a dedicated ground wire. Metal-clad cables are designated like Romex cable—so a metal-clad cable with three insulated wires (black and red for hot, white for neutral) plus an extra insulated green ground wire is known as 10/3.

For the purposes of this project, I assume that you have a main circuit panel or subpanel in your workshop or garage, and that service is activated. If you are building a new shop or garage, get yourself to the point where you have a service panel in the shop before starting this project.

Tools needed:
- Flathead screwdriver
- Carpenter's pencil or Sharpie-type marker
- Power screwdriver/drill
- Metal-clad cable cutter

Supplies needed:
- Lengths of flexible metal-clad cable (10/3, 8/3, or 6/3 as necessary) sufficient to span the distance you need
- Bag of red plastic anti-shorts that install between the wire and every break in the MC cable; a small bag with 8 to 10 anti-shorts is usually included with a spool of MC cable
- Junction and receptacle boxes
- Junction connectors and metal-clad cable supports
- Plugs, switches, and fixtures (as necessary)
- Roll of electrical tape
- Circuit breaker of appropriate amperage for your wires and designed for your panel
- Box of screws to attach components to the wall

Follow these steps:

1 Carefully plan and measure your circuit from the panel to its end. Note where to install any junction boxes or switches. Then use your pencil to mark the walls or ceiling where each component goes. Measure and note the distance between each fixture.

2 Determine the amperage of your circuit—this defines the gauge of cable you need according to your local code. In general, choose 10/3 for 30-amp circuits, 8/3 for 40-amp circuits, and 6/3 for 50-amp circuits.

3 Lightly tack each fixture in its desired position, and use your drill to make holes in the studs as needed to thread the cable from point to point. Run your lengths of cable now.

Metal Clad

Metal-clad cable is designed to be run on the surface of a wall. It can also be run through holes in studs or joists. Use a nail plate where the cable passes through studs if you run MC behind wall boards of any kind. ■

 Supporting Clamp

You must attach a supporting clamp within 2 feet of the circuit panel to support the metal-clad cable, and then attach clamps not farther apart than every 6 feet thereafter to the end of the run. If the cable passes through a stud or joist, that counts as a support. ■

This metal-clad cable is being run through holes in the ceiling joists. Passing through a joist or stud, or terminating in a junction box, counts as a cable support.

CHAPTER 3

4 Attach your fixtures firmly and attach the metal-clad cable into each box, using a plastic anti-short plug to make sure the cut edges of the MC cable do not abrade against the wire insulation and cause a short. Leave the outlet boxes open with the wires hanging out for inspection.

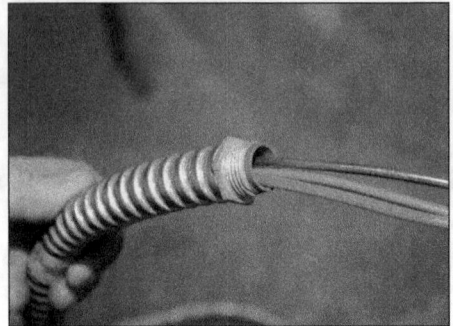

Always use a plastic anti-short wherever you cut metal-clad cable; the edges can be razor-sharp and cut right through your wire insulation.

5 After your work is inspected and approved, connect your appliance or plug. Always remember that black and red wires go to the positive (hot) terminals, the white wire is neutral, and the green wire goes to ground.

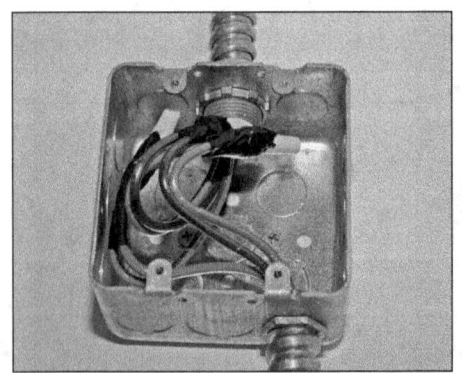

Metal-clad cables can use a variety of connectors at junction boxes. This 240-volt circuit required three wire connections: two hot and one ground. This box is covered for now, but a switch on this circuit could go here later.

6 Finally, install the covers on your fixtures and then go to the circuit panel. Make sure the power is turned off at the main breaker. Install the new 240-volt circuit breaker and label it on the panel. Attach the cable to the side or back of the panel with a metal-clad cable clamp, and strip the metal sheath off inside the panel. Route the wires to the circuit breaker and to the neutral and ground bus bars. Close the panel, reset the main breaker, and then turn on the breaker and test your new circuit.

CAUTION: Always stand to one side of the panel when turning on a breaker in case there is an unknown fault in the panel. If the breaker trips when you turn it on, you have a short somewhere in your work. Turn the whole panel off and disconnect the new circuit completely—hot, neutral, and ground—before you go looking for the problem.

Use the knockouts nearest the circuit breaker as the entry point into the breaker panel for the wires.

Most 240-volt breakers are double-wide, although there are single-wide breakers available now. The conventional double-wide breakers still cost less, so unless you need the panel space, there's little reason to spend the extra money.

ELECTRICITY AND LIGHTS

A budget T12 fixture like this one from a home supply store may cost as little as $10 and they are useful as occasional lighting over a workbench. Just grab the cord and plug it in when you need it.

I installed four of these Philips Day-Brite fixtures to the bottom of the trusses and they light up the whole shop very nicely. With reflectors and four T-8 instant-on bulbs in each fixture, they're nice and bright. You can hard-wire the fixtures, but for ease of maintenance I used plugs. Note that fixtures like these use a 15-amp twist-lock plug, and they run about $12 each at a home supply store.

Lighting Your Workshop

One of the most frustrating experiences is trying to work on a car, or any project, in the dark. You can't see the pieces you need to see, you can't find the tools and parts you need, and you can't see the things you should have seen, but missed. Lights are a critical feature in any well-appointed workspace.

There are many different options when it comes to lighting your shop. In general, new is better than old. For example, the new T8 and T5 fluorescent light fixtures are better than the old T12 lights. The number designators represent the diameter of the fluorescent tube in eighths of an inch. With this system, a T12 bulb has a 1½-inch diameter while a T8 is 1 inch and a T5 is 5/8 inch in diameter.

The thing to remember about fluorescents is that you do not want T12s. These old-style lights often require a magnetic ballast. T12 fluorescents hum and flicker, they don't work well in cold temps, and they use more power. The T8 variety uses an electronic ballast, uses less energy to produce the same light, and doesn't hum. T8 fixtures and bulbs cost a little more than T12s. T5 lights are the best of all, but they cost a lot more. T5 lights also use electronic ballast, and produce a lot more light while using less energy than a T12 or a T8.

All things considered, T8 is really the budget choice these days, as T12 is being phased out. You can still use T12 fixtures for on-demand lighting over your workbench areas, but for your main shop lights, choose T8s or T5s if you can afford them.

Incandescent Spots and Floods

Incandescent spotlights and floodlights are easy to install and the

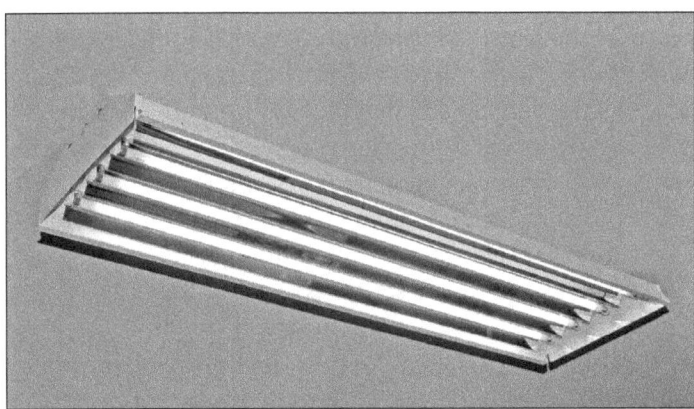

Choose a reflective multi-bulb fixture like this four-lamp unit. The T8 bulbs give more light than a T12 setup and use less power.

From the overhead-light junction box, simply run an extra set of wires to an incandescent floodlight. The ceramic bases for these bulbs are inexpensive and mount to a standard metal junction box.

HOW TO DESIGN, BUILD & EQUIP YOUR AUTOMOTIVE WORKSHOP ON A BUDGET

CHAPTER 3

Motion-sensitive outdoor floodlights save power and light up when you approach your workshop.

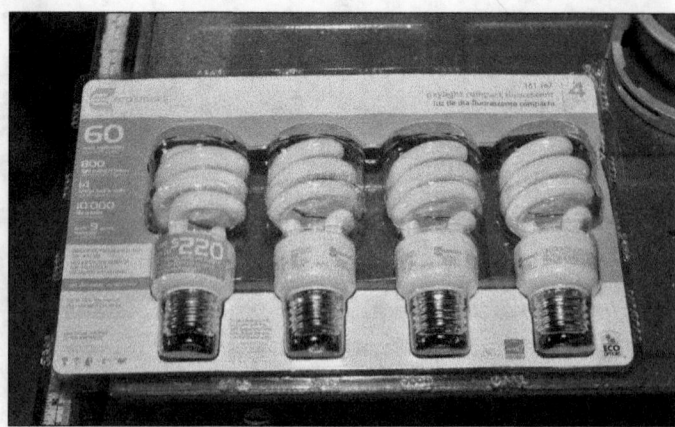

Instant-on compact fluorescent bulbs fit into traditional incandescent fixtures and use less power while delivering more light.

fixtures are inexpensive. They provide good light where you need it. If you have a particular workspace that needs light, you can focus a couple of spots on it from above and behind you for maximum effect. The downside of incandescent spots and floods is that they need to be replaced regularly and they use a lot of energy compared to other options.

Extra Lights

Sometimes the best solution for lighting a particular area is to locate an inexpensive light fixture in a low-tech way. For example, if you have a work area that you use occasionally, such as a soldering station or parts washer, you may find the most economical solution in terms of time and financial investment is simply to get a basic 48-inch T12-fluorescent shop light and hang it over the area—home supply store specials generally come with a 120-volt plug attached. Just hang the light and plug it into the wall socket when you need it—not everything has to be hard-wired and switched!

LED Lights

LED (light-emitting diode) is wonderful for shop lights. They run cool and the diodes last up to 25 times longer than an incandescent bulb. They also use about one-third the electricity of a comparable incandescent bulb

By now, just about everyone has an LED-based flashlight. You can buy them for a couple bucks at any hardware store, and the discount tool stores are literally giving them away with purchases. Many large trucks and other vehicles have gone to LED-based taillights and headlights—you can't miss an LED brake light! And the next obvious step as this technology comes down in price is to use LEDs. The higher-end tool suppliers are now selling LED droplights on reels—those could be well worth the price.

Nothing comes for free, and LED shop lights are likely to remain more expensive to buy than other fixtures. But once installed, you should be able to get years of bright, trouble-free service from LED fixtures. The list of LED applications gets longer every day.

Motion-Sensing Lights

If you work in your shop after dark, or occasionally come home to your garage in the dark, consider rigging up a motion-sensing light outside the drive-up or walk-through door. Having the light click on automatically as you approach and stay on for 5 or 10 minutes is economical and convenient. These fixtures cost about $20 at any home supply store and use a standard circuit for an external light fixture. You might have to experiment a bit to get the sensor aimed correctly, but after you set them, these fixtures generally last several years.

You can also find canister lights, at a used building materials store. These lights have a little cage and a glass jar to protect the bulb. They are great for outdoor lighting over a door and can be mated to a motion-sensor to save energy. For best economy, use a compact fluorescent bulb in the canister.

TECH TIP — More Lighting

You always need more lights than you think you're going to need. Lighting is one feature where going overboard is a good idea. ■

46   HOW TO DESIGN, BUILD & EQUIP YOUR AUTOMOTIVE WORKSHOP ON A BUDGET

ELECTRICITY AND LIGHTS

You can make a portable fluorescent work light like this one using just a few dollars worth of metal to make a stand and a cheap T12 fixture.

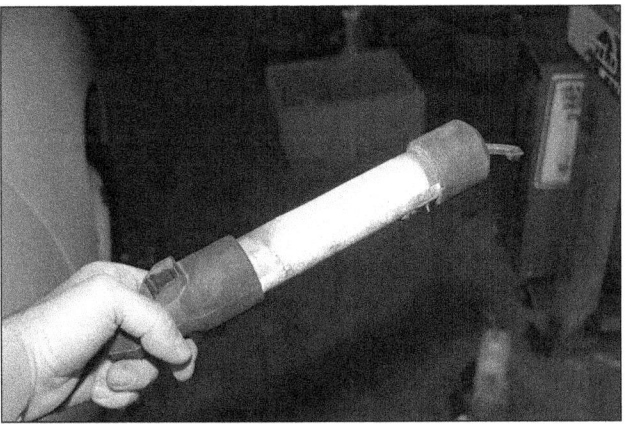

Forget traditional incandescent drop-lights—get a fluorescent drop-light mounted in a reel from the ceiling. This one has been in use for more than 15 years with the same bulb.

Portable Lights

No matter how well-lit your shop may be, you occasionally need some light in a specific place. Whether it's in an engine bay, under the workbench, or behind the brakes, you are going to need some portable lights sooner rather than later.

Mechanics' drop-lights have been around for decades, and usually require an incandescent bulb in a little cage with a handle and a 110-volt power cord. Some are made to run on 12 volts and they have handy battery clips. Incandescent drop-lights work well enough, but you need a rough-duty bulb and they get very hot.

A better and more robust solution is to look for a fluorescent drop-light—or to install a compact fluorescent bulb in a traditional drop-light. Any of these generate enough light for you to work, and they use less power and create less forearm-burning heat in the drop-light housing. The best drop-lights use cord reels, so you can install one or two hanging over your work bay in the shop and just reach up and grab a light as needed.

Another portable solution is the moveable rack of lights—like the Klieg lights used in movie studios. These have an adjustable stand that you can set up at a variety of heights and aim the lights as needed. These lights generally use 500-watt halogen bulbs, which are very bright and also create a lot of heat.

Obviously, as LED lights drop in price, they're going to be the preferred solution for portable shop lights in the future. They're available now, but the price is comparatively high for a high-quality LED drop-light.

>  **Portable**
>
> You can mount an inexpensive fluorescent light on a tripod and have a useful portable light fixture. ■

> **Light and Heat**
>
> A portable 500-watt halogen work light (such as the Northern Industrial brand) is small and costs less than $10. Not only do these portables generate a lot of light, they generate a lot of heat. If you need to warm up a small area, such as a fender to be fiberglassed or a joint to be sealed, just place one of these lights nearby and shine it on the spot and it quickly warms up to allow your adhesives to set. ■
>
>
>
> *These small halogen work lights cost less than $10 and also make effective small-space heaters.*

HOW TO DESIGN, BUILD & EQUIP YOUR AUTOMOTIVE WORKSHOP ON A BUDGET

Project: Install Fluorescent Lights

As a rule, you can never have too much light. This project installs a switched bank of Philips Day-Brite High Bay T8 overhead fluorescent lights in a shop, with provision for incandescent spotlights or floodlights focused on key locations. The Philips Day-Brite fixtures use four T8 bulbs in a 48-inch fixture with instant-on silent electronic ballasts. Because this shop needs to be extra-bright, six of the Philips fixtures will be installed.

For the purposes of this project, I assume that you have a main circuit panel or subpanel in your workshop or garage and that service is activated. If you are building a new shop or garage, wait until you have a service panel in the shop before starting this project.

Tools needed:
- Flathead screwdriver
- Carpenter's pencil or Sharpie-type marker
- Roll of twine or an electrician's fish tape tool
- Power screwdriver/drill
- Lineman's pliers

Supplies needed:
- Lengths of flexible metal-clad cable (14/2 or 12/2 as necessary) sufficient to span the distance you need.
- Bag of red plastic anti-shorts (usually included with MC cable)
- Junction connectors and metal-clad cable supports
- Junction boxes and switch boxes
- Light switches and light fixtures (as necessary)
- Box of wire nuts in the appropriate size
- Roll of electrical tape
- Circuit breaker of appropriate amperage for your wires and designed for your panel
- Box of screws to attach components to the walls and ceiling

Follow these steps:

1 Carefully plan and measure your circuit from the panel to the switch location and then to the light fixtures. Note where to install all junction boxes and switches. Then use your pencil to mark your walls or ceiling where each component goes. Measure and note the distance between each fixture.

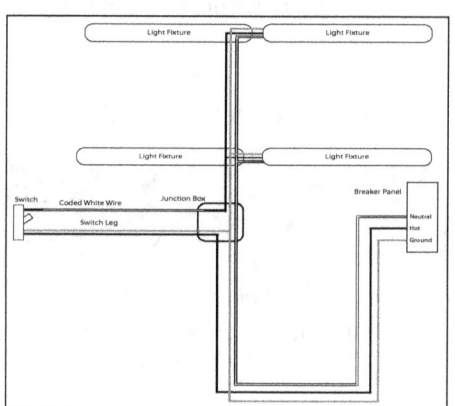

This drawing shows a basic circuit for several light fixtures. You can also run a circuit in which the hot wire from the breaker box goes straight to the switch before the junction box.

2 Determine the amperage of your circuit—this defines the gauge of cable you need to run according to your local code. Choose 14/2 for 15-amp circuits and 12/2 for 20-amp circuits.

3 Lightly tack each fixture in its desired position, and use your drill to make holes in the studs as needed to thread your cable from point to point. Run your lengths of cable now. Remember that you must attach a supporting clamp within 2 feet of the circuit panel to support the metal-clad cable, and then do the same not farther apart than every 6 feet thereafter to the end of the run.

4 Attach your fixtures firmly and attach the metal-clad cable into each box. Mount a junction box for the switched wiring in the rafters or on the ceiling and then join the cable wires using wire nuts, then run short lengths of cable to each light fixture.

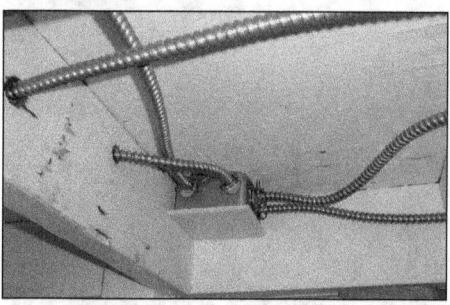

One switched line can serve many light fixtures if you split the line at a junction box.

5 Before the first bank of lights or outlet in the circuit, take a length of MC cable and run it from the junction box to the desired location for the light switch. This length of wire is called the switch leg. You "code" the white wire in the cable as black by wrapping it with black electrical tape for several inches in the switch box and in the junction box. Use wire nuts to connect the black wire in your switch leg cable to the black wire coming from the breaker and then connect the white wire in your switch extension cable to the black wire going to your light fixtures. Connect the ground wire to the circuit ground at the junction box and to the switch box. Finally,

ELECTRICITY AND LIGHTS

Code the wires at the junction box and at the switch box to use a standard piece of MC cable to wire a switch.

connect the black and white wires to the poles of a light switch.

6 Optionally, you can add incandescent spotlights or floodlights on the same switch by making more connections from your junction box. A combination of incandescent and fluorescent lights produces a nice working light with good color rendering.

7 Finally, install the covers on the switch box and junctions and then go to the circuit panel. Make sure the power is turned off at the main breaker. Install the new circuit breaker and label it on the panel. Attach the cable to the side or back of the panel with a metal-clad cable clamp, and strip off the metal sheath before inserting the wires into the panel. Route the wires to the circuit breaker and to the neutral and ground bus bars. Close the panel, reset the main breaker, turn on the breaker, and then test your new lights at each switch. Remember to stand to one side of the panel when turning on the breakers.

Garage Door Opener

If you have any kind of conventional garage door for your workshop, it's hard to go wrong with an automatic garage door opener. They cost just a couple-hundred dollars, run on a 120-volt circuit, and it's easy to find one with an external code box—you can walk up to your shop, punch in the code to raise the door. You can also buy a remote for each car you keep in the shop.

If you have more than one garage door, you might have to spend a bit more and get a couple of openers, but you can program a two-button control (or the "homelink" transmitter included in many modern cars) to open each door with a different button.

The opener requires a dedicated, always-on circuit for your garage door openers, but the good news is that it's the same as any other outlet circuit, except that you put the outlet on the ceiling or in the rafters.

About the only potential downside to these devices is that installing a garage door opener may require a "mechanical" permit and inspections. Check your local building codes and laws to be sure.

You can program an external code box for your workshop garage door; just enter the code to raise the door.

If you have a heavy steel roll-up door, you need a more expensive heavy-duty garage door opener. Standard garage doors can use the standard residential variety, but be sure to get enough remote activators to put one in every car.

HOW TO DESIGN, BUILD & EQUIP YOUR AUTOMOTIVE WORKSHOP ON A BUDGET

CHAPTER 4

WATER AND HEAT

After electricity and compressed air, the most useful service you can install in your garage or workshop is water. Heat is also nice for your comfort and protection of your cars if the weather in your area is severe. Water service requires some forethought and work, while heat is comparatively easy.

This chapter covers many of the things you can do with water service. This includes the plumbing options available to implement common water-based features such as a washbasin, toilet, or dishwasher. Many of these appliances also have an electrical component but, for this chapter, it is assumed that they are already wired, or can be plugged into a standard 120-volt outlet (covered in Chapter 3).

Installing Plumbing

In general, it's easier to get water into your shop or garage than it is to get it out again. If you have an attached garage of any size, it might already have water outlets and drains to the sewer system installed—for laundry or a washbasin, or just a hose spigot located somewhere inside.

The upside of making the effort to install plumbing is that you have access to useful facilities and equipment such as a dishwasher or professional parts washer, a hose to wash your car, and warm water to wash your hands. With a little planning, you can have a bathroom, which is a great feature in a detached shop.

Installing any kind of plumbing—either inbound or outbound—in your shop or garage generally requires a plumbing permit and inspections. Check your local building codes and laws. Plumbing is also a lot of hard work, especially if you're retrofitting plumbing to a building that doesn't already have water or sewer service.

Heat makes your shop comfortable in the winter, when you have the most time and inclination to work on car projects. It makes no sense to do that work in the cold!

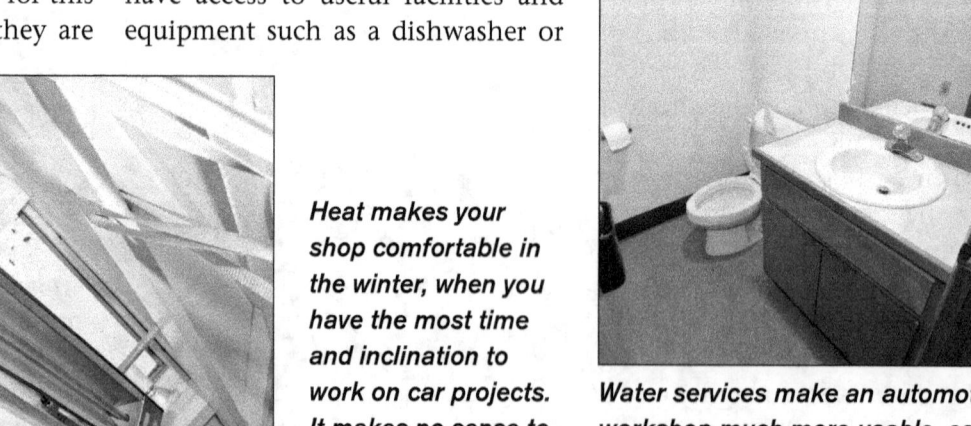

Water services make an automotive workshop much more usable, especially if it's more than a few steps to a usable bathroom.

WATER AND HEAT

Thinking Ahead

If you're building new construction, at least stub out fittings for water and sewer connections. That way the hard work (getting through the concrete slab) is done and you can fit up your plumbing at any time. ■

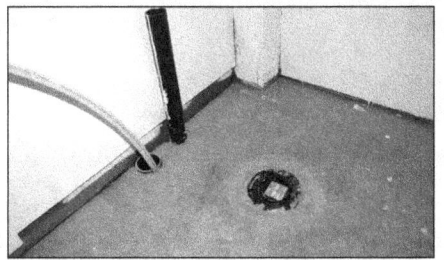

If you're having a new building put up for your workshop, put in stubs for water services even if you don't plan to use them right away. You'll be glad you did.

Fresh Water In

The first and most important step is to get fresh water into the shop. A simple spigot in the corner is far better than running a hose to the shop, but if you have the pipe into the shop to serve a hose spigot, it's a simple matter to place a master shutoff valve where the pipe comes in and then extend the plumbing to whatever services you desire.

Water generally comes into a shop or garage through 1/2-inch or 3/4-inch pipe. These use a standard thread

PEX or Pipe?

When you begin planning for plumbing, check to see what kind of plumbing already exists in your workspace. You can tie into that plumbing with a different material, or simply extend the existing style of pipe.

One newer option available is called PEX, or it is also known by the manufacturer's previous company name, Wirsbo. The company is now called Uponor.

PEX is a flexible cross-linked polyethylene pipe that is tough enough to resist some amount of freezing, though the hard plastic fittings used to connect lengths of PEX and mate to fixtures often cracks in a freeze.

The advantages of PEX are numerous. It's clean, because the material is crimped to fittings, which eliminates glues, solders, and threaded fittings from your project. Its flexibility also allows you to get your fittings right where you want them with ease. And the freeze-tolerance of the material is a big improvement over PVC or metal pipes.

The downside of PEX is that you need to invest in a crimping tool, at about $60. There are a couple different styles of crimp rings, and each of these requires a different tool. But after you buy the tools, PEX is an excellent low-cost alternative to traditional plumbing.

PEX flexible pipe reduces the amount of time it takes to install plumbing, plus it resists freezing better than PVC or metal pipes.

If there is a traditional iron pipe coming into your shop, you can put a simple fitting on it to convert to PEX for the interior plumbing. Just put the PEX fitting after the master shut-off valve.

CHAPTER 4

If you use galvanized or other threaded-metal pipe, be sure to get a supply of white Teflon-style tape to seal those joints.

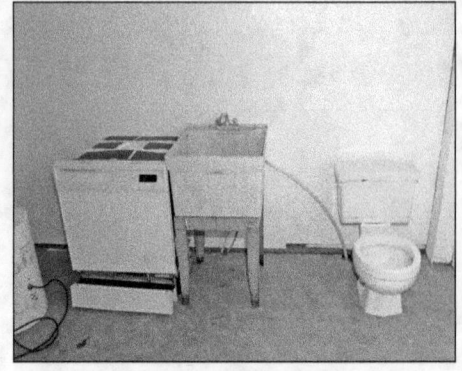

Placing all your water appliances in one part of the shop limits the distance you have to run plumbing and the potential damage area if you have a leak.

Insulation

Any hardware or home supply store sells insulation and warming cables for water lines. Insulation is generally a good idea, and warming cables are nice for winter nights and extremely cold weather. However, a basic 100-watt incandescent light bulb placed near your water pipes can effectively ward off freezing unless temperatures in your workshop drop deeply. ■

pitch called National Pipe Thread (NPT). These threads are tapered to create a good seal on plumbing when used with Teflon tape or other pipe joint sealant compounds.

When you buy pipe, you often see a bewildering array of acronyms used to describe the fittings. MPT (male pipe thread), FPT (female pipe thread), MIP (male iron pipe), and FIP (female iron pipe) are all the same as NPT. The same sizes of pipe fit together regardless of designation. The odd exception is British standard pipe (BSP). You are unlikely to come across BSP fittings at a North American home supply store, but if something's not fitting up right, that could be why.

The best plan when you're bringing fresh water into your shop is to keep all water-using appliances and services in one area. That limits the extent of your plumbing and makes finding leaks and problems much easier. For a working auto shop, you also want to run your plumbing on the surface of the interior wall if it won't disrupt things too much. In general, it will be warmer in the middle of the shop than closer to the outside wall, and you want to do everything pos-

sible to ensure that the water supply never freezes.

Inside your shop, it's a good idea to put a drain valve in the system right by the main shutoff. If you know it's going to get very cold, you can shut off the water to the shop and drain the system at this point and at the spigot outlets. Just be sure to turn off or unplug the water heater or it will cook itself dry. Also, be sure to drain the toilet tank and the toilet drain as much as possible so that it doesn't crack. The trap in your washbasin drain is another place where freezing temperatures can break a pipe.

When you put in water spigots, make sure that you can attach hoses to the spigots. You want to be able to

Cold Weather Checklist

It's a good idea to have a cold-weather checklist for your workshop that includes draining the pipes and turning on a warming light. Make sure your checklist also includes draining any water reservoirs in your cars! ■

direct the water. Also, if you plumb in a water heater, be sure to plan for a hot-water spigot—hot water used in combination with a pressure washer is the best thing for cleaning a greasy engine or underbody.

Drain Water Out

After getting water into your workshop, your next task is to get it out again. If you just want to have a hose spigot in the shop, or even hot and cold spigots, you can skip drainage as long as you're willing to squeegee or mop up spills. But if you want to have a washbasin or dishwasher-style parts washer, you must have a sewer connection.

If you have a single 1½- or 2-inch pipe connected to your house sewer

Drain Last

Install the drainpipe after you've assembled and located all your appliances. It's generally easier to figure out how high the drain should be and where it should go than it is to route your appliance drains to the pipe. ■

WATER AND HEAT

line, that's plenty. You can set up your washbasin to drain into that pipe, and you can buy a drainpipe for the washbasin that includes a fitting to drain the dishwasher. If you have a large commercial washer, it may require its own route to the drainpipe, but as long as everything points down to the drain, you can stack several appliances onto the single drain line.

Be aware that water in the drains can freeze as easily as water in the inlet lines. Drains are designed to be mostly empty when they're not carrying waste water away, so the traps are your main concern. These are designed to retain enough water to stop gases and fumes from escaping from the sewer into the air. You'll know why if you get a whiff of raw sewer air.

Most modern sewer drainpipe is made of PVC. It works well and is easy to install because it's a press-fit with glue (older iron pipe had to be carefully threaded together). PVC pipe is also inexpensive, and you should be able to plumb in several drains for about $20 worth of materials. The downside to PVC is that, because it's glued together, you generally have to cut it apart and replace it to make repairs or changes. But if you have thought through your plan carefully, this should not happen very often.

Environmental Concerns

As you use the washbasin, keep in mind that automotive workshops are full of hazardous chemicals that should never go down the drain into the environment. Sewer systems are built to handle a small amount of grease, dirt, etc., but not something like a gallon of motor oil or old gasoline, for instance, which may subject you to civil or even criminal liability. In additon to many environmental and ground water problems, putting chemicals down the drain can also result in dangerous sewer pipe explosions.

Make a rule that nothing but soap, water, and whatever was stuck to your hands go down the drain in your shop. If you use a dishwasher for cleaning parts, make sure they've been scrubbed as clean as possible to minimize the amount of crud going into the sewer. This also helps keep your dishwasher from getting clogged.

In addition to a drain to the sewer, there may be a central drain for water on the floor. These may be attached to the sewer or they may simply drain to the outside of the building. In either case, limit the amount and type of pollutants that end up going down these drains.

TECH TIP: Leave Yourself Sewer Access

Always leave at least one open end with a threaded plug in your sewer drain lines. This allows you to add a connection later, or it can provide a convenient place to insert a drain snake to clear a clog. ■

Always leave room for another connection when you create a PVC drain, so you don't have to cut your work to add something later.

Project: Install a Fresh Water Supply

This project takes a water line from a basic stub in the workshop to a finished distribution ready to supply several appliances. The procedure describes how to work with PEX pipe.

PEX uses two kinds of crimping clamps. One has a catch and the crimper simply closes the clamp until it grabs the catch. The other type is a copper crimp ring that is crushed

This style of PEX ring uses catches for tightening. It is easier to remove than a crushable crimp ring.

A copper crimp ring installs easily and quickly, and the PEX seals well.

HOW TO DESIGN, BUILD & EQUIP YOUR AUTOMOTIVE WORKSHOP ON A BUDGET

CHAPTER 4

onto the pipe and fitting. The crimping tool for these rings looks like a pair of bolt cutters—it simply crushes the ring in a set of round jaws. Professional plumbers prefer the catch type of ring because it's easier to remove later, but the tool is more expensive. (The examples in this procedure are shown with copper crimp rings.)

Cost: About $100 in PEX pipe and hardware

Time to complete: About 2 hours

Tools needed:
- Cable cutter
- PEX crimper
- Power driver
- Measuring tape

Supplies needed:
- Lengths of PEX pipe in 1/2-inch and 3/4-inch diameters
- PEX fittings and crimp rings as needed
- 1/2-inch and 3/4-inch conduit supports
- PEX bending support
- PEX water manifold
- 1½-inch construction screws

Follow these steps:

1. Locate the water inlet and make sure that water flow to the pipe has been turned off outside the workshop. If the pipe is plugged or capped, it is likely that there is water pressure behind the plug. After the water is shut off, thread a female NPT-to-PEX fitting onto the pipe. If you have a choice, choose a fitting that connects 3/4-inch PEX to a 3/4-inch water pipe. The PEX manifolds have 3/4-inch or 1/2-inch inlets, so match the manifold to the pipe you're using. If the pipe coming into your shop is already PEX, just start with that.

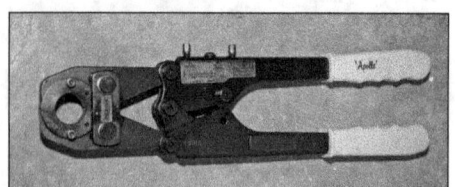

This style of PEX tool crushes the copper rings onto the PEX barbed fittings.

2. PEX pipe can be cut with any sharp knife, but the best tool for the job is a cable cutter. This is a large scissors-like device with round cutting jaws that are very sharp and heavy-duty. A cable cutter is designed to cut heavy electrical wires, but also works well on PEX because it makes a clean cut and does not deform the material. A basic cable cutter costs about $15 to $30.

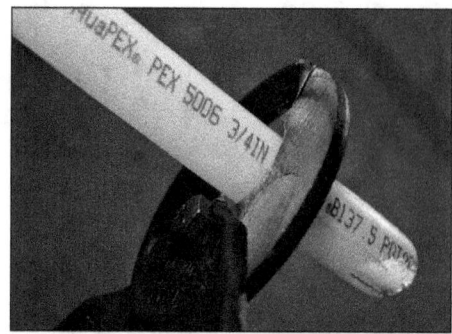

An electrical cable cutter works great to cut PEX tubing cleanly.

3. To affix a PEX fitting to a piece of PEX pipe, slide the copper crimp ring onto your PEX pipe, then press the PEX onto the barbed fitting, and align the crimp ring over the barbs. Open the jaws of the crimping tool and place it around the pipe at the ring—be sure to align the jaws to completely cover the copper ring. Close the jaws of the crimping tool all the way—you can feel the ring crush down. Then open the jaws and remove the tool.

 **Cable Cutter**

Buy a good cable cutter if you plan to work with braided steel hoses (such as Aeroquips from Eaton) in your automotive projects. Cutting braided steel sheathing without damage to the sheath is nearly impossible without this tool. ■

4. The crimping tool comes with a Go/NoGo gauge—this is a piece of metal with one or two U-shaped bites taken out of it. Some Go/NoGo gauges have a line inscribed halfway into the gap—the line should match the widest part of the crimped ring. If the gauge goes all the way onto the ring, it's crimped too far and you need to adjust your crimping tool. If it doesn't go on far enough, your ring is not crimped enough and you need to adjust your crimping tool. A different design of Go/NoGo gauge comes with two U-shaped gaps—one large and one small. The larger of the two is the Go side, and your crimp ring should fit snugly in the gap. If the NoGo side of the tool fits around the crimp ring, you need to adjust your crimping tool.

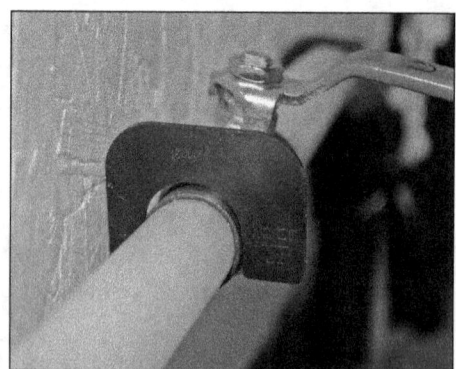

This Go/NoGo gauge is designed so that the marks on the gauge find the widest point of the crimp ring. This ring is crimped correctly.

WATER AND HEAT

5 As close as possible to the entry point to the shop, place a shutoff valve on the water line. If you prefer, you can place a shutoff valve at the pipe before the PEX connection, but the shutoff valve must come before you plumb in a manifold or any other fitting. If you live in an area where you know your workshop is subject to freezing temperatures, place a valve in line near the shutoff to allow you to drain the entire system in advance of cold weather.

If the initial run of PEX pipe is vertical, use a PEX bending bracket to force a bend to direct the PEX toward the area where you plan to have water appliances. PEX is flexible, but does not take and hold a bend. It quickly returns to a light curve if it is not held. The bending bracket makes a 90-degree bend over about 6 inches of length. Sharper 90-degree bends must be accomplished with hard plastic or brass PEX fittings, but these are more subject to damage from freezing than the PEX pipe, so it's best to minimize cuts in the pipe.

6 Support the PEX pipe to the wall with conduit supports every 2 to 4 feet. With enough supports, you can make the PEX go in a straight line, but it's okay to let it curve to its destination. When you arrive at the location to split off lines to your water appliances, fit the PEX to a four- or six-line manifold. Typically, the inlet is sized for 3/4-inch PEX, and the outlets are one 3/4-inch PEX and four or six 1/2-inch PEX. If you plan to use a water heater, plumb that appliance from the 3/4-inch outlet, and plumb washbasins, dishwashers, toilets, hose spigots, and other appliances from the 1/2-inch outlets.

7 From each of the 1/2-inch outlets, route a pipe to a selected appliance. Near each appliance, crimp on an appropriate PEX fitting to make the appliance connection. This is usually a valve with a PEX input and a compression fitting or 1/2-inch NPT outlet.

8 When your system is entirely assembled, turn on the water and check every joint for leaks. If you find a leak, cut off the PEX crimp ring and reattach the pipe with a new ring.

This copper manifold takes a 3/4-inch inlet line and splits it into four 1/2-inch outlets and another 3/4-inch outlet for the water heater. I plan to use those four outlets for a toilet, washbasin, dishwasher, and ice maker in a refrigerator.

Because PEX doesn't hold a bend, you need to use a bending bracket to make fairly sharp turns, or cut the PEX and use a 90-degree fitting.

PEX Fittings

The Shark Bite brand of PEX fitting uses push-on connectors that seal to PEX and are easily removed by hand. They don't cost much and the convenience is amazing. ■

Shark Bite fittings simply press onto the end of the PEX pipe and release by pulling on the plastic collar. What's amazing is that they don't cost much more than conventional fittings.

Project: Install a Wash Basin

Cost: About $50 for the faucet, pipes, and flex lines, plus the cost of the wash basin

Time to complete: About 2 hours

Tools needed:
- Crescent wrench
- Pliers
- Carpenter's pencil

Supplies needed:
- Wash basin and stand
- Faucet
- 1/2-inch faucet to 3/8-inch compression fitting flexible faucet lines
- Basin strainer
- Tailpiece (with dishwasher drain fitting, if needed)
- P-trap
- Plumber's putty or pipe joint compound

Follow these steps:

1. The easiest way to begin is to turn the basin over on your workbench or table. Install the strainer first, using a generous amount of plumber's putty or pipe joint compound to seal the drain. Use your crescent wrench to snug this fitting down, but don't pull too hard. Then install the tailpiece pipe to the bottom of the strainer. This piece can generally be put on by hand—again go snug, not too hard. If you chose to install a dishwasher, note the direction of the dishwasher fitting on the tailpiece and make sure it points toward the dishwasher.

You can see the strainer attached to the basin, and the tailpiece threaded onto the strainer. Because drain water is not under pressure, these just need to be a little more than finger tight to avoid leaks.

2. Install the faucet and tighten it into place, then attach the flex lines. Use a small crescent wrench to snug these lines. Make sure the flex lines reach to the valves. But if you cut it a bit short, PEX water lines are generally easier to move around than fixed pipe; or you can cut another length of PEX and redo the valve line.

Flexible faucet lines attach under the washbasin and to the Shark Bite valves on the end of the hot and cold PEX lines.

3. Install the P-trap to the tailpiece. This goes on by hand with compression fittings, so you have a little bit of leeway in where it points and its exact height. The P-trap generally comes in two pieces—a U-bend piece and a pipe designed to go horizontally to the drainpipe at the wall. The pipe going to the wall should extend past the back of the washbasin.

Gently push the washbasin to the wall and use a carpenter's pencil to mark where on the wall it hits. Also, note how far behind the washbasin the P-trap extends. When the drainpipe is installed, it sticks out from the wall a little bit, and you can trim the P-trap pipe so that everything is snug against the wall.

4. Route the drainpipe and attach it to the wall, then trim the P-trap pipe to fit. This is generally another compression fitting. If the drainpipe is already located, note that you can buy longer tailpieces, or cut the tailpiece to get the P-trap pipe to the right height for the drainpipe.

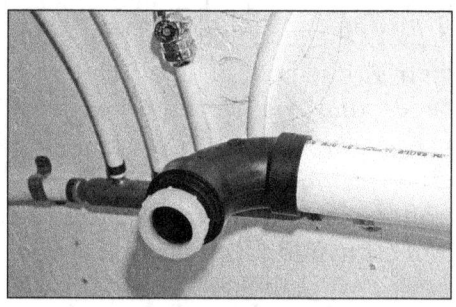

When you know how high the P-trap tailpiece stands, you can route the drainpipe to it. That's a simple compression coupling to fit the 1½-inch P-trap and tailpiece to the 2-inch drain pipe.

Plastic Fittings

Choose smooth plastic fittings for the drains. Metal fittings are subject to corrosion from water and soap. The accordion-style flexible drainpipes collect soap, grease, and grunge, and they clog more easily, so avoid them. ∎

WATER AND HEAT

5 Connect the faucet lines to the hot and cold water supply valves. If the valves include a collar and a little brass ring for copper pipes, you can discard those because the 3/8-inch compression fittings on the flex lines attach directly to the water supply valves.

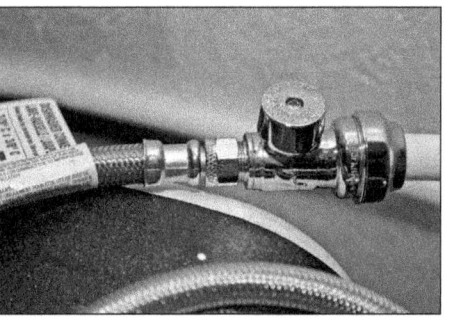

6 Finally, screw or otherwise attach the washbasin to the wall for stability.

The Shark Bite valves end in a 3/8-inch compression fitting, and the flex lines to the washbasin and the dishwasher are also 3/8-inch compression fittings.

Project: Install a Water Heater

If you're going to have water in your shop, you also want to have hot water. Nothing's worse than washing your hands with cold water in the winter; and hot water is great for cleaning greasy items. This project installs a basic 120-volt, apartment-size water heater.

Cost: About $30 in wood and hardware, plus the cost of the water heater

Time to build: About 1 hour

Tools needed:
- Circular saw
- Hammer and nails or power driver and screws
- Carpenter's level
- Measuring tape
- Crescent wrench

Supplies needed:
- Water heater flexible inlet and outlet pipes
- Dedicated 20-amp 120-volt circuit
- Water supply
- 2x6s and plywood, if you want to raise the water heater
- Plumber's tape to secure the heater to the wall

Follow these steps:

1 Decide where to locate the water heater. The location should be as close as possible to the point where you will use the hot water. Since the heater you're installing is not a full-size unit, you can often place it in the cabinet under the sink, but you should also consider placing the water heater under your workbench or overhead on a shelf. You don't need to touch the water heater in the general course of work, so put it out of the way.

2 If you choose to elevate the water heater, you can and should build an appropriately heavy-duty shelf out of 2x6 lumber and plywood, or some other appropriate lumber. Remember, when you lift the water heater into place, the weight of the unit itself does not include the weight of the water. (At 8 pounds per gallon, a 20-gallon water heater adds 160 pounds to its basic weight when it's in use.) Make sure the shelf is up to the task. Also use plumber's tape to secure the water heater to the wall in case of earthquake or accident. You don't need 200 pounds of scalding hot water falling on your head!

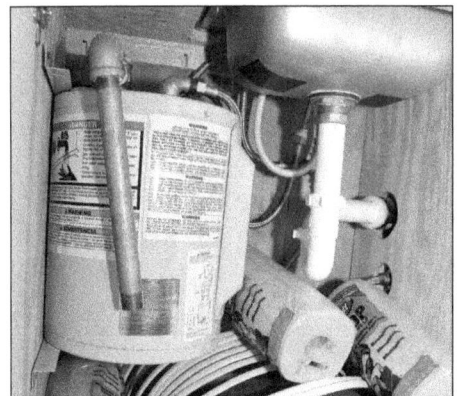

If you have a small water heater or the tankless variety, you can often place the heater under the same cabinet that houses the sink.

> **TECH TIP — Used Sinks**
>
> If you want to have a traditional bathroom sink or kitchen sink, check a used building materials store—they always have a selection of free-standing bathroom and kitchen sink pedestals. They don't cost much and they're far easier to install than building your own. ■

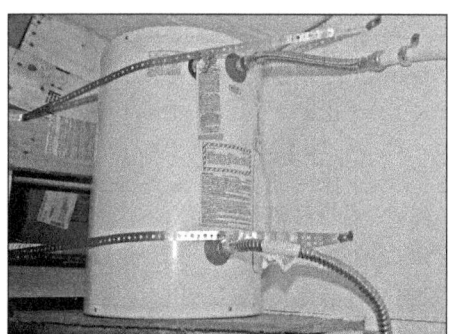

If you can't put your water heater under the sink, then put it out of the way—high on a shelf. Just be sure to strap it in place for safety.

3 Make sure you have a dedicated 20-amp circuit for the water heater—these appliances can draw a lot of power. Check the label on the heater to find out its amperage requirements. You can wire the water heater to a 120-volt outlet or hard-wire the circuit into the unit according to your preference. Any hardware store sells an appropriate cord that attaches to the heater's electrical connectors.

4 Bring the cold water line as close to the water heater as you can. A 3/4-inch pipe is best because it provides the most water to the appliance and the input pipe on the heater is usually 3/4-inch. For the last 18 inches or so, use a flexible water heater pipe. Some of these are made of shaped copper and others use a flexible braided steel sheath over a nylon pipe. All the fittings at the water heater end are NPT. Tighten the fittings to the water heater with a crescent wrench, and make the connection to the cold water line appropriate to the pipe you used on the hot water outlet, and mate the flex line to an appropriate pipe headed back to the washbasin.

5 The water heater has a pressure relief valve—this keeps the water heater from exploding due to excess pressure in the system. You should never plug this valve, but if you have problems with it dripping, you can attach a pipe to it to route the drips to the washbasin or other convenient place. You may also want to use a water heater pan if you expect drips.

Save Energy

If you're not going to use your shop every day, put a switch on the circuit for the water heater. An ordinary light switch works perfectly, and you can place that switch next to the light switches or next to the water heater. There's no sense in paying for energy to keep water hot if you're not there to use it. A water-heater blanket also helps keep the heat where you want it. ∎

Hot Spigot

You might consider putting a dedicated hot water spigot on the wall or at the basin. Get a spigot with hose thread so you can wash your car with hot water or use it to feed a pressure washer—great for greasy engines and undercarriages. ∎

Project: Install a Dishwasher

An old dishwasher can be found for very cheap or free on www.craigslist.org or you can often get a working unit from a friend. Ask around—people replace perfectly functional dishwashers all the time. If word gets around that you like old dishwashers, you'll probably have people dropping them on your front lawn. At worst, you'll have to pay $20 for a good one. Make sure that the drain line and the inlet line are included, but if they aren't or the parts are not suitable for use, new lines are not expensive.

Cost: About $40, including the dishwasher

Time to build: About 2 hours

Tools needed:
- Circular saw
- Hammer and nails or power driver and screws
- Measuring tape
- Crescent wrench

Supplies needed:
- 2x4 boards
- 1/2-inch plywood
- 16D nails or 3-inch heavy construction screws
- Dishwasher inlet kit
- Dishwasher drain kit

When you have a dishwasher, look at the parts you want to wash. If they are big, consider cutting out the plate stands from the lower basket. The upper baskets are usually removable, but keep them in case you need to wash a bunch of small parts. You can use any dishwasher detergent you like—there are rumors that some phosphate-free detergents discolor or damage aluminum parts, but reports are mixed. If that worries, you, don't use the dishwasher on any part you couldn't bear to see stained.

If you take the top rack out, you can fit some fairly large car parts in the dishwasher for cleaning.

WATER AND HEAT

Finally, use common sense with the dishwasher. If you have a part with 1/2 inch of gritty, yucky buildup on it, a trip through the dishwasher probably won't get it all off the part, but it will get enough of it off the part to clog the dishwasher drain. Scrape or brush the parts as much as possible and let the soap and boiling water dissolve the stuff you can't clean off by hand.

Follow these steps:

1 Dishwashers are made to be installed under cabinets. They're unfinished and ugly without something around them. Use lumber and plywood to build a simple cabinet around the dishwasher. Or go to a used building materials store and buy a piece of kitchen cabinet designed for a dishwasher—it serves as an additional storage shelf or a great little workstation for your bench-top parts washer.

You can build a little cabinet around the dishwasher for convenience. I'll paint this one white to match the walls before finishing this project. A used building materials store may also have a ready-made cabinet.

2 You don't need a dedicated circuit for the dishwasher, but you do need a functional 120-volt outlet, preferably on a 20-amp circuit. Make sure you have an appropriate electrical outlet for the dishwasher. Most have been hardwired into homes, but all should have connections to allow you to attach a pre-made plug cable, or you can use metal-clad cable and hardwire the dishwasher to the wires in the outlet box and omit the plug.

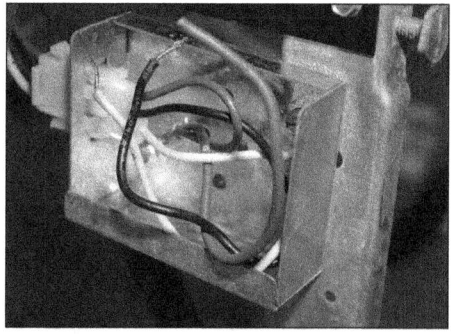

There's a little metal box on the underside of the dishwasher for you to attach a cord or hard-wired connection for electrical power.

3 The dishwasher inlet takes cold water—do not run a line from the hot water heater to the dishwasher, because the dishwasher's internal heating element is there to heat the wash water. The inlet is generally a 3/8-inch compression fitting, and copper pipes are the usual water source. But you can get flexible nylon pipe at any home supply or hardware store, and these are generally easier to install without leaks. Note the format of the inlet pipe and make the appropriate connection to the water source.

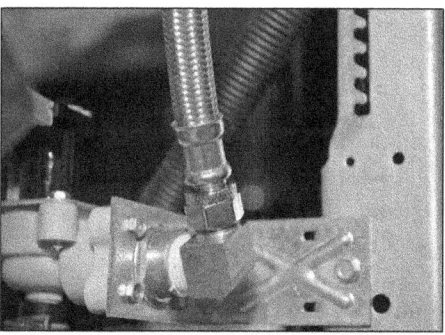

There's a little brass inlet with a 3/8-inch compression fitting for you to attach the water supply to the dishwasher.

4 The dishwasher outlet takes a flexible line with rubber ends. It's a press-fit on a barbed fitting under the dishwasher. You can run it over the side of the washbasin (with an appropriate attachment) into the tailpiece in the drain of the washbasin, or straight into the drainpipe (depending on how the plumbing is set up). If you run the drain into the tailpipe of the basin, you might need a hose clamp to get a good seal.

This white plastic fitting is the dishwasher drain outlet. Your dishwasher should come with a drain hose, but they're not expensive.

Dual Valve

You can get water to the dishwasher using the same cold-water valve that supplies the washbasin by using a dual-outlet valve—ask for one at your local hardware store.

CHAPTER 4

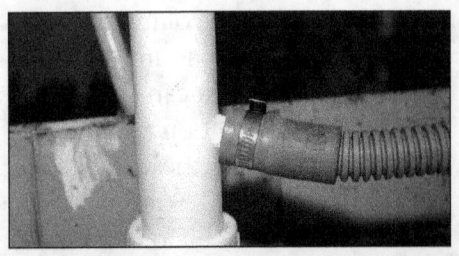

5 That's all there is to setting up a dishwasher—the connections are simple, although getting everything connected and working properly can take some creativity and work. But once it's set up, a dishwasher in your workshop should last a long time provided you don't put too much awful stuff through it.

The other end of the drain hose goes on the fitting at the washbasin tailpiece, or into the sewer drainpipe.

Keep Your Dishwasher Green and Legal

Water and detergent based parts cleaning is better than using solvents, because it generates less hazardous waste and delivers equal or better cleaning performance. It also eliminates a big fire hazard.

If you choose to use a kitchen dishwasher as a parts washer, be sure that the outflow from the dishwasher doesn't cause an environmental problem. Rules vary based on location and the nature of the sewer system, so you should call your utility company or your local city hall.

Although most water and detergent based solutions are nonflammable and nontoxic, they can qualify as hazardous waste after you use them because they may then contain toxic metals from the parts and grunge cleaned off them in the parts washer.

You can buy parts washer filters from parts washer supply companies. These remove the particulate matter and sometimes the oil from the outflow. You can dispose of the used filter elements as you would a used oil filter.

Each time you run the dishwasher, it uses between 4 and 6 gallons of water. The best thing you can do is run the dishwasher discharge into a 55-gallon drum and dispose of the wastewater when the drum is full. Waste haulers can haul the dirty water away, or your area may have a drop-off location. Sometimes, filtered wastewater can go down the sewer, but check with your local sewer utility before you put anything down the drain. Never put wastewater from the washer into a septic or storm drain system.

Heating Your Workshop

If you live in the 80 percent of the world where there is some cold winter weather, you will want some form of heat in your workshop or garage. Working in a freezing cold garage is very unpleasant and generally yields poor results. Not only are you uncomfortable, but many products like paint, glue, fiberglass, and silicone gel do not set up and dry properly in a cold or damp environment. If the temperature inside the shop drops much below 25 degrees Fahrenheit (-4 degrees Centigrade) you also risk damage to your cars, because the water in the engine, radiator, and other reservoirs may freeze.

Garage and shop heaters come in four basic types: natural gas, electric, propane, and kerosene. Electric heaters are the least effective at warming, but are also the easiest to install. Natural gas heaters are usually the least expensive to operate. Propane works well, but costs more than gas, and you have to refill the tanks from time to time. Kerosene also works well, but is less convenient and smellier to deal with than propane or natural gas. And, of course, there is also the woodstove option.

A good scenario for working in a garage attached to your home is to use natural gas. Just make sure there's a vent in the warm-air plenum and you're done. Or, see if you

An industrial natural gas heater is the best, most efficient solution for shop heat, but they're expensive to install, and you must have gas service to use one.

can run a duct from the furnace in the house to the garage. Many modern homes have heat already ducted to the garage, especially in places with severe winter weather.

Fan-forced electric wall heaters are commonly available in the $100 to $300 range, and these put out about 15,000 to 20,000 BTUs on 20 to 30 amps of 240-volt electricity. That's sufficient to take the chill off in a two-car garage, but not much more than that. There are also smaller 120-volt heaters, but these are not suitable for even single-car garage spaces—you'd be better off with an indoor space heater from the hardware store. If you do choose to install a 240-volt heater, be extra careful about distance to combustibles—including fuel fumes. Make sure you install ventilation as well as heat.

Another easy option is to use propane in portable bottles. Depending on the size of your shop and the kind of weather you have, you can get by with a 5-gallon bottle and a 15,000-BTU tank-top radiant propane burner. These are often available at outdoor supply stores. The downside of any exposed-flame heater is that it uses oxygen in the workspace and it has an open flame. Again, ventilation must go with this kind of heat.

For larger shops or colder weather, consider a convection heater with 30,000 to 200,000 BTUs. You also need a larger propane bottle (20 gallons or so) to use one of these conveniently, but they effectively heat a 1,500-square-foot workshop in minutes. This is the most cost-effective option for heating large spaces, but you still have an open flame.

For maximum heat, you can get a forced-air propane or kerosene heater. These look and sound like jet engines, and they really kick out the heat—up to 400,000 BTUs—but they use fuel more quickly than convection heaters and have an open flame.

If you are planning to use a natural gas or propane heater, the installation tasks are difficult enough to make hiring a professional a really good idea. The upside of a natural gas or propane heater is that they are efficient and produce very good heat. But the downside is that leaks or failures can be catastrophic. It is critical that all pipes and junctions be completely sealed, or you will have a gas leak. A professional gas plumber is a good investment in this case. If you end up running the control circuit for the thermostat, the electrical control lines to a gas furnace are usually 15 amps at 120 volts, using 14-gauge wire or 14/2 Romex.

If you have time to let the shop warm up every time you head out to

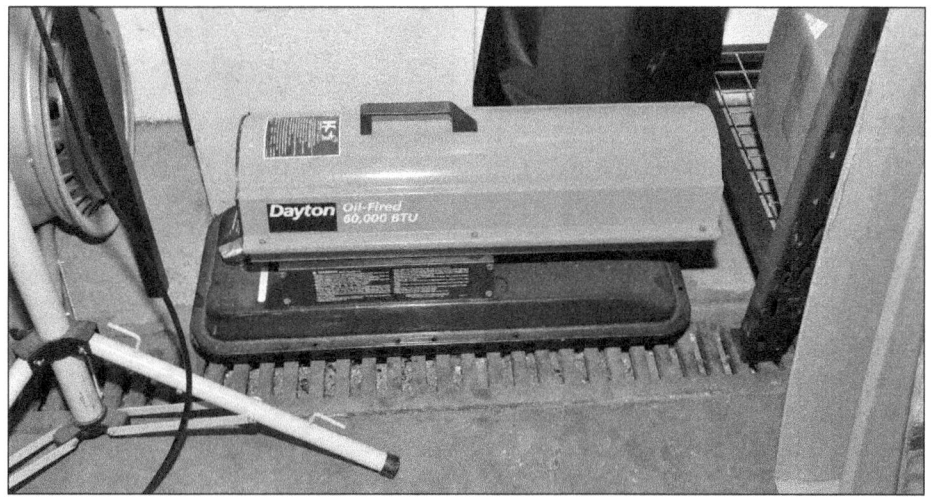

These kerosene-fired blast heaters work really well to heat a space, but you do run the risk of open flames and liquid fuel near your cars.

A 120-volt electric wall heater is easy to install, but not energy-efficient and not powerful enough to heat a large space. However, with its auto-thermostat, it can keep your pipes from freezing.

A propane heater like this one can heat a big shop, and be stored when it's not in use, but you risk having an open flame in your workshop.

CHAPTER 4

> ### Burn Clean Wood
>
> Don't ever burn "dirty" wood in a woodstove. This primarily means wood that has been painted or treated with creosote. Creosote is that sticky, smelly, black goo that's put on telephone poles to keep insects and water out of the wood. Creosote builds up in the chimney and eventually catches fire, and can burn down your shop. ■

> ## Insulation is Your Friend
>
> One thing you should definitely install in your shop is insulation. Ordinary household, paper-backed pink fiberglass insulation is all you need, but you should try to get the most R-value you can reasonably get into the walls and roof. Insulation helps keep the shop cool in the summer and warm in the winter, cuts down on the heating bills, and helps protect your cars against temperature extremes.

Even a basic fan helps ventilate a workshop, and if you use an open-and-close vent with the fan, you don't lose too much heat in winter.

This vent is way up high—great for venting hot air in summer, but it also vents the heat from this shop in winter.

work, you might prefer a woodstove. Many shops are heated with wood, and it works very nicely, but it takes a long time (more than an hour in most cases) to get a fire going and warm up the space. You also need a ready supply of dry wood. So depending on your situation, a woodstove might make the best economic sense. One note of caution: Woodstoves cannot be shut off when you leave for the night, so you need to be extra sure they are installed safely according to building and fire codes and that they are working correctly.

You can usually plan on needing a "mechanical" permit and inspections if you are installing any kind of permanent heater in your shop or garage, whether it's gas, electric, propane, or a woodstove. Check your local building codes and laws to be sure.

Providing Ventilation

Ventilation is critical in any workshop or garage where you work on cars. You are likely to generate exhaust gases, paint fumes, raw gasoline fumes, fiberglass fumes, and solvent fumes at various times, and you don't want to breathe any of them. An active ventilation system can be as simple as a vent with an electric fan on a switch, or simply one box fan set up to pull fresh air from a window and another to send air out the opposite side of the shop.

Installing any kind of ventilation system generally requires a "mechanical" permit and inspections. Check your local building codes and laws to be sure.

If you need to clear fumes, install a basic weather-resistant ventilation fan. This setup includes an electric fan on a switch and a vent that keeps rain and snow out of the shop. Mount the vent and fan up high where they can vent hot air in summer and rising fumes at any time.

A wall-mounted exhaust fan with a shuttered box works well because the blast from the fan opens the shutters when it's in use, but the shutters fall closed when the fan is

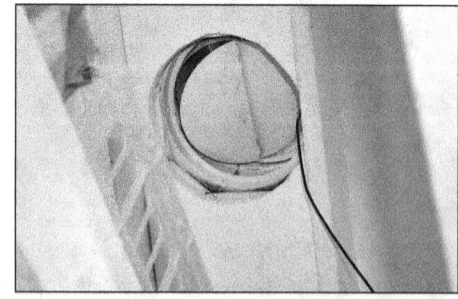

This is a pipe to a conventional roof vent, but equipped with a flue valve so it can be closed off in winter to retain heat.

A Low-Cost Air Circulation System

If you install it right, you can use a box fan in the rafters to circulate heat in the winter and provide a cooling breeze in the summer. Simply mount the box fan at an angle to direct air from the ceiling area (where heat rises) downward to the working area, and plug the fan into a switched outlet. Especially in a high-ceilinged shop, you don't want to spend a fortune to warm the rafters in the wintertime while you freeze on the floor. In the summer, circulating the air in the shop helps keep it cool. Just be aware that this system is only circulating the air that's already inside the shop—it doesn't help you if that air is full of carbon monoxide.

If you have high ceilings, that's where your warm air goes. Just rig up a box fan in the rafters to blow that warm air back down where you're working.

turned off. You can get a small version of these fans for less than $200 and they range in size from about 12 to 40 inches square. They use very little electricity and can be installed on a 15-amp 120-volt circuit. The larger fans may run on a 20-amp 240-volt circuit and cost up to about $750.

Choose where to install the ventilator, measure the circuit from the panel to its end, and then use the standard circuit procedure to run the wiring. It's best to put ventilation fans close to the source of fumes or dust, or up high to vent hot air and pull cooler air into the shop.

Pay close attention to the amperage requirement of the ventilator fan—this defines the gauge of wire you need to run according to your local code. Most 120-volt ventilator fans can be wired on a 15-amp circuit with 14/2 Romex wire.

Some vent fans have a simple on/off switch, while others use more elaborate control mechanisms. If your fan requires a special speed controller, wire it into a box at a convenient height and location, usually near the light switches.

This powerful and elaborate ventilation system is appropriate for a full-time paint booth. Filters go in the framework, and the fan discharges all the fumes created by constant painting.

CHAPTER 5

COMPRESSED AIR AND WELDING

In the previous few chapters I talked about the basics—getting walls, electricity, light, water, and heat into your work area. For many people, that's all they need. But here are some additional projects that you may find useful if you spend a lot of time in your workshop or you want to undertake more ambitious projects.

Installing Compressed Air

After lights, compressed air is probably the most frequently installed service in an automotive workshop. Air tools make many of the tasks far easier—especially if you're involved in any kind of restoration that requires taking apart assemblies that may not have been apart in decades. Compressed air allows you to mount and fill tires, remove or install nuts and bolts in a flash, run a nibbler or a shear, blow dust and crud out of any assembly, operate a paint spray gun, operate an abrasive blaster to clean parts, and use a plasma cutter, among many other uses.

Most hobbyists buy a compressor that can fit under the workbench. These are affordable, they work great for light duty, and they plug into a standard 120-volt outlet. That's fine as far as it goes, but these can't do much more than run an impact wrench or a spray gun on a light-duty cycle. Powering a blast cabinet or a tire mounting machine is absolutely out of the question. There is a little more expense and work involved in buying and installing a larger compressor, but if you plan (or hope) to use more intensive tools, you won't look at the big compressor and wish you'd bought something less powerful.

Air compressors come in all shapes and sizes. Be sure to get a powerful enough one to meet your needs. There are a few design considerations to help you choose.

64   HOW TO DESIGN, BUILD & EQUIP YOUR AUTOMOTIVE WORKSHOP ON A BUDGET

COMPRESSED AIR AND WELDING

How Much Compressor Do You Need?

The first step is to figure out how big a compressor you really need. To figure out the size and power of the compressor to buy, you need to look at CFM (cubic feet per minute) and maximum pressure in PSI (pounds per square inch). This figure is usually printed on the compressor and should be included in the machine's advertising and literature. You also need to look at the tools you want to run and think about how much you plan to use them.

When you go compressor shopping, you notice right away that compressors are more often rated and sold based on their horsepower, and you need to know that this is a misleading statistic. Also remember that the CFM ratings placed on a compressor by the manufacturer are generally optimistic. And that rating is the amount of air that the compressor sucks into the intake to be compressed, not the amount of air that comes out of the hose.

The other thing to realize is that the air usage requirement printed for most tools assumes a very light duty cycle—which is to say, perhaps using air 10 to 15 percent of the time. So if the compressor's manufacturer is overstating its ability to produce compressed air, and the tool-manufacturer's ratings are understating the amount of air they actually need for intensive use, you need some overkill on the compressor.

You should buy a compressor for your maximum needs. A free-standing abrasive cabinet designed for home shop use can require as much as 10 to 15 cfm at 80 or 90 psi. That calls for a 240-volt, belt-driven, 3.5- to 5-hp, 60-gallon, vertical-tank compressor, which you can get for about $400 at any big-box home supply store. However, if you're just planning to run a 1/2-inch impact wrench from time to time and use an air nozzle to blow out dust, and maybe air up a few tires from time to time, you can be perfectly happy with a 120-volt 4-gallon "hot dog"–style unit that produces 3 cfm, located under your workbench.

The bottom line is: For any kind of serious automotive work with air tools, and absolutely if you're running an abrasive blast cabinet or other free-standing tool, you need a 240-volt compressor pumping more than 10 cfm with a tank of at least 60 gallons.

Choosing a Compressor

There is a bewildering variety of compressors on the market, but it's easy to choose a good one. The first big difference is between direct-drive and belt-driven compressors. The names are completely descriptive: In a direct-drive unit, the electric motor directly drives the pistons of the compression pump. In a belt-driven unit, the motor drives a wheel that holds a flexible belt driving another wheel attached to the compressor pump.

This may seem like a small difference, but when you look at the assemblies, the belt-driven compressor pumps tend to be made of heavy cast iron, and they are substantially larger than the direct-drive units. When they're running, the direct-drive units are far noisier than a belt-driven unit because of the lighter weight and smaller size of the compressor pump. Plus, the direct-drive units turn the compressor pump at the electric motor's speed, while the belt-driven units can use different-size wheels to reduce the drive ratio and get some mechanical advantage (like using a lower gear in your car) to make life easier on the electric motor.

If you just need to air up tires occasionally and maybe run a small paint gun, a little compressor under your workbench could be just what you need.

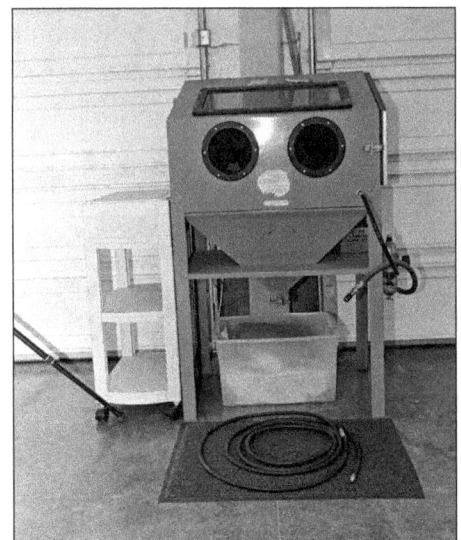

If you have to run a major air tool like this abrasive blast cabinet or a bunch of air tools, you'll likely want a larger compressor.

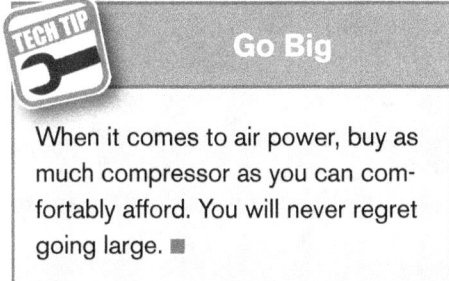

Go Big

When it comes to air power, buy as much compressor as you can comfortably afford. You will never regret going large. ■

HOW TO DESIGN, BUILD & EQUIP YOUR AUTOMOTIVE WORKSHOP ON A BUDGET

Most good belt-driven compressors big enough to be useful are the vertical-tank variety with 60- or 80-gallon tanks. But there are good belt-driven compressors in 240 or 120 volts with horizontally-mounted tanks of 20 to 40 gallons.

Direct-drive units are usually advertised as being oil-free—which is to say, you don't ever have to add or check the oil level in the compressor pump. That seems like a good feature, but direct-drive units do not actually last as long or work as well as a belt-driven unit. Look for a belt drive, and then check the size and construction of the compressor pump. You want to see big, heavy, cast-iron cylinders and a notation that the pump sleeves are also made of cast iron. Also, on the day when the electric motor fails, you can easily replace a belt-driven-unit motor, but that's not necessarily the case with a direct-drive motor.

Among high-end industrial compressors, you also have the option of buying a multi-stage machine or a compressor that uses a mechanism other than pistons to compress the air. The difference between a single- and multi-stage compressor is fairly simple: A single-stage compressor sucks in room air and compresses it into the tank in one step. A multi-stage compressor compresses the air once its in a bank of pistons, and then transfers the air to another set of pistons that further compresses it and stores it in the tank.

The advantage of a multi-stage system is that the tank pressure rises much faster to a higher level than a single-stage compressor. But the tradeoff is that a multi-stage compressor is far more expensive—about five times as expensive. Unless you're in a commercial/industrial environment, you don't need a multi-stage compressor or an exotic compression mechanism.

Location of Compressor

The appeal of a small compressor is that it doesn't use up much valuable working space, but even if you have a big compressor, you don't have to let it dominate the space. Compressors are noisy; so they are often placed outside the shop in a protected shed, or in a well-insulated closet inside the garage or shop. As long as the compressor's heat can't build up around it, an isolated space is great for a compressor.

All things considered, the best place for a compressor is outside. But a compressor is an expensive piece of hardware, so you do need to protect it from the elements. A simple shed nicely does the trick. Plumb the air lines through the wall into the shop and leave the compressor on, or put it on a switch located right by the door. That way you can fire up the air at the same time you turn the lights on.

One word of caution about putting your compressor outside—you might annoy the neighbors if it's a noisy unit and you use it a lot, especially if you like to work late into the night or if you leave it turned on and it roars to life at 3 am. So if the garage or shop is near the neighbors and you want to put the compressor out back, be sure to build that shed with some fiberglass insulation to keep the noise down.

This is a good compressor for an automotive hobbyist. It costs about $400 at a home supply store. It's a belt-driven unit at 3.5 hp and 10 cfm. The tank is 60 gallons and the cylinder is heavy cast iron.

Notice how the electric motor is connected directly to the compressor engine? That's a quick way to recognize a direct-drive unit. This one has a good cast-iron compressor engine, but that direct-drive motor is noisy.

If you can lift it without killing yourself, putting your compressor out of the way vertically is one way to open up space. It would be even better if it were in a shed outside.

COMPRESSED AIR AND WELDING

Hard-Line Air Plumbing

The best way to use a large vertical-tank compressor is to plumb air lines throughout your shop. You can't easily move the compressor, and it's probably hard-wired rather than using a plug, so you might as well run pipe to the places you want to use the air.

The advantages of hard-plumbing the air system is that you can easily attach multiple tools where you want to use them, and you can use inexpensive flexible air lines for the short runs. You can permanently plumb in larger fixtures like abrasive blast cabinets and tire mounting machines with shutoff valves. Also you can easily plumb water drains and oilers into the lines. There is really no downside to hard-plumbing the air system except for the expense and time required to do the work—and that's not a big problem.

For a budget installation you can use 3/4-inch Schedule 40 PVC pipe and glue to create an air system. Don't use PVC pipe rated lower than Schedule 40. You really don't want the pipe to crack or blow up when it's under pressure. Schedule 40 PVC is rated for 289 psi in 3/4-inch pipe and 270 psi in 1-inch pipe. Schedule 80 PVC is rated much higher—413 psi in 3/4-inch pipe. Most compressors, even cranked up as high as their safety relief valves allow, won't get past 150 psi. Still, the PSI ratings of PVC pipe are tested on new pipe, and like all plastics, PVC becomes brittle over time and loses its ability to hold pressure. You should be able to outfit your shop with Schedule 40 PVC for less than $100.

Heavy-duty and long-term air system installations are often done with galvanized or black steel pipe. This works well because it can be threaded and unthreaded if you want to extend or reduce the system. But the water in the compressed air rusts the pipes over time, and you can't bend iron pipe, so you're limited to the bends you can put into the system with pipe fittings. Iron pipe is also more expensive than PVC and heavier, so it's more difficult to hang on the wall. Copper pipe rated for pressure is also used, and this is great stuff. But it's expensive and it must be soldered together.

Newer materials like Rapid-Air nylon tubing, AirNet pipe, and Duratec pipe are the way of the future, but they cost a little more

A clean PVC-pipe air system on the surface of your walls can be functional and look good at the same time.

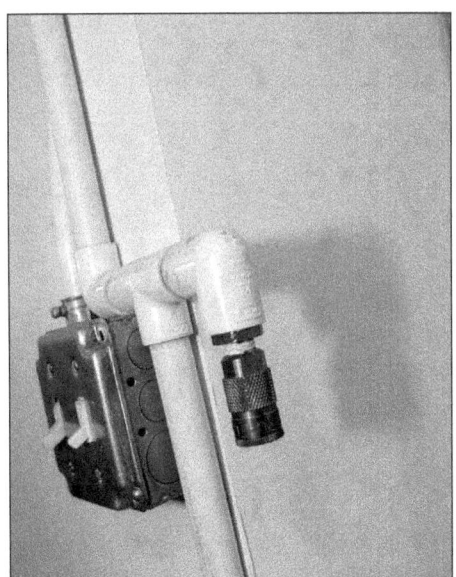

Hard-line plumbing for air lines is nice because you can put air connections all over your shop and use shorter air lines.

Galvanized pipe holds pressure really well and doesn't often leak. Getting everything to the right length is often difficult, and eventually it rusts.

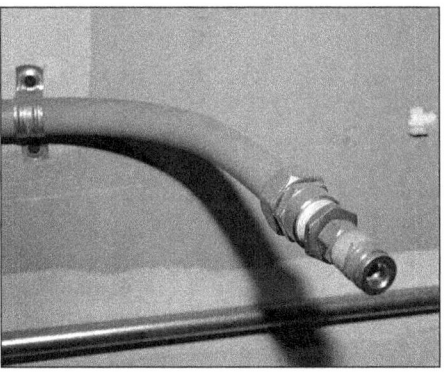

Duratec pipe is amazing stuff for air lines, but you pay quite a lot for it. Still, if you save your money, it's not a lot more expensive than a decent compressor.

CHAPTER 5

than the old-school solutions. Air-Net pipe is powder-coated aluminum, and it's not designed to be bent. It can cost $400 or more to outfit a shop. Fittings are push-on with hand-tightened compression nuts. RapidAir tubing is made of nylon, so it bends easily and the system uses push-on fittings. You can outfit your shop with RapidAir for about $300 or less.

Duratec is amazing stuff, with an aluminum tube coated inside and out with high-density polyethylene (HDPE). You can bend it by hand and it won't crimp, and it uses removable fittings. Duratec is so good that it's even approved for use in medical facilities. It costs about $600 or more to install Duratec in your shop, but you will love it.

When you plan your air system, think about stations where you want to use air, and plan for a quick-disconnect fitting at each station. Don't forget to put a few overhead where you'll be working on cars. It's great to just reach up, grab an air hose, and plug in a wrench.

The rules for plumbing an air system are simple:

- Make sure there is a low point to the system with a valve opening at the low end to collect condensation and drain the resulting water. Put a slight tilt on every long-running tube, angled down toward the drain. Water collectors and filters in the lines are a good idea.
- Put an oiler in the line ahead of outlets where you plan to use air tools such as impact wrenches, shears, and drills. These tools need to be oiled regularly because of the water vapor in the compressed air.
- Use the same style of quick-release connectors throughout your shop. This is not a safety issue, just convenience.

Soft-Line Air Plumbing

The easiest and cheapest air plumbing you can have is to simply attach the air hose to the compressor and coil it neatly when it's not in use. Just make sure that the hose reaches anywhere you want to work, including out the door of the shop into the parking area.

For an upgrade to the coil of hose on the floor, consider a hose reel. Even shops with a full hard-line air plumbing system often keep a hose reel connected. This is simply 50 or 100 feet of quality air hose wound on a big spool. There's a connection at the center to allow the reel to spin

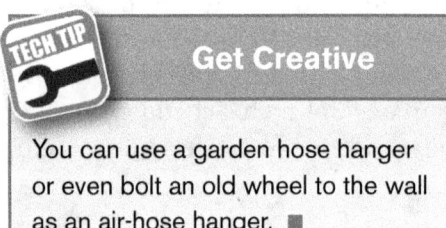

Tech Tip: Get Creative

You can use a garden hose hanger or even bolt an old wheel to the wall as an air-hose hanger. ■

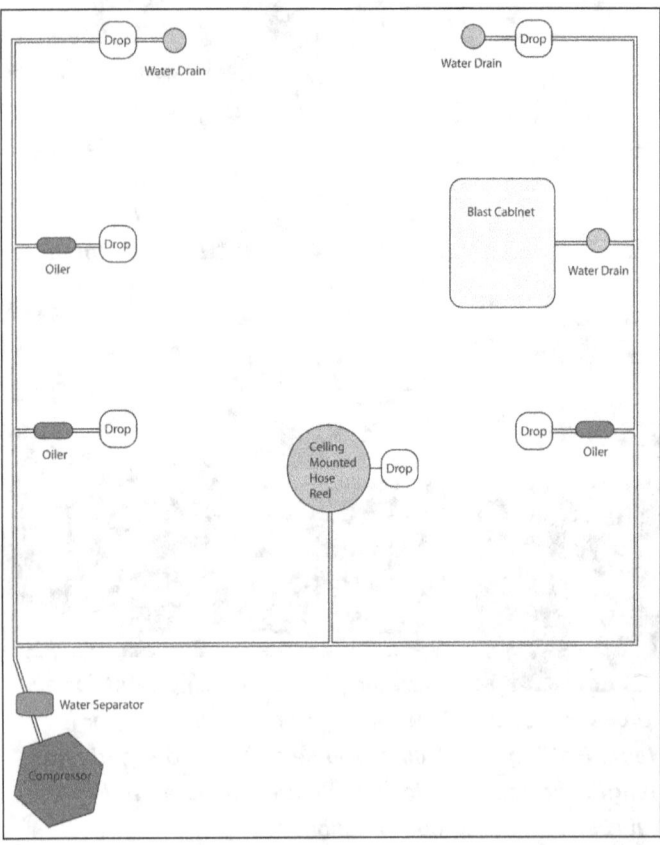

Plan out your air system in advance so you know how much pipe and what supply of fittings you are likely to need.

A hose reel costs less than $100 and makes storing your air hose a snap.

and then a length of hose to connect the reel to the compressor or air system. When you need the hose, just grab it and pull. Then crank it back onto the reel when you're done. Most hobbyists use hose reels for years and many never get around to all that complicated plumbing work.

One expense that's worth the money is for high-quality air hoses. Buy the best air hose you can get and it will last you for years or even decades. You can run over it with a car or brush it across hot metal and it will take the abuse. Avoid the coiled plastic air lines that are sold in bargain stores. That material is easily cut, burned, crimped, and crushed, and the end fittings often come loose. The exception is that you might want to have one or two cheap plastic hoses to use for jobs where you know you might damage the air hose.

Quick-Release Connectors

A decision that everyone faces is what style of quick-release air connectors to use. Once you choose a style, you're locked into that style unless you replace all the connectors, so it pays to choose wisely. There's really only one good choice—use the standard "industrial interchange" style because it's the most commonly used. If you buy or borrow an air tool and it has a quick-release plug on it, it is likely to be an Industrial style. You'll find the same thing if you plug the tool into an air source.

This is a little bit counter-intuitive, because there are also two "automotive" styles of plug. The Tru-Flate or Type G style is often used in professional auto shops, and there's certainly no harm in choosing this style if you're starting from scratch. There's also the ARO (developed by ARO Manufacturing Company) style, which looks very similar to the Industrial style, but doesn't lock into the female end of an industrial coupling. There are also a bunch of other styles, used mainly for hydraulic or other purposes.

Even within the industrial style, there are substantial differences between fittings made by different manufacturers, and they won't always work well together. The failure modes range from a little extra air leaking to random popping apart of the connection. If you're a beginner with compressed air, it's best to buy a lot of couplers and a big lot of plugs from the same manufacturer all at once, and then use those as long as possible.

There are a number of "universal" female-end couplers now on the market, and these accept industrial, ARO, and automotive Type G plugs. Apart from a tendency to leak a little more air than usual, there's no reason to not buy these couplers and use them with whatever plugs you may have.

Air Plug Types

The industrial interchange plug goes by a lot of names, including "Standard" and "Type D" couplings. But if you look for 1/4-inch NPT plugs manufactured to Military Specification (Mil-C4109), that's the right part.

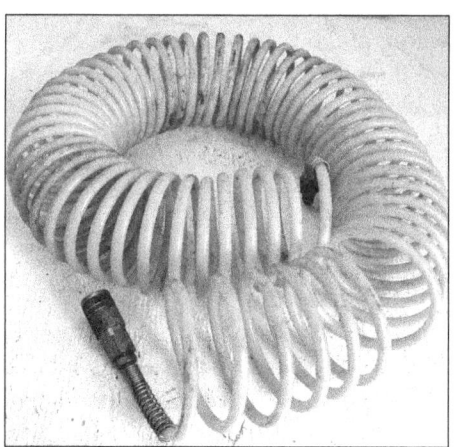
Plastic hoses tend to kink, and they melt if you touch them against something hot. It's a good thing they only cost about $5, and you can also trim them past the damaged portion and reinsert the barbed end fitting.

These 50-foot top-quality air hoses cost $20 each, brand new. At that price, why bother with a cheap plastic hose?

Here are some typical air fittings. The one on the left is a larger 3/8-inch Series-B industrial fitting. The one in the center attached to the inflation chuck is the one you want to use—an industrial Series-A 1/4-inch fitting. On the right is the female side of the industrial coupling.

CHAPTER 5

Project: Install, Wire and Plumb a Compressor

This project installs a compressor with hard-line plumbing and a soft-line hose reel. The compressor installed in this project is a 240-volt upright model, hard-wired to a dedicated 30-amp circuit using flexible metal-clad cable. The distance from circuit panel to compressor is approximately 30 feet.

Cost: $60 to $250, plus the price of the compressor

Time to complete: 2 hours

Supplies needed:
- Compressor
- Wire and conduit
- Conduit supports and connectors
- Junction boxes and switch boxes as needed
- Circuit breaker
- Air couplings
- Schedule 40 3/4-inch PVC
- PVC primer and glue
- Galvanized iron fittings
- Hose reel and air hose
- Bolts or screws for hose reel mounting
- Construction screws

Tools needed:
- Flathead and number-2 Philips screwdrivers
- Tools appropriate to your conduit type

Check Permits

You may need to get a "mechanical" permit from your local planning department to install a hard-wired compressor. Check your local laws to be sure. ■

- Hacksaw
- Power drill/driver and drill bits
- Crescent wrench

Follow these steps:

1 Determine the amperage requirement of the compressor—this defines the gauge of cable you need to run according to your local code. In general, choose 12/3 for 20-amp circuits, 10/3 for 30-amp, 8/3 for 40-amp, and 6/3 for 50-amp circuits.

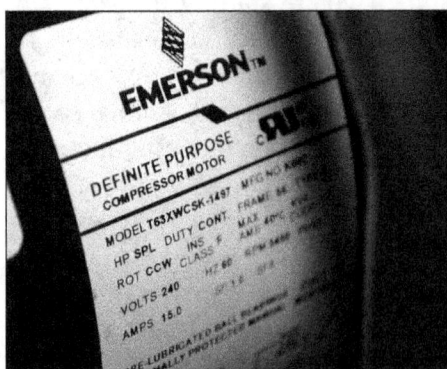

Read the sticker on the electric motor that drives your compressor. It tells you the amperage drawn by the motor. Make your circuit more capable than your compressor requires.

2 Position the compressor where you would like it to stay, and carefully plan and measure the circuit from the panel to the compressor. Note where you plan to install any junction boxes or switches, and then use a pencil to mark the walls or ceiling where each component goes. Measure and note the distance between each fixture. Place each fixture in its desired position, and use the drill to make holes in the studs or walls as needed to thread the cable from point to point. Next run the lengths of cable. Don't forget to support the cable within 2 feet of the panel and at least every 6 feet to the compressor.

Metal-clad cable works well for compressors. You can also buy the individual wires and a length of flex conduit and pull your own metal-clad cable. But don't forget to pick up anti-abrasion plugs for the ends of the conduit!

3 Locate the electrical connection box on the compressor. This is usually a small plastic box held to the compressor with a screw. The on-off switch is usually located on or

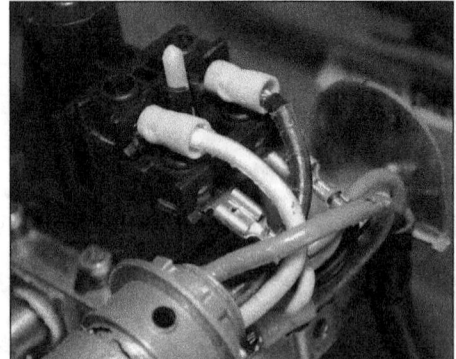

The white and black wires in this 240-volt circuit are both hot. The white one should be wrapped in black tape to code it as a hot wire. The green one goes to ground.

70 HOW TO DESIGN, BUILD & EQUIP YOUR AUTOMOTIVE WORKSHOP ON A BUDGET

COMPRESSED AIR AND WELDING

near the box. Open the box and follow the installation guide instructions for making the connection.

4 Close the compressor connection box and go to the circuit panel. Make very sure the power is turned off at the main breaker. Install the new 240-volt circuit breaker and label it on the panel. Attach the cable or conduit to the side or back of the panel and route the wires to the circuit breaker and to the neutral and ground bus bars. Close the panel and reset the main breaker, then turn on the breaker and test the new circuit by turning on the compressor. Don't forget to stand to one side when you throw the switch. Most compressors have a brief break-in period when they should run without pressure, so this is a good test.

5 Turn off the compressor at the breaker and start plumbing the pipe from the port provided for the air line. This is generally a 3/4-inch NPT-threaded hole, but may be larger or smaller depending on the unit. Smaller compressors may come with an air coupler already installed. This usually is an industrial interchange format, but check to be sure. Start the plumbing with galvanized or black iron pipe, because this is easily removed later without damage. Use some kind of thread sealant such as Teflon tape or liquid pipe thread sealant or the joints may leak. Take the plumbing to the nearest wall before switching to PVC or some other pipe.

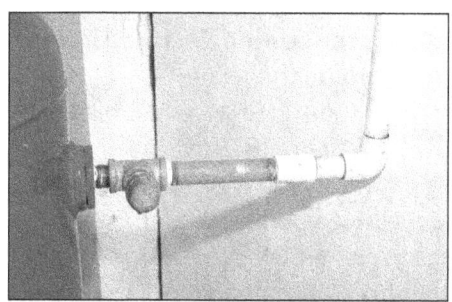

Make the first piece of your hard-line installation out of galvanized pipe. That way you can remove the cap to add more hard line without breaking or cutting the PVC.

6 Once at the wall, run the PVC or dedicated air pipe upward to the ceiling or attic—or simply far enough to get to where you want the air without being in the way. Rafters and joists are a good place to run air lines because the line is easily attached to the wood. You'll want supports at least every 6 feet or so.

Support the PVC air line with conduit support straps at least every 6 feet.

7 Use 3/4-inch PVC Tee fittings to drop air-access points where you want them—usually this is over working bays and at the workbench. If you have free-standing tools that use air, such as a blast cabinet or air-powered tire mounter, drop a coupling near those tools as well.

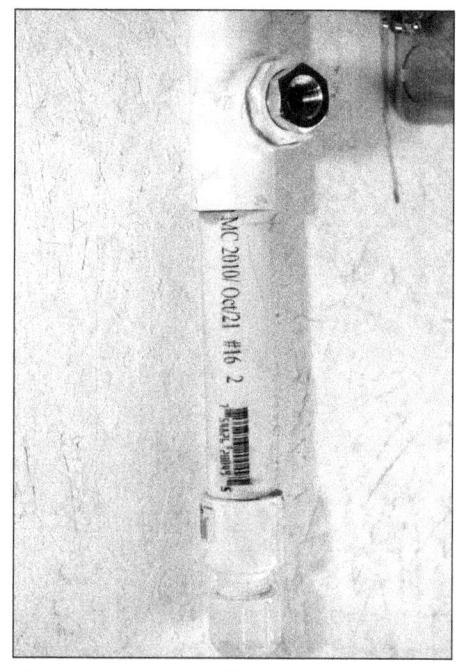

You can use a tee fitting to drop an air line from the ceiling. Use a brass reducer to get to 1/4-inch pipe thread for the air connector. You can also put an extension on the bottom with a cap to use as a simple water drain.

8 When you put in an air coupler, note that most couplers use a 1/4-inch NPT fitting, male or female, but you're likely using 3/4-inch PVC for the pipe. You need to reduce this, generally with a 3/4- by 1/2-inch elbow and then a 1/2- to 1/4-inch brass reducer fitting.

9 Be sure to plan for drainage. Compressed air generates a tremendous amount of water, especially if you live in a humid climate. As a rule, you want the system to have a little drop from one end to the

Drain Valve

Make sure you can get to the compressor's drain valve conveniently. The compressor needs to be drained of water in its tank at least once a week, and it's a good idea to leave that valve open when you're not using the compressor. ■

CHAPTER 5

An in-line water collector is a good idea; it makes it easy to drain the condensation out of the system.

Pro Grade

Professional air compressor sales and service businesses have better drain valves that cost about $20. The ones that come on most hobbyist-level compressors tend to be cheap and get gummed up and stuck very quickly. ■

Gasket Sealant

A little silicone RTV gasket sealant works wonders on barbed press-on fittings. Don't torque down the hose clamp too tight. ■

other, so the water flows to a drain. A drain can be as simple as a PVC cap on a short extension from the air couplings. The initial run of pipe drains back into the tank and you can use the bottom drain on the tank to eliminate that water.

10 Mount the hose reel in a convenient location near a hard line. Ideally, you should place the reel where you won't bump into it all the time, but where it's easy to unreel the hose. Spring-loaded hose reels can go overhead, but if you have to crank it to recoil the hose, make sure you have space to do so.

11 Make an appropriate connection to the tail of the hose reel. The hose reel tail may have a 1/4-inch NPT fitting, or it could be bare hose requiring a barbed fitting and a hose clamp. You may need to make a longer hose or use a purchased hose if you plan to install the hose reel farther than a couple feet from the line.

12 Connect the hose reel to the compressor and let the system build up pressure. When the compressor turns itself off, note the total PSI in the system—there's usually a gauge on the compressor. You can adjust the PSI, usually by turning a screw under the cap with the electrical connections, but be sure the circuit breaker is turned off before you open that cover. Also, be very cautious about increasing the pressure beyond the manufacturer's specification, usually 90 or 125 psi. Never disable or eliminate the emergency pressure valve; you could end up with a disaster at worst and a broken compressor at best.

13 Test the system with your most demanding air tool. If it works, you're ready to go.

You can use the air system with just a hose reel for as long as you like, and then upgrade to a hard-line air system. But you might find that the hose reel works well enough that you don't need to spend the money—this is especially true if you do most or all of your work alone. If there's only one person using tools, you can get by with just one connection.

Many automotive hobbyists get by with a simple hose reel for years, and never feel the need to plumb hard lines into their system.

HOW TO DESIGN, BUILD & EQUIP YOUR AUTOMOTIVE WORKSHOP ON A BUDGET

Building a Paint Booth

Being able to paint your own car is a source of tremendous pride, and it is well within the range of projects achievable in a standard one-car garage. Even if you don't need to paint a whole car, most automotive hobbyists frequently need to paint a variety of parts for dress-up purposes. And if you have a paint booth, you can get practice painting non-automotive things such as mailboxes and other household items. When you can reliably put a candy-apple finish or a set of killer flames on a mailbox, you're ready to graduate to a car. Plus you'll be the envy of your friends and you'll never again wonder what to get someone for a birthday present. It's a win-win situation.

Why Not Rent?

From a practical perspective, unless you plan to paint things frequently, you may find that it's far more advantageous to rent a professional paint booth when you need one. Ask around in your area and you're likely to find several available booths suitable for painting cars. You can typically rent a paint booth by the hour, and it comes with compressed air. You supply the paint and the sprayer, and it keeps dust, mess, and overspray away from your tools, your other cars, and everything else in your shop.

You may also be able to obtain access to a paint booth through your local community college or high school auto shop program. Many community colleges teach classes in body and paint work—they typically offer evening and weekend adult education classes for far less than you would pay to rent a facility, and you also get the benefit of instruction.

Infrastructure Requirements

The first thing to realize about painting is that it's dangerous and requires its own infrastructure. Paint, and specifically the solvents in paint, is usually toxic to some degree—you need to bring fresh air into the paint booth and evacuate the fumes constantly or you can be killed. Paint solvents are also generally flammable, so you need to make sure that fire safety has been perfected—especially if you're sharing the garage with your household furnace or water heater.

Also you need a lot of light to get a clear view of the paint work. The general light level you need to change spark plugs won't do for painting. You need to have a lot of light, and ideally it should be of varying light temperatures so that you can see colors well.

In addition to light, ventilation, and fire safety, you need compressed air in quantity if you want to paint in a booth. Aerosol cans are expensive for the amount of paint you get; the paint is generally not a good-quality product; and it would take cases of spray cans to paint a car. So even if you could get the kind of results you want from spray cans, they're never a good choice for anything much bigger than a mailbox or more important than the inside of a trunk. So you can plan on using a large upright compressor of at least 3 hp and 60-gallon capacity to power a decent, gravity-fed spray gun. You only have to buy those pieces once.

Local Laws

Your local laws may have a lot to say about painting in your garage or workshop, especially if you live in an urban area. Painting has air-quality implications. While there are generally allowances for amateurs, check your local airborne-toxin venting laws.

Protect Your Surroundings

If you're like most amateur mechanics, you don't have a separate space in which to paint your car, or to handle the paint prep. Preparing for paint and then painting is a messy business and involves lots of dust and overspray.

Cover absolutely everything in your shop with plastic drop cloths. These cost just a couple dollars each at a home supply store, so buy more than you think you need. Be sure to tape down the edges, because paint spray really has a way of getting on everything in the vicinity. If you're working in the same garage that houses your favorite car, or your home's laundry facilities, you need to be extra careful to protect the area and items you don't want to paint; or better yet, move the project out of that space entirely.

Before you decide to build a paint booth in your garage, consider renting a professional paint booth to get top results and leave the mess somewhere other than your workshop.

CHAPTER 5

Project: Create a Full-Size Paint Booth

This project creates a simple paint booth suitable for painting items inside or outside your garage or workshop. Although you can theoretically get a whole car into this kind of booth, you should rent a professional paint booth if you're painting a whole car. This booth is certainly suitable for shooting a coat of basic black on frame or suspension components, or other items where you want good results but which won't be judged as closely as your car's body finish.

Cost: $60 to $100

Time to build: 60 minutes

Supplies needed:
- 4 side-outlet 90 three-way fittings in 3/4-inch PVC
- 2 side-outlet Tee four-way fittings in 3/4-inch PVC
- Thirteen 10-foot lengths of schedule 40 or 80 PVC pipe
- 4 heavy-duty 3.5-mil 10x25-foot plastic drop cloths
- 10 to 20 carpenter's spring clamps
- Duct tape
- 3/4-inch pipe supports
- 25x25-inch square furnace filter

Tools needed:
- Hacksaw
- Power driver and screws
- 24-inch shop fan

This project specifies 3/4-inch Schedule 40 PVC pipe because the example paint booth was built in a workshop and was well-supported from the ceiling. But you could use schedule 80 PVC, thinwall metal conduit, or metal fence pipe of the same outer diameter for more rigidity and build the project as a standalone. Weigh down the legs with concrete construction piers if you build outside. As a rule, the larger the diameter of the pipe, the stiffer it is. PVC has the advantage of being lightweight and cheap, plus you can always use it for plumbing later. You can assemble this structure with PVC cement and make it more-or-less permanent. But since the pieces hold together just fine without the cement, you could break the whole thing down and store the corners in a box and bundle up the pipes.

You need to purchase the four "side-outlet 90" corner pieces and the "side-outlet Tee" fittings from an online vendor. Your local home supply store is not likely to carry these because most of them are "furniture grade" and not NSF (National Sanitation Foundation) rated for plumbing use. The fittings used in this example came from www.flexpvc.com for a total of $27, including shipping.

As you read through the steps, you can see that changing the size of the structure is simply a matter of cutting the pieces of pipe to the desired length. The smaller the structure, the more solid it is. You can make the booth stronger by purchasing more side-outlet Tees and making shorter spans. Or you could buy twice the number of side-outlet 90s and side-outlet Tees and more lengths of PVC and tie together the bottom of the structure as well as the top.

Follow these steps:

1 Determine the size of the booth you wish to build. You have enough junctions for a booth 10 feet wide, 10 feet tall, and 20 feet long using 13 10-foot lengths of pipe. However, the booth is stronger if the spans are shorter.

2 Place the side-outlet 90s at the corners of your work area. If your work area is outdoors and there is wind, tie the structure to concrete construction piers to keep it from flying away. Put the width and length spans of PVC pipe in place to make the top of the frame.

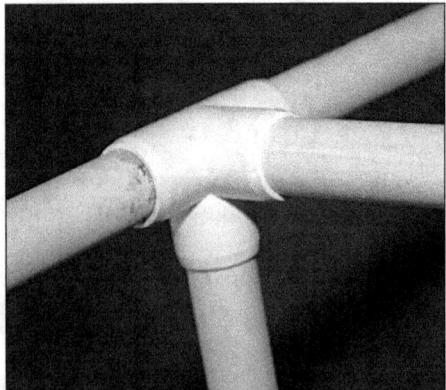

A side-outlet tee is not a fitting you can usually find at your local shop, but they are widely available on the Internet.

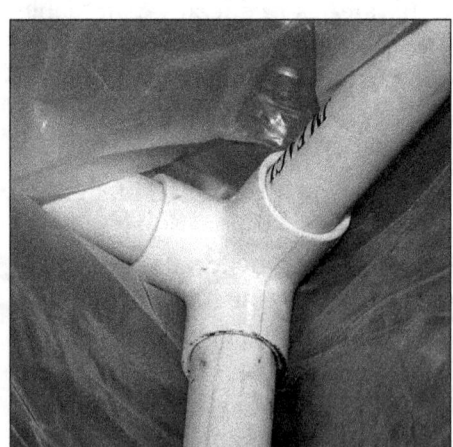

Side-outlet-90 fittings can be purchased in plumbing grade and furniture grade. For a paint booth, it really doesn't matter which ones you get.

COMPRESSED AIR AND WELDING

3 Schedule 40 PVC is quite flexible, so you should build this paint booth inside if possible. Tie the upper frame to the ceiling using standard 3/4-inch plumbing pipe supports. These use two construction screws and hold the top frame to the ceiling nicely. Put the screws in loosely at first, so you can move the pipe and get the plastic sheeting over it, and then tighten them when you have everything ready.

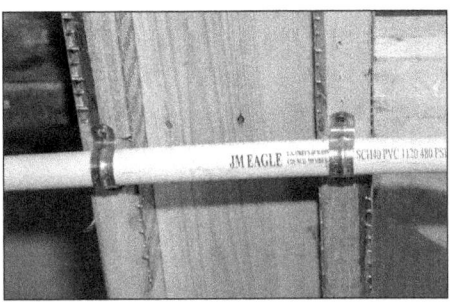

If possible, you always want to support the paint booth frame. Use Schedule 80 PVC, a larger diameter of pipe, or get extra corner fittings to stiffen your structure.

4 Put the legs onto the structure one side at a time. If you're anchoring the frame to construction piers, you can stick the bottoms of the legs into the holes in the piers and shim the legs firmly in the holes with soft wood shims. If you have attached the upper frame to the ceiling, you can insert the legs as you go. If the ceiling is less than 10 feet high, you may need to cut the pipes to fit. You want a good solid fit, because the legs also hold down the bottom edge of the plastic booth walls.

5 Cover the structure with plastic drop cloths, using spring clamps or duct tape to secure the plastic sheeting to the structure. The exact method of attachment depends on the size of the structure and the size of the sheeting. Be sure to anchor the sheeting under the legs and concrete piers.

6 For ventilation, cut a hole in the sheeting at one corner and duct tape the furnace filter to the intake face of the shop box fan. Place the fan in the hole and duct tape the sheeting to the fan. The idea is for the fan to suck air through the furnace filter and out of the booth. You can allow fresh air to come in through slits in the sheeting or place another furnace filter over a hole for air intake. The fan should create a slight vacuum in the booth, but nothing too drastic—about 1/10 of 1 psi—but it should move air through.

For a really fancy setup, you can use Tees and elbows and a little more PVC pipe to create a frame at the bottom of a leg brace for the box fan.

The idea with this paint booth is to create a low-cost painting area that keeps the paint off your tools and workshop surfaces and keeps dirt off your work. You can set this booth up inside your garage or shop, in a driveway, or on any flat piece of ground.

Use cheap carpenter's spring clamps to hold the plastic sheeting on the top of the frame.

You can simply tuck the plastic sheeting under the legs of the booth to hold it down.

You can see how the booth frame goes together inside the garage and how the car fits inside it with plenty of room to spare.

You can upsize this booth to fit any car if you support the frame from above. The 3.5-mil plastic sheeting comes in 10- by 25-foot lengths, and you can use as many sheets as you need.

Project: Create a Benchtop Spray-Painting Box

This is an adaptation of the full-size paint booth project (above) that creates a simple benchtop paint box suitable for painting smaller items with spray cans or an airbrush. This project was built using some of the same PVC pipe and fittings, plastic sheeting, and the filter and fan assembly. You can also use a basic household fan for this size of booth. If you have painted your car, you can recycle the materials from that booth into a benchtop unit at no cost.

Cost: $40

Time to build: 1 hour

Supplies needed:
- 8 "side-outlet 90" three-way fittings in 3/4-inch PVC
- 3 10-foot lengths of schedule 40 PVC pipe
- Heavy-duty 3.5-mil plastic drop cloth
- Duct tape
- 25x25-inch furnace filter

Tools needed:
- Hacksaw
- 24-inch household box fan

This project uses 3/4-inch Schedule 40 PVC pipe. As with the full-size booth, you can assemble this structure with PVC cement and make it more-or-less permanent. Again, since the pieces hold together just fine without the cement, you can break the whole thing down quickly. And changing the size of the box is simply a matter of cutting the pieces of PVC pipe to the desired length.

Follow these steps:

1 Determine the size of the box you wish to build. The box is stronger if the spans are shorter, but anything up to a 3-foot cube is absolutely stable. For this project, the box is 25 inches tall, 25 inches deep, and 37 inches wide. This is a large-enough working space to paint valve covers, a mailbox, or a small automobile wheel up to about 15 inches in diameter.

2 Cut the height and depth lengths of PVC from the 10-foot lengths. Cut eight 24-inch lengths of pipe, and four 36-inch lengths. You should be able to get all of the lengths out of three 10-foot lengths by cutting two short and two long pieces out of two 10-footers, then four more short lengths out of the third. You'll have one 24-inch length left over.

You can downsize the same paint booth design to fit on your workbench for spray painting purposes, plus it makes a nifty light booth for taking photographs.

3 Place four side-outlet 90s at the corners of the work area. Put the width and depth spans of PVC pipe in place to make the base rectangle of the frame. Then build the top rectangle the same way, using four more side-outlet 90s. Then install the vertical posts and place the top frame on the posts.

4 Cut a section of one of the plastic drop cloths sufficiently large (100 inches by 60 inches) to wrap around the long axis of the structure and enclose one end. Position one corner of the plastic at a corner of the structure to start—the plastic should overlap the opposite corner by a couple feet. Tape the edge of the plastic to the frame and wrap it all the way around and tape the plastic sheet to itself. You should have about 4 inches of overlap. Then trim the overlapped end so that only one sheet of plastic 25 inches square can be taped over that end. Leave the other end open for now.

Cut the plastic sheeting so you don't have a lot of excess, and simply duct tape the plastic to the frame and to itself. Cut slits in the front to pass objects through and put your hands in to paint.

5 At the open end, duct tape a 25x25-inch furnace filter in the opening. This size of filter is unusual enough that a grocery store probably won't have one, but any home supply store will. Place a box fan with the intake side against the filter and duct tape it in place. The idea is for the fan to suck air through the furnace filter and out of the paint box.

COMPRESSED AIR AND WELDING

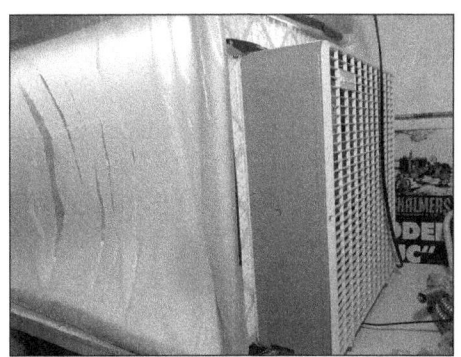

A basic household box fan works for the benchtop design. Use a more powerful shop fan for the car-size booth.

6 Cut a series of slits 2 inches apart in the front face of the sheeting for air intake and access. You can fit quite large objects through the sheeting this way, and you can get the paint and your hands into the box to work while still preventing paint from escaping. The fan should create a slight vacuum in the box, but nothing too drastic—about 1/10 of 1 psi—but it should move enough air through to suck the plastic inward a bit.

7 Place a cool fluorescent light over the top of the box. The plastic is translucent, so it disperses light very nicely. You can also use this paint box as a photographer's light booth.

You can replicate this design in virtually any size—but since box fans are generally 20 to 24 inches square and the 25-inch air filter size makes a useful space, this size works well on most workbenches. The plastic is easy to replace when it gets coated with paint.

Setting Up Your Shop for Welding

Welding and metalworking are a frequent part of the automotive hobby, and they're easy to do in your garage or workshop if you have the right equipment and working space set up. If you get the right gear and observe a few basic safety precautions, you are ready to go. To begin, let's look at the types of welding and metal cutting that you're likely to use.

MIG and Flux-Core Wire-Feed Welding

The most common welding technique used in automotive applications is wire-feed or MIG welding. MIG stands for metal inert gas and is so named because the welding gun issues a small cloud of gas such as argon or krypton to protect the molten steel from oxygen while welding is taking place. The gun also directs a feed of consumable wire into the weld, taking the place of the electrode or welding rod in other types of welding.

You do not have to use gas to use wire-feed welding. The least expensive welders on the market use "flux-core" wire to generate the oxygen-free environment required for a good arc weld. This wire has the same sort of material inside that stick welders place on the outside of welding rods. Flux-core wire-feed welding is relatively easy and inexpensive, and so it is often used in non-critical applications.

A MIG welder using inert gas to protect the weld area can be operated in AC or DC mode and with either polarity, depending on the material being welded. Aluminum requires AC operation for best results, while DC straight polarity yields a smoother weld, less splatter, and generally better results on steel. You can buy an inexpensive 120-volt wire-feed welder for about $150 and add the gas bottle later on when you can afford it. 240-volt MIG welders are substantially more expensive, but they turn up on the used market all the time.

Plasma Cutting

In recent years, the price and availability of plasma cutters has brought them within reach of the automotive hobbyist. A basic plasma cutter now costs about $600 and cuts up to 1/2-inch steel using just ordinary household 120-volt electricity and compressed air. Anyone can get good results with one of these units, and they're rapidly replacing oxy-acetylene rigs.

A plasma cutter uses an arc to melt the metal and then a stream of compressed air to blow out the molten material and make the cut. This

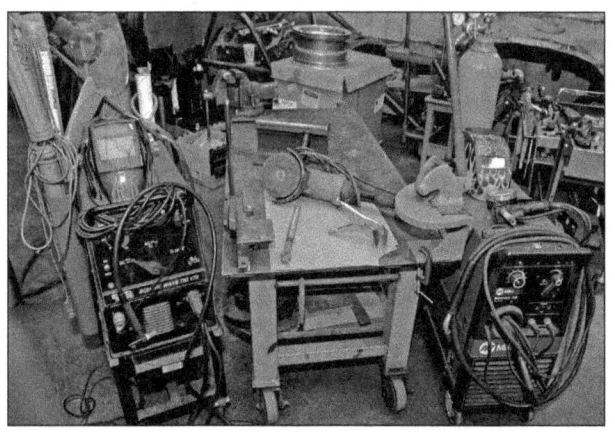

MIG and TIG welders are the state-of-the-art tools for automotive welding projects. You can find these on the used market at good prices, but they're still expensive if you're not going to use them all the time. For small and occasional jobs, choose a 120-volt wire-feed welder instead.

yields a precise cut with less skill and lower operating cost than an oxy-acetylene torch. An inexpensive plasma cutter allows you to make the kind of detailed and precise cuts that cannot be achieved with an abrasive or saw.

Oxy-Acetylene Gas Welding

Oxygen-acetylene welding is the oldest of old-school welding. With the prevalence and low cost of electric welding today, gas welding is becoming a lost art. But hot rodders, race car builders, and home mechanics can make good use of gas welding and cutting in projects. A well-formed gas weld with the proper rod is strong enough for most automotive purposes. Professionals shy away from gas welds on structural or safety pieces such as roll bars because gas welding can oxidize metal, removing carbon and leaving the welded area brittle. However, it's just the ticket for many repairs. And with a basic oxy-acetylene rig purchased from www.craigslist.org or the used equipment shelf at a local welding shop, you can cut and weld.

Cutting with an oxy-acetylene torch is easy if you don't care about extreme precision, but it is harder to make precise, clean cuts than if you use a plasma torch. The advantage of torch-cutting is that you're not limited to straight lines as with a chop saw, and you can cut thicker materials more easily than with a Sawzall or Skil saw. The downside of oxy-acetylene is that getting good results takes practice and, depending on how much you use, the gas can get expensive.

Be careful when considering a classified ad deal on gas welding gear; if the bottles are rented or out of date, you can be in for extra expense if the bottles require replacement or recertification. (Welding gas bottles must be certified every 10 years.) If you buy an older welding kit, find out if the bottles require recertification before they can be filled. Certification generally costs about $20 per bottle. Often a local welding shop simply charges you the $20 and trades your bottle for a new one. Often it's cheaper to buy a basic torch kit, find a good nearby welding shop, and rent the bottles from the store. Remember that you are restricted to having rented bottles filled at that shop.

TIG Welding

TIG welding is also known by the trade name Heliarc welding. TIG stands for tungsten inert gas. Like MIG welding, the welding gun issues a cloud of inert gas to protect the molten metal from oxidization. But a TIG gun uses a non-consumable tungsten electrode to create the arc, and you use uncoated welding rod similar to that used with an oxy-acetylene welder to feed material into the weld. TIG welding is known for its capability to weld delicate or thin materials. TIG is especially associated with welding aluminum. The downside of TIG welders is the price. Even a basic TIG setup costs about $1,000.

Stick Welding

A traditional, stick-based arc welder (called a "buzz box") is one of the least expensive tools you can buy to get started with welding. You can use one of these boxes to do a wide variety of projects. It takes some skill to get a pretty weld with a stick welder, and they're not as precise as a wire-feed or TIG welder, but with a bit of practice, you can get good results on structural pieces such as when building a trailer. These welders are not generally precise enough for delicate work such as on sheet metal, although you can get small rods that allow you to work with thin plate.

Plasma cutters have dropped in price to where they're affordable by hobbyists. Once you've used a plasma cutter, you'll never want to use anything else.

A good, old-fashioned oxy-acetylene rig still has its place in the hobbyist workshop, but be careful to store the bottles properly.

 **Oxy-acetylene**

It's generally a good idea to have an oxy-acetylene setup around, even if you're not that good with it and you don't use it very often. You can use it to weld, braze, and heat up frozen parts with a rosebud tip. If they find a good deal on the used market, few people ever regret buying an oxy-acetylene rig. ∎

Stick welders are the most common welders to find in the classified ads. They are inexpensive and sturdy. The most basic stick welders are AC-only and straight polarity. Better models allow you to select both current and polarity. All stick welders allow you to set the power level, from about 30 to 225 amps for a basic shop/farm model, up to several hundred amps for a top-of-the-line unit.

Brazing and Soldering

A close relative of oxy-acetylene gas welding is the process of brazing and soldering. Simply put, brazing and soldering do not melt the pieces of metal being joined, but use low-melting-point metals such as lead, tin, copper, silver, brass, and bronze to "glue" the pieces together. Most automotive brazing and soldering is done with an oxy-acetylene or propane gas torch, and the most common use is sealing fittings to a radiator, fuel tank, or oil tank. For soldering wiring, the best tool is a basic soldering iron.

Welding Safety

Welding is more dangerous than most things you do in your automotive workshop, and it requires special safety gear. Mostly, this is because welding involves extreme heat, but you're also at some risk for radiation burns from the welding arc if you use an electric welder, and you can damage your eyes by looking directly at any welding flame.

Getting hurt is no fun at all and an injury can put your projects on indefinite hold, so it's important to purchase good safety gear and then use it as designed at all times.

Welding Helmets, Masks and Goggles

First on the list of required safety equipment is high-quality eye protection rated for the type of welding you're doing. A pair of sunglasses simply is not enough protection, and you can damage your eyesight permanently if you don't use appropriate protection. All good-quality welding lenses protect your eyes from ultraviolet and infrared radiation as emitted by the welding process, and that's something your sunglasses just aren't designed to do.

Fortunately, appropriate protection does not have to be expensive. A basic welding helmet (often called a hood) with replaceable lenses costs about $30 and just a few dollars more for a complete selection of lenses. Also, most welders you buy come with at least a basic helmet or handheld mask, which is usually enough to get you started.

The lenses used for welding are numbered in ascending order by the amount of light they block. Thus, a number-8 lens allows more light to pass through than a number-12 lens. In general, as the amperage of the welder increases, so should the lens number. For example, depending on the amperage being used, a TIG welder requires a lens from number-10 to -12, and a MIG welder from number-10 to -13. Stick welders require lenses from number-9 to -14. Lighter lenses can be used for gas welding and brazing. The standard lens that comes in most welding helmets is usually a number-10. Follow the recommendations in the welder operator's manual.

No matter what brand of helmet you choose, make sure that it is lightweight and fits you well. You'll be wearing it a lot; if it's uncomfortable or unwieldy, you'll be tempted to weld without it, and that's a bad choice.

The cheapest welding around is an old-fashioned stick-based arc welder. Unfortunately, it's tough for a hobbyist to get good results with one of these, and you can forget about welding sheet metal with it.

TECH TIP: Welding Fuel Tanks

If you're going to work with a fuel tank, you must empty it of all flammable gasoline and fumes. The best way to do that is to remove the tank from the car and fill the tank with water before welding. If you take a torch to a fuel tank that still has gasoline fumes inside, it will explode. If you have a MIG or TIG setup, you can also fill the tank with an inert welding gas mixture.

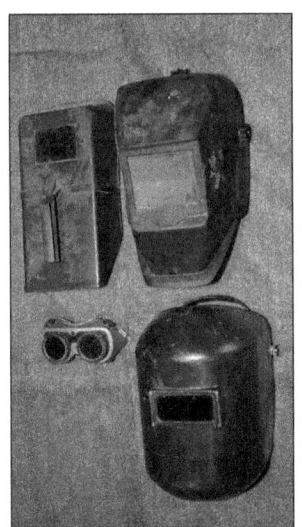

Welding eye protection comes in a variety of styles and lenses. Buy an auto-darkening helmet appropriate to the type and intensity of welding you're doing. You'll never regret the investment.

CHAPTER 5

Welding Lenses	
Lens Rating	Activity
2–4	Propane soldering and brazing, some spot welding
5–9	Oxy-acetylene welding, higher numbers for cutting
10–11	Stick welding up to 75 amps, MIG welding
12–13	Stick welding at 75 amps or more, TIG welding
14	Stick welding at 400 amps or more

Use Aloe Vera

If you plan to do a lot of work with hot metal, whether it's welding or just working around hot exhaust pipes, an aloe plant on the shop windowsill is a good addition to your first-aid kit. Just cut off a chunk and rub its juice straight onto any burn. It kills the pain, soothes the wound, and aids in healing. ∎

Hand-Held Masks and Goggles

Many low-cost welders come with a handheld mask rather than a welding hood. These masks can be handy for working in close quarters, but you should be aware that the radiation from stick, MIG, and TIG welding is dangerous for your skin as well as your eyes, so you should cover all your skin to avoid suffering welding "sunburn." This means that you really do need a full helmet to cover your face and neck. A hand-held mask or set of goggles does not provide the necessary protection for arc welding of any kind. If you are using oxy-acetylene gas, a set of goggles or a handheld mask is sufficient.

Auto-Darkening Helmet

With most helmets, you have to position the welding tip, then flip down the lens before you start to weld. An auto-darkening hood allows you to see what you're doing right up to the moment you strike an arc, and then the lens turns dark within 1/1,000 second as you begin to weld. The better auto-darkening helmets cost more than $200, but most serious welders choose these hoods because of their convenience. Bargain tool stores sometimes carry less expensive auto-darkening hoods, but these trade off features for low cost. The low-cost auto-darkening helmets work just fine, however, and they can be a good choice for the hobbyist welder.

Better auto-darkening helmets allow you to set the total sensitivity and the re-lightening delay. The lens sensitivity setting is intended to prevent nearby welders from darkening the helmet. With a fully adjustable helmet, you can also set the lens rating for the work you're doing. Setting the re-lightening delay allows the helmet to re-lighten shortly after you stop the arc, protecting your eyes from residual glow but allowing convenient work.

Gloves

A good set of leather welding gloves is a basic part of your safety kit. Buy several pairs, because gloves get lost more than anything else in a shop. Any kind of animal-skin gloves are good, but cowhide seems to be the toughest against heat. Pigskin works well, but the surface tends to be more porous and the gloves do not last as long as cowhide.

Special TIG welding gloves are made from thinner material to provide greater tactile sensitivity. This helps when TIG welding because the rods are finer and TIG is often used for welding very fine sheet-metal or other delicate tasks.

Never use any kind of synthetic material for welding gloves, as they may melt or catch fire. Some welders keep a supply of thick cotton gloves, which may catch fire if used carelessly, but are much less expensive to replace. Wool gloves are even better; they smolder but do not catch fire.

Some welding gloves come to the wrist, but traditional welder's gloves are insulated and have a skirt to protect your forearms. These are most useful when you have to work in a very hot area or you have another reason to protect your forearms, but you trade off dexterity for insulation.

Owning a variety of high-quality gloves allows you to choose the best option for any given job.

Coat/Apron

As mentioned before, the radiation from arc welding is dangerous for your skin as well as your eyes. Welding also frequently involves splattering molten metal, so you really want to protect your entire body from burns. A good coat or apron (or both) is an important part of your welding safety kit. Most welding aprons are made of leather and work very well. Though it does burn, cotton clothing is preferable because it's easily extinguished and, unlike synthetics, does not melt onto your skin. Wool is even better than cotton because it does not catch fire, and military surplus stores have 100-percent-wool pants and coats at low prices. If you're not sure of the material, cut off a small bit and try to light it with a match—if it melts and burns, it's synthetic and not wool.

Hat/Hair Control

Your hair is flammable. Because you're likely to have your head near the welding project, it's important to cover your hair and your scalp when welding. Cotton is the preferred material for a dedicated welding hat. Any welding shop offers inexpensive beanie-like hats that do not interfere with a welding helmet and protect your scalp from splatter and sparks. As always, avoid synthetic materials because they burn and melt.

Welding Supplies

A welder generally comes without supplies. One exception is that wire-feed welders have a small spool of flux-core wire. If you're buying on the used market, ask what supplies come with the welder because they're not cheap.

MIG and Wire-Feed Supplies

If you plan to use a wire-feed welder on steel, you have two basic choices for welding wire: flux-core and solid metal. Flux-core wire includes its own welding flux, a material that burns and creates the air-free area in the vicinity of the weld. The flux also forms a crust over the surface of the weld that you need to chip or brush off as the weld cools. If you try to weld over the crust, some of it becomes trapped as a bubble in the weld, which reduces weld strength and looks ugly.

The benefit of flux-core wire is that you don't have to deal with a bottle of gas. You just plug in the welder and start working. The downside is that flux-core wire requires AC operation and produces a lot of smoke and splatter. Flux-core is also not recommended for welding thin (20-gauge or less) materials. With a small bottle of MIG gas (generally argon or a mixture of inert gases) you can work using DC and get a much smoother weld. Common flux-core wire choices for automotive work include Lincoln NR-211 or any wire that meets the American Welding Society (AWS) E71T-GS standard.

For best results in MIG welding, you need the right kind of gas to keep oxygen and nitrogen (98 percent of ordinary air) away from the weld. There's a price range among different welding gases, and of course the better formulations are more expensive. You can use pure carbon dioxide (CO_2) and it works, but you get better results with a gas with 75-percent or higher argon content. For aluminum or other non-ferrous welding, you want 100-percent argon or helium, but these pure gases are not suitable for welding mild steel. To weld stainless steel, a small amount of hydrogen or another reactive gas is added to a basic argon/carbon-dioxide mixture. You can also purchase "three-way" welding gases that include some combination of helium, argon, carbon dioxide, and a small amount of oxygen.

For the vast majority of automotive mild steel welding, an 85-percent argon and 15-percent carbon-dioxide gas mixture is a good choice. A local welding shop can make a recommendation about alternate mixtures for specific purposes.

Most mild-steel MIG welding wire is made to the ER70S AWS specification. ER70S-3 and ER70S-6 are the most commonly used mild-steel MIG welding wires, and the -6 variation is generally considered easier to use. These specifications include elements in the alloy that allow the wire to flow well and create a good, solid weld.

If you plan to weld aluminum, you absolutely need a bottle of argon or helium gas. Aluminum oxidizes easily and one of these protective gases is a requirement. You also need aluminum wire and special rollers to push it. The most popular aluminum selections are a solid-core 4043 or 5356 alloy. The 4043 wire is the most popular and easy to work with. The 5356 alloy is harder, and should be used when you plan to anodize (color) your work, because 4043 weld material does not take color well.

Obtain or make a leather welding apron. If you have access to large scraps of leather from a tannery, you can make an apron in an hour.

MIG welding uses an inert mixture of Argon and other gases to keep oxygen away from the weld. This is absolutely critical to a safe and solid arc weld.

If you plan to weld aluminum regularly, you also want to invest in a spool gun. Because 4043 aluminum wire is soft, mounting the wire spool right on the gun allows a shorter wire travel, which is easier on the wire and reduces breakage and jams.

If you plan to weld stainless steel, you need stainless-steel wire. The most popular alloys for stainless welding are 304, 308, and 316. You also need a special gas formulation. Gas for stainless welding includes a small amount of hydrogen or oxygen.

TIG Welding Supplies

TIG welding rods are similar to those used in oxy-acetylene welding in that they come in lengths of straight rod in sizes from 1/16 to 1/8 inch. Like MIG welding wire, TIG rods are available in a variety of alloys based on the material to be welded. There are three main rod formulations for mild steel, known as S6, 70S, and 80S-D2. Steel welding rods have a thin layer of copper plating on their surface to resist rust and prevent puddling. Most TIG welding is performed using 100-percent argon gas, but mixed gases also work well. Remember that with a TIG welder, you should also stock a supply of the tungsten points for the welding gun.

Oxy-Acetylene Supplies

There are a tremendous number of choices in oxy-acetylene welding rod. When working with mild steel, most welders choose the copper-coated RG45, RG60, and RG65 rods. Each of these has a slightly different formulation, but all work well in an automotive-steel context. You can also get a variety of specialty rods made of bronze (for brazing), aluminum, stainless steel, and other materials. Many of these rods are flux-cored or flux-coated for brazing.

Stick-Welding Supplies

There are a wide variety of stick welding rods available on the market, each optimized for a different kind of welding. Because a stick welder has only a power adjustment, you use different rods to meet various different welding requirements. For example, if you're welding something very easy to work with—such as clean, new metal, well-fit with no gaps—choose 6013 rod. This formulation is easy to work with, easy to clean, and generally gives good results when everything is in order. If you have gaps to fill, 6012 is a better choice. A local welding shop can advise you on the best rods to use for your particular project.

Preparing to Weld

It's one thing to buy a welder and plug it in; it's quite another to start welding. Start smart and work on some scrap pieces for a while before you weld on something that counts. You might consider taking a class at the local community college or skills center as well. Education purchased from a school is much cheaper than the school of trial and error.

To create a strong and good-looking weld, you need to have good technique, but it's just as important to prepare the project. The best welder in the world can't get good results if the piece isn't cut, cleaned, and supported properly. Use the information below to ensure that your shop's welding station is set up to succeed before you start.

Controlling the Mess

When you plan your welding space, think about ease of cleanup—welding is a messy business. A concrete floor is best, but if you have a nice floor coating you might consider things such as putting a lip on the welding table or a catch-pan under the cutting zone.

If you're grinding and cutting near a valuable car, consider buying or making a simple portable screen or using the paint booth setup to keep errant mess from getting on your car. Welding slag and grinder abrasive are horribly damaging to paint.

For welding aluminum, the best tool is a spool gun loaded with aluminum wire. This way, you don't have to re-thread the main welding gun every time you want to weld a different material.

TECH TIP — Transporting Bottles

Always use, transport, and store your welding bottles in an upright position. Acetylene is dissolved in acetone when it's placed in the bottle—if you put the bottle on its side, the acetone can get into the valve and then into the regulators. If your bottles have been on their side, stand them up and let them stabilize for an hour or so before you attach the regulators and try to use them. ■

COMPRESSED AIR AND WELDING

Supporting Your Work

When the metal is fitted properly and cleaned of all scale and impurities, you're ready to position the parts. It's important to get the parts positioned correctly and securely before you start welding. This is where it's handy to have a welding table to prepare the parts.

If the parts are long, you may need additional stands to support them at either end and at one or more places in the middle. You can buy or make variable-height welding stands (sometimes called a "dead man") using threaded rod and a tripod stand. You can also use sawhorses, tables, stacks of boxes, or anything else that is available. The important thing is that the parts must be held firmly in the proper orientation. Parts sometimes move when you start to weld, and cutting the pieces apart to try again is extremely tedious.

Don't be afraid to tack-weld the parts to the welding table. If you have a selection of carpenter's squares, protractors, or magnetic angles, measure in every possible way to make sure that the right angles are square and that everything fits and lines up the way you planned.

Preparing Your Environment

It's more difficult to weld in full daylight because the light from the sun gets into your mask and limits your ability to see the weld. Also you can't see the glowing metal as readily in the full light of day. It's best to weld indoors if you can do so safely; or at least weld in a shaded area where you can see what you're doing through the mask.

Wind is also your enemy when you're welding. Wind blows away the shielding gases from a MIG or TIG welder, and even from flux-core wire or the flux on a stick-welding rod. On the other hand, your welding environment should be well-ventilated to replace the smoke and fumes from welding with fresh air. Again, indoor welding is best, provided you aren't creating a fire or ventilation hazard.

Get your safety gear together. It's often tempting to just make a tack or run a short bead without your protective gear, but that's precisely when you get burned. Keep your safety gear with your welder so it is close at hand when you're ready to weld.

Make sure you've selected the appropriate grade/number of lens before you begin to weld. If your helmet is auto-darkening, make sure its settings are appropriate for the type of welding you're about to perform.

Welding Accessories

One of the great things about welding in your auto shop is that it gives you a fantastic excuse to make a bunch of accessories. Making these items is great welding practice. So before you run to a welding shop to put all this on your credit card, think about building some or all of them yourself—you'll save money and impress your friends. And if you screw it up, no one needs to know.

Welding Cart

Unless you set up a dedicated welding station, you want the welding gear to be mobile. If you set up a welding station, you often find that you need to take the welder to the project, so making the welding gear easily mobile is a good idea. The welding kit includes the welder, basic safety gear, some pliers and cutting tools, welder's magnets, and probably a supply of welding rods. The best way to keep all of this stuff close at hand is to put it on a roll-around welding cart.

Oxy-acetylene rigs use two-wheeled stand-up carts about the size of a set of golf clubs, and these generally provide a tray for the spark striker

When you measure and mark a piece of wood (or anything) for cutting, make an X on the waste side of the cut, and then cut the piece so that the edge of the cut comes to the line, but the width of the cut is taken up on the waste side. ∎

A "dead man" support is handy when you want to support something while you weld on it.

An indispensable technique for determining squareness in a rectangle is to measure diagonally across the rectangle. You can measure the corners all you want and still end up with a cockeyed rectangle—but when you measure in an X-pattern across the diagonals and the measurements are the same, the corners are well and truly square. ∎

CHAPTER 5

and spare welding tips, as well as a place to store welding rods. Larger stick welders generally provided a space to stash some welding rods and, because they're large, they probably already have wheels attached.

Wire-feed and smaller MIG/TIG welders and plasma cutters need a welding cart. This is a chance to get creative and make a cart that suits your needs, or you can get by very nicely with an inexpensive shop cart purchased at a discount tool store such as Harbor Freight.

Welding Table

If you plan to do welding on a regular basis, consider creating a welding table or devoting a section of your workbench as a welding table. The critical factor that distinguishes a welding table is that the table top (and ideally the whole table) is made of steel. This has a number of advantages, most notably that you can tack-weld your work to the table, and then break or grind the tacks away when you're done. Another advantage is that you can place the workpiece on the table and connect the welder's ground clamp directly to the table edge. The contact between the workpiece and the table is enough for conductivity, and you don't have to worry about the ground clamp on the workpiece.

You can make a steel-topped welding table or bench with a wood frame, but for obvious reasons, you need to be careful how close you put the combustible wood to the parts of the table that are likely to get hot. Really, it's just as easy and not much more expensive to make a welding table entirely of steel, and it's good welding practice to build one.

An inexpensive roll-around cart, such as this one from Harbor Freight, works well with a small 120-volt welder. It holds masks, tools, spare wire, magnets, clamps, and everything else you need.

Another feature you might want to add to a welding table is a cutting zone. This area is simply a framework with several replaceable strips of metal placed edge-up to support your work. The idea is that you can cut the piece and do some damage to the metal strips, but the majority of the molten steel and slag falls through the strips to the floor. Just make sure the floor isn't flammable. When the metal strips are too badly damaged for further use, simply cut them out and replace them. Easy.

 **Get Off the Floor**

It might be tempting to weld by placing your workpiece on the floor, but this can be dangerous. If there's any water soaked into the concrete, the heat from the weld can flash that water into steam and the force of the steam could explode a small chunk of concrete, sending shards your way. This really happens, so make a welding table—it's easy and nicer to work on than the floor. ■

A welding station is a good idea if you plan to weld more than a few times a year. Make it entirely from scrap metal, and you can do it yourself for just a few dollars.

This welding station can be put together in about 4 hours using an inexpensive wire-feed welder and some basic tools.

COMPRESSED AIR AND WELDING

Project: Build a Welding Table

If you plan to do significant welding, you want a steel-topped table. This basic structure is strong enough to hold just about anything you might want to weld.

For the purposes of the project, I assume you're using a 120-volt AC wire-feed welder with flux-core wire. But you can undertake this project with a stick welder or oxyacetylene setup and still get good results if you know how to weld with those tools. A MIG or TIG welder makes the job quicker, easier, and cleaner.

Cost: About $100 in box steel and a thick top plate

Time to build: About 4 hours

Tools needed:
- Chop saw
- Carpenter's level
- Carpenter's square
- Measuring tape
- Wire-feed welder
- Welding safety gear
- Welding magnets

Supplies needed:
- 3 8-foot lengths of 1.5-inch .095-wall square box steel
- 10-foot length of 1.5-inch .095-wall square box steel
- 30x50-inch plate of 1/2-inch or thicker mild steel

The following instructions provide measurements and dimensions for a small (30-inch deep x 50-inch wide x 32-inch tall) table made of 1.5-inch .095-wall box steel topped with 1/2-inch steel plate, but you can easily create a larger model by extending the relevant dimensions.

Follow these steps:

1 Get a supply of 1.5-inch .095-wall square box steel. For this project, you need three 8-foot lengths and one 10-foot length. The overall lengths are important to avoid waste. Metal supply yards may have the material in 20-foot lengths, but they generally make at least one cut without an extra charge, and this makes the pieces easier to carry home and use.

2 For the basic project, you can make 90-degree cuts. This leaves the ends of the tubes open. For a more advanced project, you can make 45-degree cuts on the pieces that comprise the basic rectangle and close the holes. Use a chop saw or hacksaw to cut the steel into the following lengths. Make sure all pieces of a given length are identical:

- 48-inch lengths (cut two 8-footers in half)
- 24-inch lengths (section an 8-foot length)
- 30-inch lengths (section a 10-foot length)

3 Clean up the cut ends on a belt or disc sander, and put a slight bevel on the outside edges. This helps provide the weld a place

Make sure you have space in your fit-up to fill with enough weld material for a strong joint.

to build up without protruding much past the original size of the tube. Give them a nice bevel but don't take too much material off—you need enough remaining to make a solid weld.

4 Take two 48-inch lengths and two 24-inch lengths and arrange the base rectangle on the welding table or another flat surface, such as a solid workbench. Put the 24-inch pieces on the inside, so the total measurement is 48 inches wide by 27 inches deep.

5 Use welder's magnets, a carpenter's square, a carpenter's level, and a tape measure to make sure the rectangle is true. You can check for true in any rectangle by measuring on the diagonals. Both diagonals measure the same when all the corners are at 90 degrees and the lengths of the pieces are correct. There may be some gap at the joints, but that's not too important; you can fill that with weld.

Make sure you get good penetration with your welding heat. You want this table to be strong and stable.

6 Carefully tack-weld the four pieces together—just enough to hold them in place. Then measure again to make sure you didn't disturb the angles. If all is good, then start running beads. Alternate corners and measure the angles again after each bead. You'll be surprised how much the structure moves as you weld. When you have the rectangle in place, put a third 48-inch length running up the middle of the space for more support.

After you build the basic framework, you can put the heavy tabletop on the structure.

7 Use welder's magnets and a carpenter's level to set up one of the four 30-inch pieces vertically at a corner of the rectangle. Tack-weld it and re-measure with the level. Then repeat this step for the other three corners. Remember to tack-weld only at this point—no beads.

The legs are just welded onto the basic framework—make sure they're all the same length!

8 Go over the structure with the squares, levels, and tape measure. The structure should be level and the four posts should be square against the corners. If any piece needs adjustment, a few light blows with a lead or bronze hammer should adjust it. It's okay if you break a tack weld or two; just re-level and re-tack the piece. If everything is good, weld beads on all the appropriate seams. Weld alternate corners, sides, and so on, until all raw edges are welded. Alternating helps stop heat-warping.

9 Trim 3 inches off the two remaining 48-inch pieces to fit between the legs at the back of the structure. The remaining 24-inch pieces should fit between the legs at the sides of the structure. Place these supports 12 to 15 inches from the ground. This leaves the front open for you to sit at the table on a shop stool or chair.

Supporting the legs with more braces helps keep the table sturdy and motionless while you work.

10 When finished, you have a basic box to support the table. Center the plate of steel on top of the table and weld it in place. There should be 1½ inches of overhang on the front and back and 1 inch of overhang at each end. You may also want to drill some holes in one corner to bolt on a machinist's vise, or weld on some hooks to hang other tools such

You only need to put a few stitch welds in place to hold the tabletop to the frame.

as a chipping hammer or wire brush. Other common fitments include a section of tubing used as a "holster" for the MIG, TIG, or wire-feed gun. The attachments you put on the welding table are limited only by available space and your imagination!

When you're done, you can easily bolt a machinist's vise to the corner of the welding table for convenient work.

If your table is a little on the short side, just grab some scrap steel and tack-weld it to the bottom of the table legs for some additional height.

11 As an alternative design for the table top, many welding tables use a half-and-half design with part of the top made of solid plate and part made in strips. The advantage to this design is that it's easy to clamp or bolt parts to the center of the table. You can also cut with a plasma or gas torch right on the table top if you position the cut over a gap in the table. You can also fit part of a bent or right-angle piece in the gap while you work. To implement this design, get some box tube or U-channel steel and space the pieces about 1 inch apart for half of the table surface, and use a plate for the other half.

CHAPTER 6

CREATE AND ORGANIZE STORAGE SPACE

Almost as important as the space where you work is the space you devote to stashing spare parts, supplies, tools, and everything else that ends up in your shop. This space needs to be compact and efficient, because that frees up more space for you to work, or to put more cars in the garage. Also, you want to be able to lay hands on your stuff quickly when you need it—nothing is more frustrating than spending an hour of precious shop time searching for a part you know is there somewhere.

We all know the basics of storage and organization. It's implementing what we know and then maintaining that organization that poses the problem. The benefit of organization is that we can keep our collection of stuff in the smallest possible space and get to it when we need it. The downside is that it requires an investment up front to create the space and create the organization system.

Many automotive hobbyists have a huge inventory of spare parts. If you work with any kind of rare or no-longer-made car, you likely spend time scouring swap meets, www.eBay.com, and www.craigslist.org looking for parts, and you may have parted out a few cars. You may even be known as the go-to person in your area for your chosen make and model. If this describes you, you're in far greater need of a storage and organization solution than the average hobbyist.

Limited space is the key concept to remember—every square foot you devote to storing stuff is a square foot that you can't use to park a car or to create pleasant elbow room when you're working. If you look at the photos of dream garages, they're always spacious, with the cars nicely positioned in the room and any workbenches and storage units neatly organized. Compare that with your experience of most people's garages—they tend to be tightly packed, with stuff crammed into every corner.

In a limited-space situation like a single- or two-car garage, stuff is always stored in every available space, but it can be neatly organized to deliver the best results.

An organized and tidy garage is a much more relaxing and pleasant place to work. The key is to make a system that works for you and that you will be motivated to maintain. It doesn't have to be expensive to be functional.

CHAPTER 6

When your shop is disorganized, you can spend more time looking for parts and tools than actually getting work done on your car. Consider this pile of fastener boxes. It's a big step-up from a coffee can full of random nuts and bolts, but it could be a lot better.

Compare this setup to the pile of loose boxes—every bin is labeled and the parts are clearly visible so you know when you're running out. A set of bins like this costs about $20.

Installing Cabinets and Shelves

You can never have too much storage space. Your car stuff will expand to fill every available space you create—it's simply an axiom of the hobby. To maximize floor space, you need to go vertical—you need to put stuff where you can't park cars, and that generally means overhead.

When you're designing a work space, lay out the storage area with tape on the floor, and measure your storage boxes and stuff to make sure that the shelf design works for your needs. For example, if you have a bunch of chrome bumpers or body panels, the shelf design needs to be sized for those items rather than for a stack of plastic tote boxes.

If your stuff mostly fits in totes, you should pick a particular size and style and get a whole lot of them. If you find them on sale, you can usually get the standard sizes for about $5 per tote, and it's generally a good idea to buy 20 or so—spend the $100 up front and then you're set for quite a while.

When you have the boxes, you can plan the shelves to fit the boxes. Make the shelves one or perhaps two boxes high, and give yourself a couple inches of open vertical space. A standard, large plastic storage container is about 16 inches tall, so 18 inches of space is a good solution. Some boxes are about 14 inches tall, and you can either reduce the shelf height and maybe get an extra row on the wall, or use an 18-inch space

Labeling is as important as sorting your parts. You can never remember exactly which box a part is in if you have spent the money to buy a whole bunch of similar boxes. Invest a dollar in a Sharpie-type marker and label every container.

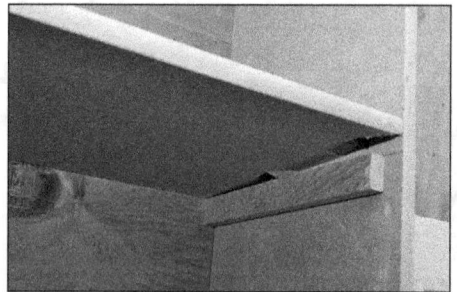

Avoid cheap shelves made of particle board. This is just sawdust mixed with glue, and it has very little strength. The material absorbs moisture and starts sagging almost immediately. Particle board also breaks easily. Also look at the shelf support, which won't hold much weight in a working garage.

Before you start sawing wood, see what your plans look like on the ground by laying them out with tape. You're looking for any potential problems fitting everything into your shop while it's still easy to change the plans.

88 HOW TO DESIGN, BUILD & EQUIP YOUR AUTOMOTIVE WORKSHOP ON A BUDGET

and stick long items on top of each row of boxes.

Another issue to consider when planning for shelves is the total weight you're going to place on them. If you use thin plywood or pressed sawdust boards, you'll find that they sag over time with comparatively little weight. Compressed sawdust boards also absorb water very effectively, so if your shop gets damp at all, they lose their integrity over the course of a year or two. Car parts tend to be heavy, so plan to make the shelves on the sturdy side. Putting the parts in plastic totes helps distribute the weight. But if you have a 4- or 6-foot span between vertical supports, you want 2x4 or 2x6 construction, which holds up over time.

Wall Cabinets

If you want to install built-in cabinetry, consider old kitchen cabinets salvaged from homes being remodeled or demolished. You can buy these at building-supply recycling stores or at the Habitat for Humanity ReStore. Kitchen cabinets work great over workbenches as a place to stash chemicals, gaskets, and books, and a place to keep your stereo from getting dusty.

For free-standing cabinets, old gym lockers are good. You can buy used heavy-duty filing cabinets with roller bearings at a used office furniture store or from the government. They're very durable.

If you do find wall cabinets to hang, be sure that you hang them to carry all the weight you plan to put in them. Anchor the cabinets solidly to the stud wall or they may fall off the wall.

Cheap Metal-Framed Shelves

One method you can use to build some sturdy, low-cost shelves using a metal framework is to use a combination of flat metal bars and angle iron. Many workshops have variations of this design. Use 1/8- or 3/16-inch-thick by 3/4- or 1-inch-wide flat bars of mild steel, and 3/4-inch by 3/4-inch angle iron, again in mild steel, so the shelves aren't unreasonably heavy. It's easy to make these shelves 6- or 8-feet tall, 2-feet deep, and 4-feet wide.

The best place to get angle iron on the cheap is at a metal yard—every city has at least one. This is a business that buys up odd lots of metal and sells it by the pound. They usually have "new" metal as well, but at a higher price. If you just need some 6-foot sections of angle iron, plus some 2- and 4-foot lengths for

If you want a finished look without breaking your budget, head to a used building materials store, and find some white cabinets. This whole bundle of cabinets was $20.

> **Tech Tip — Weight Consideration**
>
> Consider the weight of the items when you choose tote boxes. Brake discs, crankshafts, and other heavy items can easily overload a plastic box (or your ability to pick up the box) if you put more than about 50 pounds inside. If you have heavy stuff to store, choose smaller boxes and stack them two-high on standard shelves.

The most basic storage is cardboard boxes, and these certainly have their place. But they absorb water, get bashed up and dirty, and they really don't work for heavy items.

These plywood totes hold anything you can fit inside them and easily last a lifetime.

> **Tech Tip — Bargain Shelves**
>
> You can often find great bargains on sturdy shelves, cabinets, and other supplies at a government-surplus-goods sale center. Every state or provincial government has one of these; many counties and cities have surplus sale centers too. Prices tend to be low and the items are generally built to last.

Angle Iron

If you can find it, get some angle iron that already has holes in it every few inches, so you can easily adjust the shelves. ■

These sturdy shelves are made from plain angle iron, drilled and bolted together with some 2x2 wood and some plywood. If you find a good supply of angle iron at a bargain price, these are easy to make.

The shelf support is bolted to the vertical support, with a wood support bolted to the angle iron and the plywood on top.

Don't Go Too Cheap

One thing you want to avoid is the ultra-cheap shelves that are stamped out of very light sheet metal. They are wobbly from the moment you assemble them and there's nothing much you can do about that except screw them solidly to the wall. But the real downside comes when you try to put anything heavier than a coffee cup on them—they bend if you put even moderate weight on them, and then they're even weaker than they were before. They look terrible and eventually they dump your stuff on the floor. Plus they're not much cheaper than buying angle iron and assembling tough shelves.

Plastic shelves of any kind are even worse. Generally these are injection-molded and while they assemble easier than stamped sheet-metal shelves, they're even weaker and they become brittle and break before long. If you're storing more than balsa wood on the shelves, it's far better to go tough.

These are the cheap metal shelves you often find for sale. They start to bend immediately and don't even hold a load of half-used spray cans. And the cheap hardware they come with tends to come loose over time. You could spend the same amount of money on angle iron and get much better results.

Perhaps the worst of all are injection-molded plastic shelves. These are handy for storing boxes of styro peanuts, but not much else.

CREATE AND ORGANIZE STORAGE SPACE

shelf supports, you can usually grab those out of the scrap bins and pay very little (as low as 25 cents per pound) for them.

You'll need your toughest drill and 5/16-inch metal-boring bit, a good supply of 1-inch-long 5/16-inch machine bolts with washers and nuts, and some plywood for the actual shelves. You can also use a welder if you want a more permanent attachment between the metal parts.

The design is simple: four pieces of angle iron on end are the vertical supports, and short segments of angle iron are bolted in place as the shelf supports. Put a diagonal strap of flat iron on the ends to add stability to the structure. You can make the shelves out of scraps of plywood. Use 3/4-inch plywood and the shelves can hold just about anything. As a nice dress-up, you can use small carriage bolts to hold the plywood to the shelf supports, but it's not necessary.

Meat Rack and Gorilla Rack Shelves

One popular option is to simply purchase metal-framed shelves or shelf systems made entirely of welded metal wire—the latter are called "meat rack" shelves because they're easily washed, making them popular with butchers and grocers. Meat rack shelves are also good for an auto shop because they look good and hold a lot of weight. You can even get them with rollers if you want to move the shelves around. The downside of meat rack shelving is that it's comparatively expensive.

Gorilla Rack is a trade name for stamped metal shelves. These are a popular choice for home-based workshops. These systems usually cost about $70 for an 18-inch-deep by 4-foot-wide rack. The shelves are adjustable within limits, and the assembly is made from sturdy painted metal. Everything slides together and locks; and these are generally useful and neat-looking units.

The downside of Gorilla Racks is the medium-density fiberboard (MDF) shelving included as part of the kit. This material just doesn't hold weight very well over time, and the boards start sagging immediately. Moreover, the particle board absorbs water. So if your shop gets damp at all, the material will swell and disintegrate.

This doesn't mean Gorilla Racks are a bad idea—you should simply

Flip it Over

If your MDF shelves have sagged in the center, you can get a little more life out of them by simply flipping them over and putting a little less weight on them.

Meat rack shelves are nice looking and handy, but they tend to be expensive. If you find some on the used market, the shelves are adjustable and they hold a medium amount of weight.

Gorilla Racks are the standard for automotive hobbyists. They hold a lot of weight, especially if you get rid of the standard particle-board shelves and replace them with 3/4-inch plywood. Gorilla Racks are a great value and look tidy in your shop.

You may be able to find wooden shelves on the used market or, if you want a nicer look to your garage, you can spend more money to get new ones.

be prepared to cut a piece of 3/4-inch plywood for reinforcement or replacement of the original shelves. It helps if you use the racks exclusively with totes to spread the weight around and you should always limit the weight you put on the unsupported center of any shelf.

> **TECH TIP — Wall Attachment**
>
> Shelves work best when they're attached to the wall, and you can make that attachment with a few L-brackets or short straps.

Custom Shelves

If you want your garage to be a display area, you can make some very nice custom shelves and still not spend a lot of money. These shelves were

This overhead shelf incorporates some nice features. It hangs from ceiling rafters by chains, so only minimal wall support is necessary. It has a white underside to reflect light onto the workbench, and it's placed to accommodate a standard tote.

No-Cost Workbench and Shelves

These shelves were made using large packing crates obtained free from a local business. If you can find a business that receives large items in wooden crates, you can likely obtain a few of them at a bargain price, or they may even be happy to give you as many as you want.

Some of the boxes were the perfect size for a spacious workbench—2 feet deep by 3 feet wide and 6 feet long. For workbenches, I turned these on their sides with the open end facing out, and then cut some scrap plywood to make benchtops. A few nails later, I had a set of sturdy workbenches.

In the case of the shelves, these crates were tall and wide and not too deep, so they work well for shelves. You can hide the fact that you're using recycled crates by putting some cut oriented strand board (OSB) or plywood on top as a shelf surface. Because these are going to be tall, it's also best to affix them to the wall behind so they don't fall over.

Another option for free shelves involves using shipping pallets. You can often get these free from companies with a surplus stack of them.

A standard pallet is 40 by 48 inches, and if you cut it in half by sawing through the main 4x4 side supports, you have a sturdy double-layered shelf that is 24 inches deep by 40 inches wide. Then simply add some vertical supports—you can even use another half-pallet turned on its edge—and you have some free weight-bearing shelves.

If you keep your eyes open and are really lucky, you may run into people giving away free workbenches. There is a whole section devoted to free stuff on www.craigslist.org, or sometimes you run into a company that is going out of business or cleaning out its working areas.

Not the most beautiful shelves in the world, but they're strong and they were free. These shelves started life as packing crates, and they are simply stacked up and screwed to the wall.

This workbench was part of a giveaway from a company that was upgrading its facilities. Keep your eye on www.craigslist.org for this kind of windfall. Along with this bench there were several useful items including shop tables, shelves, and a moveable staircase.

built by a professional cabinet maker for his auto shop using a high-quality hardwood-based plywood kit. You can source this material, on occasion, at a used building materials stores, or from someone remodeling and selling their old shelves on www.craigslist.org.

The shelves assemble easily, and the pre-drilled vertical supports make it easy to choose and change the shelf heights. Because they're hardwood ply, they hold more weight than you can put on MDF or even regular plywood shelves. They look elegant and the best protection for shelves like these is a simple coat of Varathane to guard against stains.

For another design, consider hanging a shelf from the ceiling joists with chain. You can make the shelf as nice as you like, and it's a good place to store light-to-medium-weight totes. And if you paint the underside white and hang a light from it, you have a great reflective surface to maximize your bench light.

Project: Build Heavy-Duty Wood Shelves

These shelves are simple, sturdy, and capable of holding anything up to a four-cylinder engine. You can vary the height between shelves when you build them but, once built, you have to disassemble them to make changes. These shelves are built entirely out of stud-quality 2x4 and 2x6 lumber. You can make upgrades such as using pressure-treated hemlock or other better wood with fewer tendencies to bend and warp, but the standard cheap lumber works just fine.

Cost: About $200 in wood and hardware

Time to build: About 8 hours

Tools needed:
- Circular saw
- Hammer and nails or power driver and screws
- Wood chisel or flathead screwdriver
- Carpenter's level
- Masking tape
- Measuring tape

Supplies needed:
- 4 10-foot 2x6 boards
- 16 12-foot 2x6 boards
- 4 8-foot 2x4 boards
- End-mount strong ties or scrap 2x4s for end supports
- 16D nails or 3-inch heavy-construction screws

For this project, I made each shelf space 24 inches high to accommodate the storage tubs or just about any kind of box. Each shelf space plus its supporting boards is 25½ inches tall. So a shop with a 9-foot ceiling can accommodate an 8-foot-high section of shelves with four shelves, with the top shelf providing 6 inches of space.

I made the shelves 24 inches deep, so the tubs can be placed perpendicular to get the greatest number into the space. I chose 24 inches because it fit well in the shop space and it works out nicely with four 2x6 boards (each 5½ inches wide) and the 1½ inches deep of the outer 2x6 vertical support. That gives you 22½ inches of shelf, 1½ inches of outer support, and 1/2-inch of free space that always gets eaten up by the natural bending of the shelf boards.

You need to adjust the instructions in this project to fit your shop space; I had two spans to fill with shelves. The left-hand span was about 4 feet wide, and the longer span was just under 12 feet between vertical 6x6 posts in the installation location, so I planned for an additional vertical support halfway along the span. I definitely wanted to take advantage of the big 6x6 posts set in the concrete at either end. This project gives instructions for the larger span of 12-foot shelves. The smaller one is just a reduced version of the same plan.

The wall backing was painted sheets of 7/16-inch OSB on top of 2x6 studs, so there was plenty of solid material for attaching the shelves to the wall. These shelves won't win any design or beauty awards, but they'll carry any load for as long as this workshop stands. I painted them with low-cost paint from the recycled building supply center, to give them a finished look.

The bottom of the trusses (triangular roof supports) in this shop building were 9½ feet from the concrete floor, which gave me 24 inches of space between each of four shelves, with 18 inches of space above the top shelf. I was able to mount two of the vertical supports inside two trusses, because the trusses were also made of 2x6 lumber, so there was a perfectly sized space inside each truss. This made for a nice, clean installation. The vertical supports that were not placed inside the trusses are simply screwed to roof joists. That connection only has to help the vertical support stay vertical—it doesn't bear any weight.

When you design your shelves, look at the situation in your garage or shop, and find the best way to hold things steady. Sometimes you may need to anchor to the wall or to rafters. If you can't easily use

Cut Correct

When you're measuring any board (or anything) for cutting, make an X on the waste side of the cut, and then align the blade so that the cut comes right to the edge of the line and the width of the cut is taken up on the waste side. This technique helps prevent that "I measured twice, but it's slightly too short" problem from occurring. ■

construction screws, consider using Simpson Strong-Ties, which are sheet-metal brackets designed to be screwed to different surfaces and provide a strongly supported mounting point. Strong-Ties are inexpensive and give your work a solid, professional look.

I cut two 2x6 vertical supports tall enough to fit into the trusses at about 10 feet and one more about 9½ feet for the center support. Then I cut sixteen 2x4 horizontal shelf supports at 24 inches long. At either end of the shelves, these attached to the vertical 6x6 posts. In the center support, I used a combination of Strong Ties and scraps of 2x4 screwed through the wall board into the studs for support.

Then I stacked up sixteen 2x6 boards at 12 feet long, but trimmed the boards that went closest to the wall a little shorter to fit the space between the 6x6 posts. I used two 1-pound boxes of 3-inch gold construction screws, plus a few nails here and there and some 1⅝-inch screws for attaching the Strong Ties to the wall.

Follow these steps:

1 Lay out your shelf plan on the floor with masking tape. This

Here's the bare wall in my new workshop. I put 16 feet of shelves along here, with five 2-foot-high spaces supported by 2x6 boards. This should hold about 45 standard totes when it's finished. That ought to be enough for now.

shows you how much room the shelves really take up. Do this step with cars and other gear actually in the garage, if possible, so you can get a true sense of clearances. Carefully measure all dimensions, especially the verticals.

2 Decide how to support the outer vertical posts. If possible, it's great to tie them to the ceiling for support while you build the shelves.

I started by putting OSB against the insulation and studs and then painted it. You don't have to have the paint too perfect; it's going to be hidden. I also test-fit the vertical supports into the trusses.

Thereafter, the structure of the shelves provides support and the floor bears the weight.

3 As an optional upgrade, you can cut notches in the vertical supports to inlay the 2x4 horizontal supports. To do this, lay out the vertical end supports, mark them 24 inches from one end, and make a series of cuts with a circular for 3½ inches. Each cut should be 1½-inches deep. With a wood chisel, cut out the pieces of wood until you have a nice, even notch. This supports the weight on the horizontal supports better than simple screws. Then measure another 24 inches from the end of the channel, make another channel, and so on for each of the shelf supports.

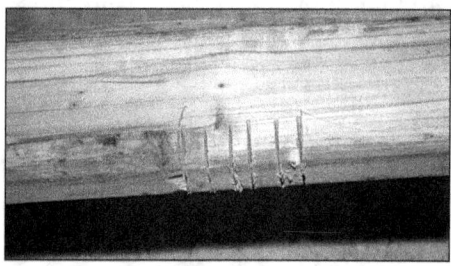

To notch a board without a router or dado bit on your table saw, just make a series of cuts with your circular saw and chisel out the wood with a wood chisel or even a flathead screwdriver.

When the shelf supports are fit into the notch and painted, no one has to know it was done the cheap way.

CREATE AND ORGANIZE STORAGE SPACE

4 Set up and support the vertical posts and use the carpenter's level to ensure that they are straight up and down. It's best if you can attach the supports to the ceiling or roof, but any method that keeps them vertical works.

5 Decide how to support the wall side of the shelves. If there are studs or vertical posts, these are good tie points. If you have smooth walls, make sure you can screw into a stud or other strong support, and use Strong-Ties or screw a length of 2x4 to the wall at the appropriate height to support the horizontal shelf supports. You can also set up additional vertical posts next to the wall and tie them to the ceiling in the same way as the outer vertical posts, and screw those to the wall.

6 Assuming that you can screw to the wall, set the Strong-Ties so the horizontal shelf-support tops are at 24, 48, 72, and 96 inches above the floor. You should measure and mark these points on the outer supports as well. Then screw the horizontal supports to the ties and the vertical supports. Use at least two screws—they have to hold a lot of weight. Make sure the horizontal supports are level and even with each other and that the vertical supports stay vertical.

7 After the basic framework is assembled, you can lay in the shelf boards. If you have end posts as I did, you may need to cut the boards closest to the wall a little shorter. For example, if your construction uses 4x4 posts on 12-foot centers, you have to take 3½ inches off the 12-foot board to fit it between the posts. The remaining boards can be laid in at 12 feet long. You can decide whether you want to nail or screw the shelf boards to the horizontal supports. If you're going to have a lot of stuff on the shelves, you really don't need to do that, but it adds stability if you don't have it well-tied to the wall. If the boards have bends in their length, you may have to pound the last one into place—this is a good thing, because it keeps everything solid and tight.

8 For the final step, paint the new shelves. It looks nice, doesn't have to be top-quality paint, and seals the wood from absorbing moisture or oil.

The four shelf supports are notched into the outer vertical support and nailed to a 4x4 post. The vertical support is screwed to the roof truss.

Finally, I laid the shelf boards in place. They don't really need to be nailed or screwed down, but you can if you want to.

The finished shelves look great and hold just about any kind of weight you can fit in there. Counting the floor, there are five storage spaces 2 feet deep by 2 feet tall.

Ultra-Solid

If you want things to be ultra-solid, get out the drill and wood-boring bit and use a 5/16 or 3/8-inch carriage bolt to attach the horizontal and vertical supports together. ■

HOW TO DESIGN, BUILD & EQUIP YOUR AUTOMOTIVE WORKSHOP ON A BUDGET

Make Your Own Totes

You can make your own boxes in any size with some basic 1/4-inch plywood and 1x1 strips of wood. Simply cut the plywood in the desired side, top, and bottom dimensions; cut the 1x1s to match; and then assemble the box with 1¼-inch drywall screws.

For example, the box shown is 12 inches deep by 18 inches wide and 16 inches tall. To build this box, you need a half sheet of plywood and a couple of 8-foot lengths of 1x1 wood. Out of these pieces you cut:

- 2 pieces of plywood 12 by 16 inches for the sides
- 2 pieces of plywood 18 by 16 inches for the front and back
- 2 pieces of plywood 12 by 18 inches for the top and bottom
- 4 pieces of 1x1 16 inches long for vertical supports
- 4 pieces of 1x1 10½ inches long for top and bottom side supports
- 4 pieces of 1x1 16½ inches long for top and bottom front and back supports

Screw the top and bottom supports to the top and bottom pieces, and then screw the vertical supports to the four sides of the box. Screw the bottom into place, so you can simply put the top on the box and it stays in place. Use a drill and a saber saw to cut handholds in the sides.

The total cost of this tote is about $12. That's about twice the price of a plastic tote, but this box easily carries the heaviest engine or brake parts without deforming or cracking. And if you make a set of these boxes, they fit well on a shelf together.

Use some extra pieces of 1x1 to make a tight-fitting lid.

These plywood totes are easy to make. Use pieces of 1x1 for the corners and screw the plywood to the lumber. If you measure and cut right, they go together in moments.

You can use a saber saw and a drill to cut some handholds in the side, or just use your drill and insert a piece of rope with knots at the ends for handles.

CREATE AND ORGANIZE STORAGE SPACE

Project: Build Lightweight Wood Shelves

If you don't need sturdy shelves, you can build some very nice ones with lighter wood and less support. These shelves are designed to hold lightweight totes only. Shelves this light would likely pull loose from the walls or sag if subjected to boxes filled with heavy car parts.

Cost: About $100 in wood and hardware

Time to build: About 4 hours

Tools needed:
- Stud finder
- Circular saw
- Hammer and nails or power driver and screws
- Carpenter's level
- Measuring tape

Supplies needed:
- 3 10-foot 2x6 boards for vertical supports
- 8 8-foot 2x2 or 2x4 boards for wall and outer shelf supports
- 2 4x8-foot sheets of 1/2-inch CDX plywood for shelves
- 16D nails, or 3-inch heavy construction screws

These materials produce a set of shelves 8 feet wide, 2 feet deep, and 10 feet tall, with 4 shelves at 2, 4, 6, and 8 feet off the ground.

The design is simple—follow these steps:

1. Use a stud finder or measure to find and mark the vertical studs on the wall. This step is critical, because drywall is simply not strong enough to hold any substantial weight. You must find the studs and attach the shelves to them.

2. With the stud centers marked, screw a series of 2x2 or 2x4 boards to the wall horizontally at the shelf heights you want. You can size these to fit your favorite totes or any height you choose. Be sure to screw into every stud to maximize support.

3. Cut the plywood shelves to the depth you want. Because these are lightweight shelves without a lot of center support, it's best to limit shelf depth to 18 inches. Use 1/2- or 3/4-inch plywood for good support strength (1/4-inch plywood is too flexible to support any kind of weight).

4. Cut a set of 2x6 vertical supports to the height of the room. In a finished area, this should

The locations of the studs are carefully marked on the wall behind this support and on the support itself.

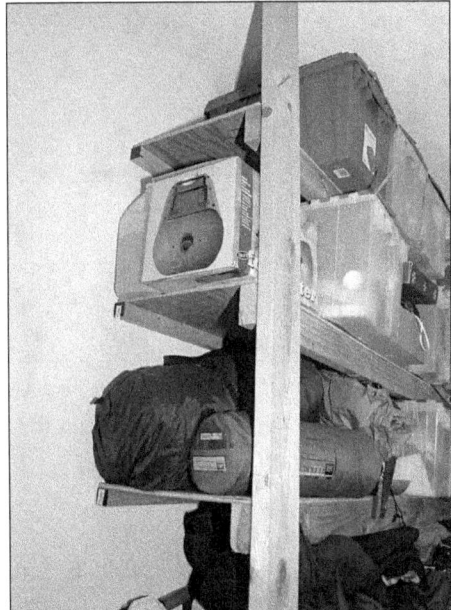

These shelves hold quite a bit of weight but not heavy car parts. The important thing is that the wall-side supports absolutely have to be solidly anchored to the wall studs, or this assembly will pull right out of the wall and fall over!

The vertical supports are 2x6s, with the outer horizontal supports made of 2x4s. You could add strength to this design by installing some short 2x4s to span the distance from the wall support to the outer support.

go from floor to ceiling. But if you don't have a finished ceiling, attach to the rafters or joists. With this design, it is critical that you attach the outer vertical support to the ceiling, hopefully into a solid joist. If you have access to the attic or joist area, attaching the vertical support to the ceiling from above is a clean-looking way to make the connection.

5 Screw a series of 2x2 or 2x4 shelf supports to the vertical supports at the same heights as the wall supports.

6 Slide the plywood shelves into place. With this design, it is important to screw the plywood to both the wall side and the outer shelf supports, because plywood sags in the middle over time, and you want to keep everything attached or a shelf may fall.

7 As an optional extra support, you can cut some short lengths of 2x2 or 2x4 and place them under the shelves. Attach these extra supports to the wall side and outer shelf supports every 4 feet or so.

Sixteen Inches

Most modern construction places studs on 16-inch centers. Happily, 16 inches is also a little longer than the length of a framing hammer. If you have found a stud, you can start looking for the next one by simply laying the hammer against the wall. Be aware that some buildings use 24-inch centers—pole barns often use horizontal 2x6 supports, placed with the flat side towards the wall, every 2 feet up the wall. ■

Here's a different take on metal shelves. These are 12-inch-deep frames without the shelves on them, and they work great for tires. Because you can adjust the height of the supports, you can fit any size tires in these.

This tire rack is supported to the wall by chains and heavy enough to hold a full load of tires. Put a piece of plywood up there and it's a good storage shelf.

Storing Wheels and Tires

Creating a convenient place to store extra wheels and tires is a great way to free up space and give your shop a professional look. Wheels and tires are bulky, and if they're nice, you don't want to just stack them outside in the weather. Show cars have a special set of ultra-clean shoes, and race cars have at least one extra set (and generally more) of competition tires. If you have rubber to store, consider making a tire rack.

Tire racks need to be extra sturdy; wheel/tire combinations generally weigh about 30 to 50 pounds each. Two sets can weigh up to 400 pounds, so always build accordingly and watch for signs of stress as you load the rack.

You also want to be able to lift those heavy tires onto and off the rack without dislocating your shoulder or dropping them onto the hood of your car, so plan the height of the tire rack to match your comfortable reach. Generally, you want the rack to be just over your head, but not too far above that.

CREATE AND ORGANIZE STORAGE SPACE

Project: Build a Low-Cost Tire Rack

This is a simple design for a low-cost and sturdy tire rack. It's best to mount this to a 6x6 or other solid vertical post, but you can install it to any sturdy vertical post. The design uses about 12 feet of basic 2x6 cut at an angle and enough 1-inch galvanized water pipe to make two spans of the width of the rack. If you go more than about 12 feet wide, you should add a center brace as well.

Cost: About $40 in wood and hardware

Time to build: About 1 hour

Tools needed:
- Circular saw
- Hammer and nails or power driver and screws
- Power drill and 1/2- and 1-inch wood-boring bits
- Carpenter's level
- Measuring tape

Supplies needed:
- 12-foot 2x6 board
- 16D nails or 3-inch heavy construction screws
- 2 1/2-inch bolts 10-inches long with washers and nuts
- 2 pieces of 1-inch galvanized pipe long enough to span your installation

The great thing about this project is that it costs very little, but looks clean and professional, and the design holds a lot of weight. You may want to change some of the measurements in this procedure to accommodate tires of different sizes. Small 13-inch wheels and tires suitable for older foreign cars have a smaller overall diameter than tires for larger cars, so size your tire rack appropriately.

Follow these steps:

1 Cut the 12-foot 2x6 in half, making two 6-foot lengths. Then cut off 30 inches from each of them at a 45-degree angle. Cut so that the longest side of the short piece is 30 inches. Then cut the square end at an opposite angle of 45 degrees, so that the piece sits up against the supporting post.

2 Place the square end of one of the long pieces perpendicular to the wall next to the supporting post at the height you want the rack. Make sure the long side of the piece is on top, and then drill a 7/16-inch hole all the way through the long end at the middle of the post. Place a 7/16-inch carriage bolt through the hole and tighten it. Repeat at the same height on the other post.

3 Take the short end, place it up against the post, and move it until the outer end is matched up with the long horizontal piece. Put a couple of construction screws or a 5/16-inch lag bolt through the bottom to hold it in place. Then use a 1-inch wood-boring bit to drill a hole through both pieces of wood. Repeat on the other side.

This design for a tire rack costs almost nothing. It was made with a couple pieces of 2x6 and some old water pipes that were laying around. The only new money spent was to buy the long carriage bolts to pierce the 6x6 posts.

The outer support is simply nailed to the post. Geometry is working for you here, transferring the weight to the post.

Drill through the 2x6 and through the 6x6 and put in a heavy carriage bolt with washers and a nut on the other side. That's what's holding all the weight.

HOW TO DESIGN, BUILD & EQUIP YOUR AUTOMOTIVE WORKSHOP ON A BUDGET

CHAPTER 6

4 Slide a piece of 1-inch pipe through both holes, spanning the distance between the supports. You can leave a little bit hanging on either side. With a saw, cut a notch in each horizontal support just in front of the posts, and lay another piece of pipe into the notch. It doesn't have to be deep—just enough to keep the pipe from moving around. You may choose where to place the notch to accommodate tires of different sizes.

The outer pipe goes through a hole drilled in the boards to be both a tire support and a fulcrum for the two wooden pieces. The inner pipe just sits in a pair of notches to help support the tires.

Workbenches

Your workbench is a critical part of your workspace. This is where you do a lot of delicate detail work, so you want to be sure that the bench is at the optimum height for you (or whoever works there). Obviously, the best height for someone who is 5-feet 2-inches tall is different from the height for a 6-footer, so spend some time testing benches of different heights and find what works for you.

Remember that bench-mounted tools generally have a working height somewhat above the bench height. A section of bench designed to support power tools may need a different top or design than a bench designed to allow you to solder or assemble small parts. Don't forget the fact that you work on some items from the top and others from the sides, so you may decide you really need a few benches of different heights for different purposes.

Another important factor for workbenches is that they are rock solid. A wobbly bench is no bench at all. So make sure that the bench is heavy, attached to the wall, and solidly standing on the floor. Most workbenches are built in place for precisely this reason. As nice as premade benches look, they are generally lighter and designed to stand free; unless they are well-attached to a wall, they move when you don't want them to.

The good news about benches is that you don't have to spend a lot of money to get a nice working surface. Some of the benches with a good "wow factor" cost less to build than you might expect.

Basic Workbench

The first step up from making a workbench out of free packing crates is to purchase a used kitchen counter from a recycled building supply store. These stores always have a large supply of used kitchen counters, and they make great workbenches for a

> **TECH TIP — Quick Bench**
>
> If you have drawers and need a little temporary workbench space, just pull out a drawer and put a scrap of plywood on it. ■

Homes being remodeled create a steady supply of old kitchen cabinets suitable for a workshop. If you don't like the color—just paint them.

CREATE AND ORGANIZE STORAGE SPACE

Counter Space

Most kitchen counters are lower than you want for a workbench, so to get a kitchen counter up to the right height, build a sturdy stand underneath. Depending on the height you need, this can be another place for storage or just a good way to keep your nice cabinets off the wet and dirty floor. ■

This entire set of top and bottom cabinets was on sale at a used building materials outlet for $100. That's a matching workbench and wall cabinets for less than the price of a stack of 2x6 lumber. You'd need to come up with a benchtop, but an old door or a piece of plywood would look nice and be perfectly functional.

variety of reasons. The first reason counters work well is that they tend to have laminate tops built over particle board, so you can mount bench tools to them, or work directly on the nice surface.

Another reason that kitchen counters work well as workbenches is that they generally come with a useful combination of drawers and cabinets built underneath, and you can often find matching wall cabinets at the same time in the same store. Your shop can have a finished look as nice as the inside of a house for about the same price as building a bench out of lumber.

Sometimes the counter drawers and cabinets at a used building materials store come separately from the counter top, which allows you to build a heavy-duty top out of lumber and plywood and still get the benefits of the finished cabinetry above and below.

Project: Build a Low-Cost Heavy-Duty Workbench

The classic workbench is a heavy-duty item, built in place, and securely mounted to the wall. This kind of bench is great for mounting tools like a drill press, bench grinder, or hydraulic press, and it's also a great place for general-purpose tasks.

Cost: About $200 in wood and hardware

Time to build: About 8 hours

Tools needed:
- Circular saw
- Hammer and nails or power driver and screws
- Carpenter's level
- Measuring tape

Here's the finished project. This bench holds any amount of weight and features more storage underneath. It is 27 feet long to accommodate a great number of bench-mounted power tools and adequate working space. It's painted white to reflect light and look tidy.

Supplies needed:
- 18 12-foot 2x6 boards
- 12 8-foot 2x6 boards
- 16D nails or 3-inch heavy construction screws
- 1½-inch heavy construction screws
- 2 sheets of 1/2-inch CDX (construction-grade) plywood

This project uses more wood from the same stack of cheap 2x6 stud lumber I used for the heavy-duty shelves, and also uses some 1/2-inch plywood for the bench top. And because I have a good supply of low-cost white paint left over from the wall project, I plan on painting it white for good light reflection and a clean look.

This benchtop is 42 inches above the floor—a good height for a 6-foot-tall man, but likely too tall to be comfortable for most people. In general, 36 to 40 inches is a good height. If you are tall enough to use a higher benchtop, you can get a good-sized storage shelf or set of cabinets under the bench.

The bench described in this project is 24 feet long, but you could build it longer or shorter by simply changing the number of supports and boards. At one end, the bench is attached to the walls in a corner, and there is a vertical 6x6 post every 12 feet in this workshop. I used two of these posts for support and built two extra supports at 6 feet and 18 feet from the corner, so the bench is supported every 6 feet.

The bench is 30 inches deep, which is five 2x6 widths with a small gap between each board. Additionally, there is a shelf 24 inches above the floor level, and this shelf uses four 2x6 boards nailed in tightly to extend 22 inches from the wall. This provides a useful shelf while being recessed far enough to avoid hitting your shins. It allows you to sit on a stool and work with your knees under the bench.

Follow these steps:

1 Plan your wall attachments. If you have vertical posts, you can attach to the sides of the posts. But if you have only smooth walls, you can cut an extra support and screw it to the wall. If the span between vertical posts is more than about 8 feet, you should plan on an extra support screwed to the wall and use both methods.

2 Cut the outer legs 2 inches shorter than the height you want for the benchtop. In this case, I cut the outer legs to 40 inches. This is a little less than half an 8-foot board. The 40-inch height accounts for the 1½-inch height of the 2x6 boards on top of the supports and the 1/2-inch plywood surface, which creates the 42-inch total height of the bench.

3 For each set of supports you need one outer leg plus an inner leg if you do not have a building post or other sturdy wall-attachment point. For this project, cut two outer legs at 40 inches long for the two post supports, and four more legs at 38½ inches long for the two mid-span supports.

4 Cut 16 horizontal supports at 30 inches each. Two of these go in the corner at 40 and 22 inches off the ground to establish the bench and shelf heights. You might need to build an additional end support if you don't have a good corner to work with.

5 Screw a horizontal support onto each side of each post, at 40 inches off the floor, and two more horizontal supports at 22 inches from the floor. They attach to an

Door Bench

If you're looking for a nice and smooth workbench top surface, look for used household doors. Interior doors are lightweight, but tend to be smooth on both surfaces. Exterior doors may even be metal-covered for maximum durability. Place the doorknob hole toward the wall and it makes a great route for the plug wires for benchtop tools or appliances. ∎

Start building your workbench in the corner with solid supports. This one is 42 inches at bench height to be comfortable for a tall user.

The main supports are attached to the vertical posts in the shop, with the horizontal supports steadying the vertical support. This will be very sturdy when the boards are nailed to it.

CREATE AND ORGANIZE STORAGE SPACE

outer leg and are placed parallel to the post.

6 The mid-span supports use a lighter design, and you can use this design for all the supports if you do not have posts to work with. First, screw a 38½-inch board flat against the wall. Then stand up another 38½-inch board at the outer end as a leg, and screw a single horizontal support flat on top of the two boards. Screw another support to both vertical boards at 22 inches off the floor for the shelf.

This lighter mid-span support is designed to keep the boards from sagging, and it can bear a lot of weight. Note the inner support positioned against the wall. With the boards nailed in place, this is very sturdy.

7 With the framework in place, simply lay out the shelf boards and the top boards and nail or screw them into place. These boards firm up the structure and hold everything in place. If you have posts, you need to cut the boards up against the walls a little shorter to fit between the posts. You might want to notch the innermost shelf board to get around the mid-span wall supports. The top takes five boards with a small gap between each board. The shelf takes four boards, placed tightly together.

The bench is almost finished when you place the boards. You have to trim the boards against the wall to fit around the 6x6 posts. There's one less board in the shelf underneath to provide some knee room.

8 A sheet of plywood cut into three pieces of 48 by 30 inches covers 12 feet of bench. Cut a total of six pieces for this project and screw them to the benchtop for a smooth working surface. (Remember that CDX plywood has a smooth side and a rough side. Be sure to get the smooth side facing up.) If you have posts, you need to notch a couple pieces of the plywood to fit around each post. Be sure to screw the plywood to the boards every 2 feet and in the center. Each piece of plywood takes nine screws or more for a solid installation.

9 Finally, paint the workbench. It helps reflect light, looks great, and helps seal the wood against spills.

You can alter the dimensions of this project to fit your needs, but the basic design is strong and lasts for decades. You can replace the plywood if it gets chewed up over time, and the basic structure won't be harmed.

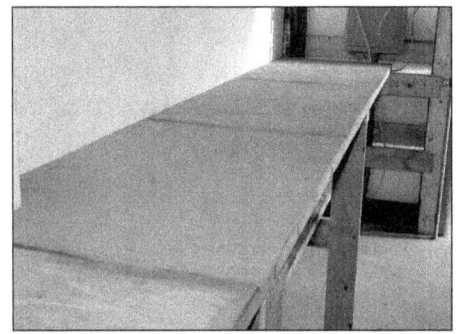

Plywood on top of the bench boards adds strength and gives you a smooth place to work or mount tools. Painting it is the final touch.

TECH TIP: Bench Paint

You might want to paint your workbench with polyurethane pickup-truck bedliner coating. This material is super-tough and stands up to all kinds of punishment. You can buy it by the quart at auto parts stores and apply it with a roller just like paint.

If you have a bunch of leftover bedliner polyurethane coating, why not put it on your workbench? It withstands all kinds of abuse and it's waterproof.

HOW TO DESIGN, BUILD & EQUIP YOUR AUTOMOTIVE WORKSHOP ON A BUDGET

CHAPTER 6

Using Attic and Rafter Space

If you're running out of storage space, it's time to look up. Most shops and garages have a lot of available and unused space overhead in the joists and rafters. If you don't have an attic already built, you can likely install one suitable for storage for just a few dollars.

With attics in general and home-built attics in particular, you want to use them for two kinds of items: things you don't use very often and things that don't weigh very much. If an item fails either test, you probably don't want to put it over your head. Engine blocks, for example, are a bad choice for attic storage, while excess fiberglass body panels are an excellent choice.

Another benefit of creating an attic is the increase in insulation. Simply separating the working area from the attic storage area creates an air space that helps to retain heat in the winter and prevent hot attic air from warming the working space in the summer. You can maximize this effect by putting in a ceiling over the workspace, then roll-out insulation between the rafters, and a layer of plywood for an attic floor. If the attic space is well-sealed from your working space, you might consider putting in passive air vents to the outside, such as those used for residential construction. But don't use these unless the attic is well-sealed, with its own layer of fiberglass insulation in the rafters. If the air in your working space can easily get into a vented attic, you'll be sending all the warm air out through the roof in the winter.

Make it Tough

The first rule for attic storage is that you need to make it as tough and solid as possible, because you really do not want things falling out of the attic onto your cars or yourself, and even if you put only light things into the attic, the cumulative weight of everything supported up there can be quite heavy. So, plan on using 2x6 rafters and at least 1/2-inch and preferably 3/4-inch plywood for the attic floor. Screwing or nailing the plywood to the rafters helps keep everything solidly in position.

You can fit rafters between roof trusses by using Strong-Ties designed for the purpose. These are stamped with a lip that goes over the top of the truss beam and then hangs alongside the truss to catch the rafter. For extra strength and stability, always put attic rafters on 16-inch centers, rather than the 24-inch centers often used for garage and outbuilding construction. This may or may not be required by the building code in your area, but it's always a good idea.

Ladders and Stairs

Once the attic is in place, you need to make some access to it. This can be as simple as an extension ladder, or as complex as a drop-down attic stair. Attic stairs are readily available at hardware stores for about $150, and they mount securely to the rafters. Just pull a cord and you can bring down and unfold a ladder that is fixed to the attic. An attic stair is convenient and a bargain if you cannot safely use an extension ladder around your cars. Ask anyone who has ever had the base of a ladder slip on a smooth concrete floor. Some people have ended up hanging out of an attic access hole with the ladder hanging on their foot, just inches from their car. At that moment, $150 for a fixed attic stair sounds like a very good bargain.

Winches and Lifting

Some garages and workshops are lucky enough to have a loft or a stand-up attic with stairs. In this case, if the attic structure is strong enough, you can put heavier items into the storage area. One way to save your back when moving items into the attic is to get a winch or crane (see Chapter 8). A floor-mounted crane with winch operation is much easier to use than carrying extremely heavy items (such as engines, or boxes of paper) up a flight of stairs or a ladder. Beam-mounted chain hoists are also handy for this purpose, if you can mount them to the roof peak. As always, be double-sure that the attic you're working with can stand the weight before you put heavy items overhead.

Gorilla Rack Workbench

Here's an idea from Jeremy Wilson of www.PopularRestorations.com for a set of really nice workbenches or worktables you can build using nothing more than a set of Gorilla Rack shelves and a piece of plywood. The super-nice part involves having a piece of stainless steel bent and welded up to make a nice table or bench top.

Gorilla Racks are available in 18x36-, 18x48-, or 24x48-inch sizes,

Truss-worthy

If you have a building built, ask your contractor about the design strength of the roof trusses. They have a weight limit that includes the existing roof materials. ■

CREATE AND ORGANIZE STORAGE SPACE

These benches and tables look far more expensive than they are. They're based on ordinary Gorilla Racks, cut in half. A benchtop of plywood and 1x1 lumber fits over the top of the Gorilla Racks, and the owner had a sheet-metal company make stainless skins for the assembly.

and all shelf kits are 72 inches tall (6 feet). If you cut a single set of shelves in half and bolt the two halves together, you have the support structure for a table 36 inches tall and 36 or 48 inches square. Simply cut a piece of thick (3/4-inch or heavier) plywood for a table top and use L-brackets to bolt it to the top of the structure. You even have a built-in shelf underneath. For extra support, screw some 1x1 fir to the underside edge of the plywood.

If you take a 24x48-inch rack and cut it in half and bolt the two halves together side by side, you have the structure for an 8-foot long, 36-inch-high, light-duty workbench with a shelf underneath. Cut a piece of thick plywood in half lengthwise and you have a benchtop. If you'd like the workbench to be taller, simply place blocks underneath the Gorilla Racks and firmly attach them to the wall. The punched-metal design of the racks makes them easy to bolt or screw to the wall.

For a luxury finish, a sheet-metal fabrication house can make nice stainless-steel table or bench tops (or borrow a long sheet-metal brake and do it yourself). Using material such as 1/16-inch stainless sheet, a fabrication shop can easily bend a crisp lip into the metal and even weld up the corners. This skin fits right over the plywood table top for an ultra-clean look.

You can see how the Gorilla Rack pieces are bolted together to form a 3-foot-square structure, and the plywood and lumber with stainless skin is simply placed over it. You also get a built-in shelf or two with this design.

Specialty Workbench

Depending on your particular projects, you may need a variety of specialized workbenches. The most common example of a specialty bench is a welding table, made entirely of steel with a thick top plate designed for both stability and electrical conductivity. (See Chapter 5 "Project: Building a Welding Table.")

Another example of a specialty bench is a flow bench, which incorporates a meter and a vacuum to test how well air flows through a cylinder head, intake, or exhaust component. Additionally, specialty benches are often designed for cylinder head porting work, fine electrical work (grounded like a welding table), soldering (fire-resistant), and ADA (Americans Disability Act)-compliant benches that accommodate wheelchairs.

If you need a special bench of any kind in your workshop, the designs shown here probably work for the basic structure, and you can modify them to your needs. The Internet is a great resource for designs, and plans can often be downloaded free or at low cost from a variety of helpful websites.

The result is breathtaking and costs just a couple hundred dollars per table or bench. Not bad compared to the price of some of the custom garage installations you can find!

CHAPTER 7

AUTOMOTIVE TOOLS

Some of the tools described here may be new to you, and others are found in virtually every home. I address the basic tools, but focus more on specialty tools that make your work easier.

Automotive work in general is a tool-intensive proposition. The most experienced and talented mechanic in the world can't do much without at least a basic set of tools, which tend to be expensive. If you plan to do your own metalwork, you need to budget quite a bit of money (and space in your shop or garage) for tools.

But on the other hand, you don't need to spend a fortune to get started and achieve good results on basic projects. While a top-quality Snap-On three-ton floor jack costs more than $400, you can purchase a good three-ton floor jack for less than $100 at a discount tool store. Used full-size jacks are available for less than $100 on www.craigslist.org and the classified ads.

Along with the big purchases, such as welders, pressure washers, and shop cranes, there are also investments to be made in wrenches, screwdrivers, and pliers. These low-cost tools can be bought one at a time and often turn up at garage sales and swap meets for extremely affordable prices. At the other end of the spectrum are specialized tools like English Wheels, sheet-metal brakes, and blacksmithing anvils. Generally these tools cost more and are harder to find.

As a general rule, buy the best tools you can afford, and generally try to get tools that are more capable than you think you need. It's frustrating and often unsafe to try to weld with a tool that is inadequate to the task at hand. When it comes to wrenches, sockets, and other tools, good equipment saves you from the time and money involved in ruined or poor-quality results. There's no shame in starting with a basic set of tools, and even if you have to build your tool set slowly, it's best to build it right.

You can use this chapter to generate a shopping or wish list for your shop, but remember that most hobbyists build their tool collection over many years, and if you're patient you can find bargains on used tools at garage sales and swap meets.

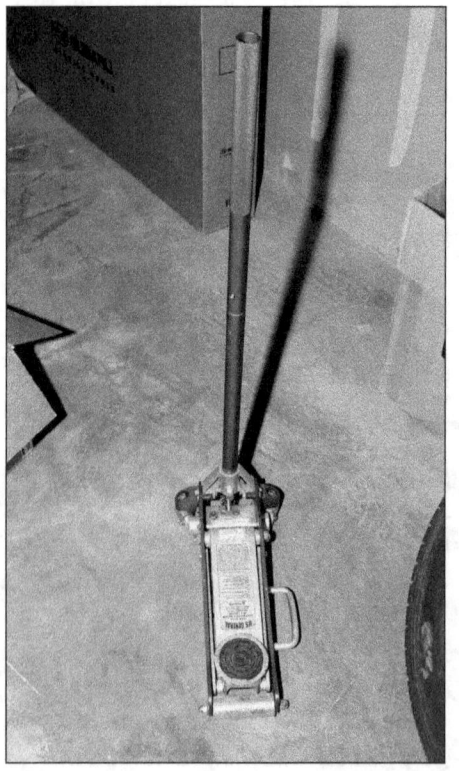

A good floor jack is a must-have tool for your shop. Strike a balance between capability and cost. This all-aluminum jack is made for racing, and some three-ton jacks are unnecessarily heavy. A two-ton jack should cost less than $100.

AUTOMOTIVE TOOLS

Know Your Bubba Ring

Roger Welsch describes the concept of the Bubba Ring in his excellent series of books on farm tractor restoration. Simply put, your Bubba Ring is a circle of friends who borrow each other's tools. If you have a group of like-minded friends, consider the benefits of purchasing only those tools that your friends don't own. If each member of a group buys a different tool, then everyone has access to a full set of tools without the expense of duplication. This works best with large, expensive tools such as MIG or TIG welders, rather than wrenches and screwdrivers, but it holds true for any tool that you don't use all the time, such as bodyworking dollies or a dual-action sander.

A Word about Renting

If you're looking at a special project or there's an expensive tool you need only infrequently such as a cherry picker or a concrete drill, you can rent large tools from many equipment rental centers. You can rent a welding setup from welding supply shops. This is often an affordable alternative to buying your own equipment, but be prepared to leave a large deposit. There are also well-equipped garages, metal shops, and paint booths that rent out working space. These businesses provide varying levels of equipment and assistance, but can also be useful if you don't have a working space.

Safety Gear

Having the right supplies is good, but the most important thing in a shop is to set it up so that safety is easy and comes naturally. For example, I keep about a dozen sets of clear safety goggles in my shop. I try to keep a set near every tool that requires their use. That way, when I go to use the tool, the glasses are right there handy so I have no excuse for not putting them on.

The lesson is simple: Be smart, play safe, and you'll have a good time.

Critical Safety: Jack Stands

Among the most important safety devices in any automotive shop are your jack stands. Amateur mechanics are killed every year when their cars fall on them. One such unlucky person was a personal friend of mine who died when his motor home fell off a jack and landed on him. Obtain a good set of extra-heavy-duty jack stands, and keep them out right next to your working space so you can remember to use them every time.

Avoid the stamped-sheet-metal type of jack stands—they don't tend to collapse, but they do frequently bend. The main problem with the sheet metal variety is that the base is not big enough and sits on only three legs, so they lack stability and may fall over.

If you have an automotive lift, that's even better; but be aware that cars can fall off lifts if they are not properly supported, and the consequences can be devastating for the car and your body.

These are the jack stands you don't want. Three legs make them prone to tipping, and the perches don't hold a car as steady. There's a reason these are for sale at a swap meet.

The jack stands you want have four legs and are made of heavy plate steel, with cast-iron perches. These last a lifetime and give you confidence.

CHAPTER 7

Safety Goggles

As mentioned in Chapter 1, obtain about 10 pairs of basic safety goggles and distribute them around your shop. Put a pair next to your bench grinder, drill press, and any other tool that can generate flying particles. Also put a pair or two in the top of your toolbox. Then remember to wear them—that's the hardest part.

Hearing Protection

Probably the most overlooked safety item in an automotive workshop is hearing protection. Workshops are noisy places, and a $1 investment in a pair of foam ear plugs helps save your hearing. If you plan to spend a lot of time in the shop, keep a stash of earplugs or external hearing protectors. Gun shops have a great selection of hearing protection designed to be comfortable for extended use. As a side benefit, reducing the noise level in your head also reduces fatigue. You can do better work for more hours if you wear hearing protection.

Shoes

You need good leather shoes to work safely around cars. Beyond the fire hazards of synthetic materials and rubber soles, you're likely to drop heavy parts from time to time. Obtain some shoes with protective steel toes if you plan to work with heavy parts such as brake discs, flywheels, engines, and so on. You can often find a good set of work boots at thrift stores for just a few dollars.

Respirator

Your workshop is likely to get dusty and dirty from time to time, especially if you plan to do bodywork or paint work indoors. You don't want that stuff getting into your lungs, so a respirator is a good piece of safety gear to have. Even if you just get some dust masks at the hardware store, they help keep the dust out of your nose, mouth, and lungs. If you have to wear a respirator for any length of time, buy a good one at a paint supply store. These have removable filter canisters. Most auto hobbyists don't need to replace the canisters very often, if ever, but these respirators fit better, filter fumes as well as particles, and are more comfortable to wear.

Fire Extinguisher/Protection

It's impossible to overstate the need for fire protection in an automotive workshop. Your household garage is full of combustibles and hot things, and it's attached to your family's home.

Fire extinguishers are not all alike—there are three classes of fire extinguisher, based on the type of fire. Class A extinguishers are meant to handle combustibles like paper, wood, and cloth. Class B extinguishers are meant to put out liquid fires like gasoline or kerosene. Class C extinguishers are for electrical fires. Because it's possible to have a fire that includes any or all of these at any time, it's best to get an A-B-C fire extinguisher. You want to be prepared to put out anything that flares up. The extinguisher industry knows this and so these are widely available.

The other thing to say about fire extinguishers is that you want several of them, and they must be big enough to finish the job. I once encountered a truck on fire and used all three 2-pound bottles in my own truck to no avail. The fire kept coming back until the fire department arrived with larger bottles. Choose 10-pound A-B-C fire bottles and get at least three of them for your shop, then keep them in accessible locations.

First-Aid Kit

A first-aid kit doesn't seem like such an important thing until you need it. A box of Band-Aids is helpful, but worse accidents have been known to happen. Your workshop hospital should start with a preassembled, large, and comprehensive first-aid kit, but then there are some things you should add:

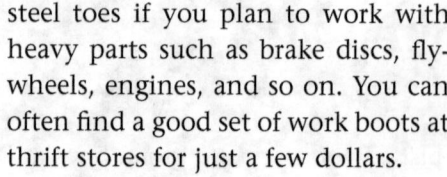

Look for the A-B-C rating on your shop fire extinguisher and plan to get your fire bottles inspected and re-certified annually.

You don't need an expensive fire extinguisher, but get a good-sized one and make sure it's A-B-C rated.

Fire Extinguishers

Have your fire extinguishers inspected annually. An extinguisher that's been sitting around for 10 years may work, or it may not. Any fire extinguisher service in your area can do this job for you at a fraction of the cost of a new bottle. ■

- Pain killers: There are some legal issues to be navigated with this, but if you have a prescription for effective pain killers, keep a bottle in your first-aid kit. If you have broken some bones or badly burned yourself, you want immediate pain relief.
- Tourniquet: If you work with knives and power saws, you run the risk of a life-threatening cut. Be prepared to stop serious bleeding.
- Clotting trauma pads: As with the tourniquet, being prepared for serious bleeding is never a waste of money. These are thick compress pads impregnated with a clotting agent.
- Butterfly closures: These are good for closing wounds until you can get medical help. In a pinch, use duct tape, but butterflies are better.
- Instant cold compress: If you don't have a ready supply of ice in your shop, an instant cold compress is a good item to include in your kit.
- Optical saline solution: You can get a bottle at the grocery store in the contact lens section. Keep it in your first-aid cabinet to wash out eyes in the event of a caustic liquid splash.
- Mouthwash: If you ever succumb to the temptation to suck-start a siphon (we've all done it) and ended up with a mouthful of gasoline, nothing clears your mouth better than some good mouthwash, followed by a cold beer.

Note that the first-aid kits marketed for home workshops are often little more than a box of Band-Aids and aspirin. Take stock of what's really there when you set up your kit. You can purchase a basic EMT/EMS First Responder trauma kit for about $70 online and it should have the tourniquet, clotting pads, and cold compresses that I listed above.

Poisoning

Another safety factor is poisoning. Even casual automotive enthusiasts work with some pretty nasty chemicals. If you have a solvent-based parts washer, a jug of antifreeze, or an automotive detailing kit, you have poisons in your shop. Make sure that these are not accessible to children or pets and minimize your own exposure by using chemical-resistant gloves, respirators, and adequate ventilation.

One final thought on safety: do you have a phone in your workspace that can call 911 with not more than a couple keystrokes? If you don't, you should get one.

Toolboxes

As soon as you start collecting tools, you're going to need someplace to put them. Shortly after that, you will need several places to put your tools, because you have a set of things that need to be close to the drill press, the welder, and other places. You will also have a set that you want to take with you in your car.

Toolboxes are often as expensive as the tools that they hold, and there's nothing nicer than a really slick rollaway toolbox with silky-smooth, ball-bearing drawer action. But a useful toolbox doesn't have to be expensive if you shop around a bit.

As with any tools, keep a sharp eye out for quality. It's better to buy

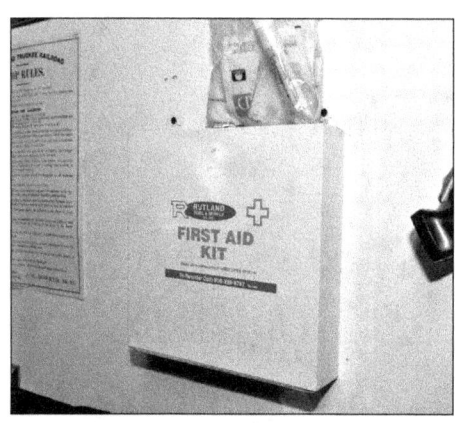

A basic first-aid kit is a good idea. Mount it in a convenient location so you don't have to dig it out when you're bleeding and in pain.

Rag Bin

Get a sealed metal rag bin. We've all heard of spontaneous combustion of oily or solvent-soaked rags. It rarely happens, but it does happen. Keep your fresh rags separate from used ones, and keep partially used rags in a sealed metal container. An ordinary, small metal trash can with a lid works great. The best habit is to keep oily and solvent-soaked rags outdoors in that sealed metal can. ∎

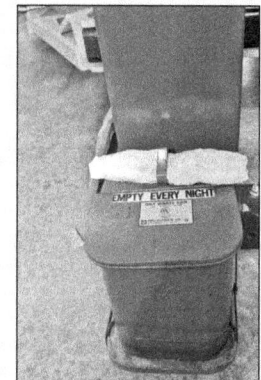

A simple rag bin like this, or a metal trash can with a lid, can help prevent fires and keep your workshop tidy.

CHAPTER 7

Glove Yourself

If you've been in a pro auto shop lately, you have probably noticed that the mechanics wear surgical-style gloves. This is not because new cars are all that delicate, but rather in response to the poisons (and general dirt and grease) that can soak into human skin while working on cars. Many of these substances are known carcinogens and potent poisons.

You can get a box of good latex or nitrile gloves at any auto supply store. In general, you want the most expensive box of gloves you can find. The price range is about $5 for a box of cheap gloves and up to $15 for the best ones. The best gloves are nitrile, which resists chemicals better than latex. The best gloves are also thicker and have some texture to increase gripping power.

While nitrile gloves keep your hands clean and chemical-free, they do not protect against burns. If you plan to dive into a hot engine bay, you want welder's gloves or at least mechanic's gloves. Mechanic's gloves are thin and tight-fitting, made from a suede-like synthetic material. These gloves were developed by professional racing teams to protect against burns while allowing mechanics to perform fine work. They cost about $20 per pair and, if you don't get them oily and dirty, they last a long time.

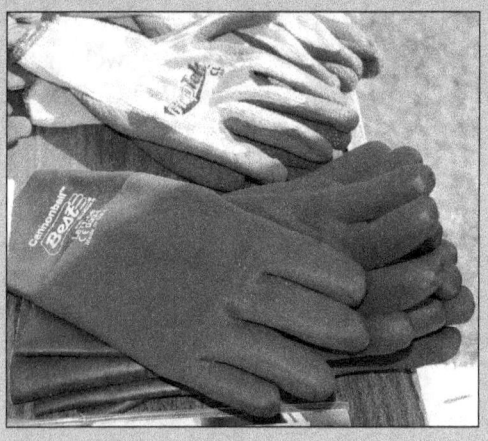

Chemical gloves are essential for parts washers and brake cleaning solvent work. Many garage chemicals go right through your skin.

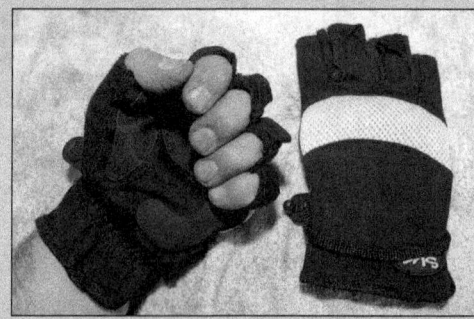

Another set of gloves to have is a pair (or several) of mechanic's gloves. These are fingerless, but you can get them in a variety of styles. They have a suede-like material that allows you to do fine work while being somewhat protected from burns and cuts.

one nice rollaway toolbox from Sears or Snap-On and use it for 20-plus years than to buy a series of annoying, cheap toolboxes.

Large versus Portable

The first decision you have to make is about the size of a toolbox. I always recommend that you get a larger unit than you think you'll need. Tools expand to fill available space, and the huge toolbox you buy today is going be full before you know it. As an added bonus, most roll-away tool chests are lockable—another measure of security.

When you find that you have a lot of tools to store, you can get a whole bunch of smaller carry-around toolboxes for hammers, files, and other sets of tools, and then keep your good stuff in the nice roll-away box. You can find plenty of bargains on toolboxes suitable for hammers and such at swap meets and in the classified ads.

A good tool chest will be with you for a lifetime, so don't cheap out and buy a box that you're going to hate for years.

Hand Tools

The first and most basic tools for an automotive workshop are hand tools. You should have a good set of these because they require no electricity or compressed air and you can generally take them with you on a road trip.

Working with hand tools can also be very relaxing. As convenient as an air-powered impact wrench is—there are many times when it's the only tool that can get the job done—sometimes it's nice to work with a silent wrench. With a hand tool, you get a much better feeling for your work. Your touch tells you when a bolt is about to strip or break, where a power tool just twists it right off.

As with any other part of building out your workshop, the first question to answer is what do you really need in the way of tools? A hot rodder or race car fabricator needs a much larger tool set than someone who just wants to perform maintenance or keep a restored classic looking good and running well.

Do you plan to rebuild engines or suspensions? Do you plan to weld or work with sheet metal and bodywork? Also give yourself an honest appraisal of your skills—are you really going to need that tubing bender? The answers tell you what level of equipment you should plan to purchase and what you should plan to farm out to professionals. But don't sell yourself short, either—it's fun to learn to use new tools. If you want to try new things, that's what your workshop is for!

Wrench

The wrench is the fundamental tool of the automotive hobbyist. They come in all shapes and sizes, and the first rule about wrenches is to buy a set of good ones and make sure you have more than one in all the common sizes (7/16 through 3/4 inch and 10 through 19 mm). Nothing is more common than a 1/2-inch bolt with a 1/2-inch nut on the other end, and you need two 1/2-inch wrenches to tighten or remove that combo.

There's a particular pleasure in using a well-made wrench. Examine a Snap-On wrench and hold it in your hand and then take a good look at a cheap wrench. You'll see and feel the difference right away. A good wrench is worth the money you spend on it and worth taking care of so that it lasts a lifetime.

Wrenches come in open- and box-end styles—get some of both because there are situations in which each is specifically required. Combination wrenches with one box and one open end are a good choice.

One set of wrenches you want to save up to buy is a good set of gear wrenches—these combine the functions of a ratcheting socket set with a box-end wrench. They are incredibly handy for getting into tight spaces and working quickly. They're usually expensive, but worth the money. To save cash, consider buying only those sizes you use most often.

Finally, you need a set of adjustable Crescent-type wrenches. Get three—small, medium, and large. They come in handy in all sorts of ways.

Pliers

After wrenches, you need to think about pliers. You want a good selection of pliers, but resist the urge to use them in place of wrenches. The world is full of useless, rounded-off nuts and bolt heads because someone couldn't be bothered to use the proper wrench and used pliers on an otherwise functional fastener.

Along with the standard slip-joint pliers, you want a set of good lineman's pliers—these have a square nose and a heavy wire cutter in the jaws. Lineman's pliers can cut most wires and flexible fuel and brake lines. Also buy a few good sets of diagonal-cutting pliers (often known as "dykes") for cutting wires and clipping plastic and sheet metal. These are useful any time you need to trim off loose ends.

The Good and the Bad

In addition to good wrenches, buy a supply of cheap, horrible wrenches and keep them in a separate box. You can generally get all you want for a couple bucks out of a box at any swap meet or garage sale. These are "sacrificial" wrenches—for loaning to unreliable neighbors, welding to 55-gallon drums as handles, and grinding down to fit into inaccessible places in old Italian sports cars. ■

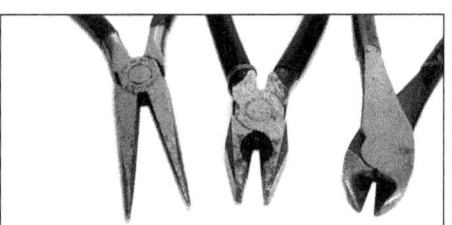

Three useful pliers you need to own are: needle-nose (left), lineman's pliers (middle), and diagonal cutters (right).

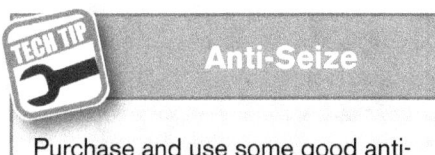

Anti-Seize

Purchase and use some good anti-seize coating to help prevent future stuck bolts. ■

For large work, get a set of plumber's pliers—not to be confused with a monkey wrench. These are known by the trade name Channel-Locks and feature a slip joint that opens the jaws to several inches. These pliers are handy any time you need to grab and hold something large, such as gripping a driveshaft while you undo its mounting bolts.

You also want a selection (from tiny ones to some fairly large ones) of needle-nose pliers for the drawer. Needle-nose pliers are always handy.

If your task list includes upholstery work, a set of hog ring pliers should be on it. These pliers have a special set of jaws to grab the staples used to attach leather and vinyl underneath a car seat. Upholstery kits often come with a set of hog ring pliers included.

Vise Grips

Vise Grips are a special type of pliers, and you should plan to purchase a selection of these in a variety of sizes. Vise Grips have a device in the handles that locks the jaws in place around the item you're gripping. There's a screw or dial in the handle that sets the jaw position and a release lever.

Vise Grips are a tool of last resort. If you have a broken stub of a bolt, a completely rounded-off nut, or anything else that just has to be grabbed at all costs, Vise Grips are the tool for it. But the tradeoff is that they mar the item being grabbed. The teeth on the Vise Grips are designed to dig in, and you can put a lot of pressure on the jaws.

Wire Stripper

Another special type of pliers is a set of wire strippers. A wire stripper and crimp tool should be part of everyone's toolbox, but an automatic wire stripper is worth a separate purchase. This tool is a comparatively new design that grabs a wire and holds it while another set of jaws cuts the insulation and pulls the jacket off the wire. This tool vastly reduces the amount of time spent stripping wires and generally makes a neater job of it than a traditional wire stripper.

Screwdriver

Every mechanic has a large supply of screwdrivers—and the same rules that apply to wrenches apply to these basic tools. You need a good set that you use only for their intended purpose—you want to keep the working end of the tool crisp and sharp. Then you need a sacrificial set of screwdrivers for those times when you need to use a screwdriver as a pry bar, chisel, hole-punch, or loaner.

Screw/Bolt Extractor

Every mechanic's nightmare is a broken stud or bolt—usually with the remains of the threaded shaft down inside a blind hole that is critical to the continued operation of the car.

When this happens to you (and it will), your only hope is an extractor. These are counter-threaded, ultra-hard pins that you wedge into the broken bolt shaft and use to twist it out. In order to use an extractor, you must drill out the center of the bolt shaft and then insert the extractor.

The problem is that if the bolt shaft was stuck hard enough to break the bolt, it often breaks the extractor as well. You then have an ultra-hard chunk of extractor stuck in the hole.

For best results with extractors, always drill out as much of the bolt as possible without marring the threads in the hole. Take your time and drill carefully, then use the largest possible extractor as gently as possible. Tap it into place—don't hammer it. Finally, prepare yourself for the possibility that you have to take the project to a machine shop to have them drill out the hole and re-thread it.

Tap-and-Die Set

Another tool for dealing with ruined threads is a good tap-and-die set. Restorers especially want to own one of these kits in both standard and metric measurements. The important thing to remember is that these kits are used to dress up and repair damaged threads—they're really not up to the task of cutting new threads that are strong and will last. If you can run a tap into a hole to clean up

Cheaters Always Win

Obtain a variety of "cheater bars"—lengths of pipe that you can put over the end of a socket wrench or breaker bar for some extra leverage. Also realize that if you put enough leverage on a socket wrench, you may break the ratchet gears or sometimes even the socket itself. ∎

Impact Sockets

Never use a standard socket with an impact wrench. An impact wrench exerts tremendous hammering forces on the socket and you can easily crack the body of a standard socket with an impact wrench. Always use sockets designed for an impact wrench. ∎

the threads, you have a much better chance of inserting a bolt to its full depth and then getting it out again in one piece later.

Socket and Ratchet

A good set of sockets and ratcheting socket wrenches is indispensible. Because of the variety of sockets, socket extensions, wobbly extensions, and specialty fittings, there's very little you can't do with a ratchet wrench. Sockets come in 1/4-, 3/8-, and 1/2-inch-drive sizes. You can get much larger sockets as well, but those three sizes cover everything you need for most automotive work.

For most automotive work, you want a set of standard sockets and a set of deep sockets. Deep sockets allow you to set nuts with more of the bolt thread showing through, which is often the need in automotive applications. A set of 12-point sockets is nice to have because these work on square (4-sided) nuts and go onto any nut more easily. With 12-points, you trade torque for convenience. A 12-point socket rounds off a nut more easily, and you can't get the same torque that you can achieve with a 6-point socket.

Good sockets are important, but even more important is a good socket wrench. Look for smooth operation and fine clicks in the ratchet mechanism. Sears Craftsman socket wrenches used to be very good, but have fallen in quality in recent years. Snap-On is the gold standard for socket wrenches, and priced accordingly.

Torque Wrench

For automotive work, you are sure to need a torque wrench sooner rather than later. A torque wrench is simply a socket wrench with a means of telling you how much force has been applied to a nut or bolt head. Torque is measured in foot-pounds, inch-pounds, or Newton-meters. The scale you use doesn't matter as long as you know what scale you're using and the proper torque value you need.

The most common mistake made with torque wrenches is to confuse inch-pounds (used with 1/4-inch-drive torque wrenches) with foot-pounds. As you might expect, there are 12 inch-pounds in a foot-pound. If a torque specification calls for 14 inch-pounds and you deliver 14 foot-pounds, disaster is sure to strike. Similarly, if you torque a nut designed for 36 foot-pounds to just 36 inch-pounds, that nut is going to come loose. Generally speaking, 3/8-inch and 1/2-inch torque wrenches are all calibrated in foot-pounds.

There are several styles of torque wrenches to choose from. Most common is a clicking torque wrench. With this style you twist the handle to the desired torque setting and use the tool like a normal socket wrench. When the desired torque is achieved, the handle makes an audible click or pop. There are also digital wrenches that show torque on a display in the handle.

Older torque wrenches had a flexible head and a needle that pointed to a spot on a scale. If you find one of these antiques, it makes a nice display at car shows, but don't use it. They were never all that accurate and by now the tool has been flexed for 40 years or more.

Finally, don't forget that a torque wrench is a precision piece of machinery. You should never allow it to get wet or dirty. Torque wrenches usually come with protective boxes—keep yours in its box in a drawer when it's not in use.

Riv-Nutters

The riv-nut (or rivnut) system is closely related to pop riveters. This tool installs a rivet with a threaded hole in its center. If you want to screw or bolt something to a sheet-metal bulkhead or firewall and have it look nice and be infinitely removable and replaceable, a riv-nut is the right tool for the job. The riv-nut tool threads into the riv-nut and crushes the rivet into the hole. Then you simply unscrew the tool and you have a threaded hole to work with.

Extension Tool

It's practically a law of nature that a dropped washer or nut falls into the worst possible place it can land. Find a few extra dollars for a set of extension tools to help you find and retrieve dropped parts from inconvenient locations.

A small mirror on an extension stick is useful for seeing around corners and into obscured pockets. If you can see where the part landed, it's always easier to get in there and grab it.

The next valuable tool is a magnet on an extension stick. Most nuts and bolts are made of steel, and if you can get a magnet down there without it sticking to the other steel all around, you can often retrieve the runaway part.

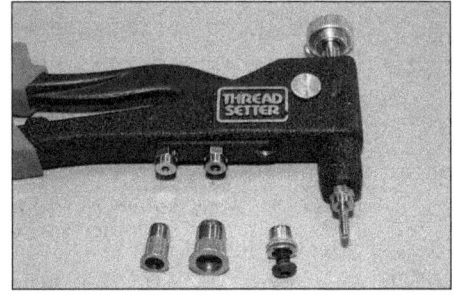

This is a riv-nut tool and a selection of riv-nuts. These are tremendously handy if you're doing your own sheet-metal work on a hot rod or race car.

CHAPTER 7

The last tool you need is a flexible grabber. This tool has a long and flexible hollow tube and a T-shaped handle. When you press the end of the handle with your thumb, three or four spring-loaded hooked ends come out of the tube. Release your thumb and the hooked ends grab the loose part and you can pull it out. Press your thumb down again to release the part and you're done.

Free-Standing and Bench-Mounted Tools

You can do a lot with hand tools, but when you start doing more and larger projects, the results will be better and easier with larger bench-mounted or free-standing tools. Of course, these tools are correspondingly more expensive than hand tools. While the prices may be intimidating, you can often find these tools for less on the used market, and you can equip your shop over time.

Automotive hobbyists are lucky to have a choice between free-standing professional shop tools and smaller versions of the same tools mounted to the workbench. The advantage of a free-standing tool is that it doesn't use up precious bench space and can be moved around as needed. The tradeoff is that a free-standing tool generally takes up more space than a bench-mounted alternative, and tends to be more expensive.

Generally speaking, free-standing tools run on the same 120-volt power as a bench-mounted tool. The exception is extremely large tools such as machining mills and lathes, which may use 240-volt current. Refer to the wiring instructions for 240-volt appliances in that case, but all 120-volt tools should come with a standard plug—make sure you're plugging these tools into a 20-amp circuit.

The list below begins with the most commonly used tools and finishes with more specialty or unusual tools.

Bench Grinder

One of the basics of any workshop is the bench grinder. These tools typically have a rough grindstone on one end and a fine grindstone on the other end. They are handy for shortening bolts, customizing wrenches, and generally removing metal from anything small enough to hold in your hands.

It's a good idea to get at least a couple bench grinders, and load up the second one with coarse and fine wire wheels to remove paint and rust from small parts. Restorers and hot rodders often use a compressed-cloth buffing wheel to put some polish on

This bench grinder is set up on a free-standing support and outfitted with a grindstone and a buffing wheel—perfect for classic car restoration.

metal parts. A stick of jeweler's rouge lets you buff almost any metal to a high shine.

Vise

By far the most common type of vise is a machinist's vise, also called a bench vise. These are typically bolted to a workbench or table, and they are designed to hold a part while you work. Most include a flat surface for chiseling or hammering, but do not use a bench vise for an anvil. If you use a hammer to beat a piece held in the vise jaws, some of the blow is transferred to the vise screw, and it won't last long under that kind of abuse.

You can get a machinist's vise in any size from jewelry (small) up to an 8-inch opening with heavy jaws. Different vises also offer a variety of adjustments to hold materials at any angle. In general you get what you pay for with a vise, but estate and garage sales are good places to find an older high-quality vise.

The other type of vise is more archaic, but also more useful. It's called a leg vise or blacksmith's vise. It's easily identified because it has a support leg that stands on the ground, while the body of the vise

A basic bench vise is a tool everyone should have. Most shops have more than one. This one is bolted to a welding table.

AUTOMOTIVE TOOLS

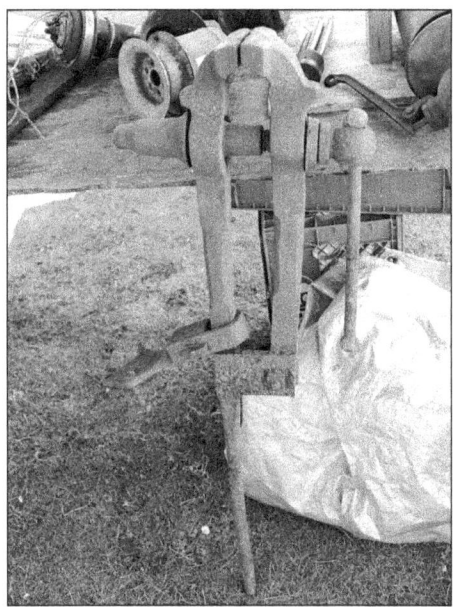

This is how you find most leg vises at a swap meet—rusty and decrepit. This one needs a spring, some de-rusting, and paint, but it's worth the money. Once you have one, you'll love it.

This is a basic cast-iron anvil, available at any discount tool center. These are handy for grommet setting and all kinds of light hammering work.

is still mounted to a bench or table. The key difference is that a leg vise is designed to be used as an anvil surface as well as to hold your work. If you find one of these, it's likely to be at a farm sale or antique store, and it is likely to be expensive. But those who use a leg vise highly value it.

Anvil

One tool that is hard to find today, but which remains one of the most useful tools you can own, is an anvil. Anvils come in a variety of sizes and designs, and even a small anvil is useful for automotive metalworking projects.

A traditional blacksmithing anvil is made of forged iron or steel, with a hard steel working face. But anvils sold in discount stores omit the hard face—you can put a dent in the working surface with any hammer. These are handy for straightening bent parts and light forming work.

It's important to set up an anvil properly. It should be mounted securely to a sturdy base such as the area directly over a floor support on your workbench or table.

If you want an inexpensive and functional anvil, you can make one out of a piece of railroad track, or you can make do with just about any large, heavy piece of steel with a flat face. Search your local steel scrap yard for a chunk that you can mount on your bench to meet your needs.

Belt Sander/Grinder

A good bench-mounted belt sander/grinder is always useful around automotive projects. These are more precise than stone bench grinders or body grinders, so they're often used for shaping small pieces of sheet metal or other parts that just need a little trimming. Belt grinders are great for removing excess casting flash and welding material.

Drill Press

Every metal shop needs a good, large drill press. Get the biggest and most powerful drill press you can afford and find a vise/clamp attachment to hold parts. The clamp is important because it's easy to get injured when a drill press grabs the part you're drilling and swings it around to hit your hands. Get a good set of high-speed hardened drill bits

Belt and disc grinders are perfect tools for shaping all kinds of parts, patches, and anything that has casting flash still attached to it.

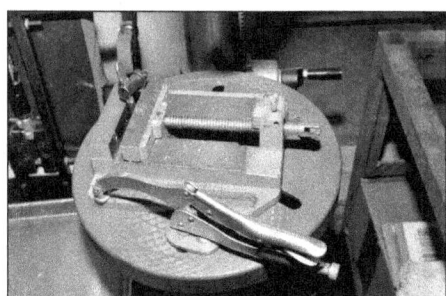

Make sure you get a selection of clamps with your drill press vise. They help prevent a drill press from grabbing parts out of your hand and swinging them around to hit you.

CHAPTER 7

with plenty of spares for the small and often-used sizes (1/4, 5/16, 7/16, 1/2, 9/16 inch, and so on). You can also invest in a set of step-bits, which have a small pilot section to start a hole accurately before the main bit cuts the hole to size.

Bandsaw

A standard bandsaw is handy for cutting aluminum and other non-steel metals. You can get by with a circular saw or a reciprocating (Sawzall) saw, but a bandsaw allows you to do finer work. Be sure that you have selected a blade that is suitable for the material you're planning to cut. A fine-tooth blade is absolutely required for cutting metal, and you get better results with hardwoods and plastics with a fine-tooth blade. Use a large-tooth blade only for cutting soft woods like pine and fir.

A variant of the bandsaw is a straight metal-cutting unit. These use gravity to pull the blade in straight cuts through metal. This tool is handy for cutting box and tube steel, but you can get results just as good with a less-expensive abrasive chop saw.

Chop Saw

A chop saw uses a circular abrasive blade to make straight chop cuts through metal. If you spend a little more on the blades you can get a carbide or diamond-tipped metal blade. The metal blade lasts longer than the consumable abrasive blade and produces less dust, but the price difference is significant.

You can also get by with an abrasive blade on a table saw or even with a handheld circular saw, but these are dangerous due to their high rotation speed. If the blade comes apart, you (or bystanders) could be injured. There are now special handheld circular saws on the market that spin at the lower speed and are designed to use the same kind of metal-cutting blades found on chop saws.

Blast Cabinet

The air-powered bead-blasting cabinet is a useful tool in the automotive shop. If you have to take paint off metal, there's nothing like a blast cabinet. You can get a free-standing version of a blast cabinet at a tool supply store. Free-standing cabinets accept anything up to an exhaust header or loose wheel.

Bench-mounted blast cabinets are usually made from injection-molded plastic, and these are great units. Free-standing and some benchtop blast cabinets usually have to be assembled from parts made of stamped sheet metal. Some foam-rubber gaskets are included, but they really don't work and these cabinets leak tiny glass-bead dust everywhere. You can get around this with a tube or two of clear silicone RTV (room temperature vulcanizing) sealant. Use the RTV to seal each joint as you assemble the cabinet.

The other thing you want to do is add a filter to the outlet vent of

A metal-cutting chop saw with an abrasive blade spins slower than a circular or table saw. This is good because it puts less heat in the metal and has less chance of breaking the blade and injuring you.

A metal-cutting bandsaw is designed to make straight cuts in long pieces of box and tube. It makes a lovely clean cut, but you can't do curves like you can with a regular bandsaw equipped with a metal-cutting blade.

A benchtop blast cabinet is good for most parts. You can take big pieces to a professional metal-stripping service for just a few dollars.

Blasting Tips

When it comes to blasting, less is often more. Don't put more abrasive material in the cabinet than is absolutely necessary to ensure a steady supply, and use the lowest possible air pressure from the compressor. If you use too much pressure or too much abrasive, the material can't move through the blast gun. ■

Go Green

Biodiesel fuel is a great natural solvent. This product dissolves grease and oil-based deposits very effectively and works well in a parts washer. ■

any blast cabinet. You're putting a lot of pressurized air into the cabinet and, as it vents out the air, it tends to carry dust and abrasive with it. A filter keeps the abrasive inside the cabinet, but be sure to check and clean it frequently.

Also be aware that the hoses and fittings that come with less-expensive cabinets are prone to kink and collapse. You may need to find some reinforced tubing at a home supply store and upgrade the cabinet.

Parts Washer

A free-standing parts washer is a good idea if you plan to perform restoration work. You may wish to put the parts washer outside because it naturally gets dirty, and if you fill it with mineral spirits, gasoline, kerosene, or diesel fuel, it could be a fire hazard.

Some free-standing parts washers use a filter system and a drum of solvent placed below the washing basin, while the lower-cost models are simply a basin full of solvent. You can get water and detergent based cleaners, but these are better used in a benchtop washer. Some high-cost units actually heat the solvent. This works great for cleaning purposes but, in addition to the cost, the heating element could be a fire danger.

Note that a parts washer uses an electric motor to drive a pump that circulates the fluid through a nozzle. Pay close attention to the solvents you put in the washer, because certain chemicals (such as acetone) immediately destroy the rubber parts of the pump. Your product documentation should tell you what's safe to use.

The highest-end parts washers are like giant dishwashers, and use boiling water and detergent to clean large parts like engine blocks. A dishwasher (see Chapter 4) simulates one of these on a small scale.

If you would rather not have a large parts washer filled with dangerous chemicals, you can always take your pieces to be washed at a machine shop or parts-cleaning business. As a rule, machine shops probably charge a little less for small and infrequent cleaning jobs, but parts cleaning businesses are a better deal for larger lots and frequent work.

Engine Stand

An engine stand is usually among the first free-standing tools acquired for a garage or automotive shop, and that's part of the reason there are a lot of engine stands out there that people can't wait to get rid of. There are two basic designs—one is T-shaped, with a single leg sticking out under the engine and a crossbar at the back supporting the vertical piece that holds the engine. T-shaped engine stands are dangerous to the point of worthlessness. With the weight of an engine up high on the stand it's very tricky to move the unit around on its casters without tipping it over and dropping the engine on the floor, or into the car's fender, or onto your foot.

The other design has parallel legs. When you shop for an engine stand,

Look for an engine stand with four feet, spaced as widely as possible. Avoid T-shaped stands at all costs.

When your engine is assembled, a cradle like this allows you to slide it under a bench without scraping the pan and to transport it safely without risk of it falling over.

consider only those stands with parallel legs, which create a broad and stable support for the engine.

A related tool is an engine cradle. These stands are designed for assembled engines that need to be stored or moved. It's simply a metal framework with engine mounts where they are needed. You bolt the engine onto one and it creates a stable base.

Shop Press

A hydraulic press is a useful tool if you plan to work with driveshaft U-joints, suspension bushings, and other press-fit items. These come in bench-mounted and free-standing sizes, and they typically use a hydraulic bottle jack as the pressure mechanism. The lowest-price versions of these tools are imported from China and found at discount tool stores. There's little reason to buy a more expensive version of this tool except that the dies and supports are better-made.

Keep a supply of short pieces of pipe and other metal shapes in a box near the press—virtually every pressing job is a custom setup. Be sure to set up your press carefully, as it's often easier to bend or collapse a part than it is to press it together straight and true. This is another task that's often best consigned to a professional machine shop if it's tricky or infrequent.

Tubing Bender

A tool related to the shop press is a tubing bender. These are often considered together because the cheapest tubing benders are a similar design—with a large bottle jack and some channeled dies that are used to press the tubing upward.

It's important to understand that these benders are useful for making non-stressed parts like bumper-mounted light bars, but they are absolutely unsafe for structural tube work such as roll bars and chassis components. This is because they work by stretching the metal at the outside of a bend, which weakens the tube at the bend.

If you plan to bend tube steel for any structural purpose, you need a quality mandrel tubing bender, which is an expensive tool. Manual tube benders start at about $300, while a professional-quality power unit costs up to several thousand dollars. But if you plan on making a lot of roll bars or tube-frame chassis, this is a good investment.

For the infrequent bender, a better solution is to have a top-notch fabrication shop bend the tubing for you. They can likely do it more accurately than you possibly could and can give you a safer part. Unless you're bending tube very frequently, farming this work out is a bargain.

Tire Mount/Dismount Tool

If you plan to work with a lot of wheels and tires, you might consider picking up a used tire mounter, often called a "buster." The old-school version of this tool is air-powered and can be bought for about $500 from a tire center or through classified ads. These tools use levers to pull the tire around and a pair of "shovels" to break the bead seals. Remember that these old-style mounters are prone to damaging alloy wheels and are usually recommended only for steel wheels with a large center hole.

A shop press is indispensable for working on driveshafts and suspension bushings. Get a good collection of metal shapes and pieces to put the pressure right where you need it.

These tube benders work well for light bars and other non-stressed applications, but don't ever use them for structural work like chassis, roll bars, or bumpers, because they substantially weaken the tube steel.

This is a proper tubing bender, but it costs a lot of money. You're better off taking your bending to a professional unless you do it all the time.

AUTOMOTIVE TOOLS

Racers who go through a lot of tires on sturdy rims often find a tire buster to be a cost- and time-effective purchase.

A modern "touch-free" tire mounter is a much more expensive tool, costing up to several thousand dollars. These tools require an electrical circuit to operate. For the hobbyist, this grade of tool makes little sense, but it is fun to use.

Tire Balancer

A tire tool that makes sense for the hobbyist is an old-fashioned "bubble balancer" for tires and wheels. This is essentially a bubble level in a cone, mounted atop a spindle. You set the wheel on the cone through the wheel's central hole and watch the bubble. The heavy side of the wheel falls; so you add weight to the light side until the bubble stays centered. Fix the weights to the wheel and you're done. These tools are inexpensive at about $100, and they are as accurate as a spin balancer. Any time your car throws a wheel weight, you can rebalance it yourself easily. Tire centers sell weights, or you can buy stick-on weights at any auto supply store.

Automotive Bodyworking Tools

If you plan to do your own bodywork or fabrication, you want some sheet-metal tools. These tend to be expensive, but they are what you need to work with this material. As with all expensive tools, if you're just an occasional user, you can usually get a fabrication shop to perform these tasks for far less money.

Body Hammers and Dollies

If you plan to work with sheet metal, you need a set of dollies and bodywork hammers. You can purchase a basic kit of body tools at discount tool stores or online, but there is no end to the variety of dollies available.

Dollies and spoons are portable, handheld anvils for shaping sheet metal. To fit a wide range of curvatures, you need a selection of dollies. These come in handy whether you're fabricating your own sheet-metal parts or repairing existing panels. They're also useful any time you need a solid backing to a part you're fitting into place.

Sheet-metal hammers are different from general-purpose hammers. They are lighter and frequently have a pick on one side of the head and a coin-sized flat surface on the other.

Hammer Wrap

Wrap a dolly and hammer face in duct tape to soften their edges if you're doing very light work on a painted surface. Be extra careful and you can avoid further damage to the paint. ■

A modern touch-free tire mounting machine is a wonder to behold, but it doesn't make financial sense unless you use it all the time. If you work with steel wheels, you're better off with an older model.

A bubble balancer is an old-school tool, but you can find them for good prices and they work just as well as a hugely expensive spin balancer. Make sure you get stick-on weights or weights designed to work with your wheels.

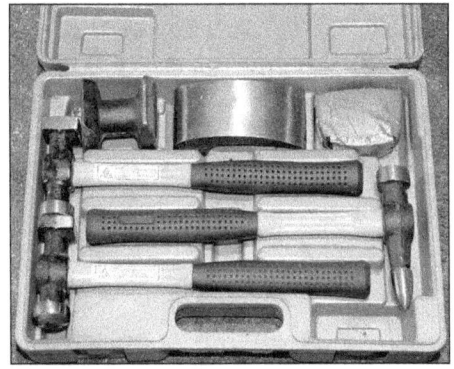
A basic bodyworking kit doesn't cost much and it's a good thing to have in your shop. Even if you don't work on surface metal, it's often nice to be able to straighten non-visible parts of the trunk, engine bay, and wheelwells. Note the dolly at top right wrapped in duct tape.

These hammers are designed for fine work without leaving marks on the surface. Consult a bodywork and painting manual for detailed instructions on using these tools on automotive bodywork.

Sheet-Metal Shear

It's almost impossible to work with sheet metal without a variety of shears. In addition to the most basic scissor-design tin snips, you can also purchase a set of "aircraft" sheet-metal shears with special designs optimized for cutting left, right, or straight. Complete sets are available at any tool store.

For extra convenience, you can also get a power shear. These are similar to aircraft shears but powered by air or electricity instead of your forearm muscles. Most power shears cut a small section from the sheet metal, so keep them to the outside of the desired cut line, and leave space between cut lines on the same sheet of metal.

Power shears work quickly, easily, and yield great results. You want to have a deburring tool handy, though, because power shears leave a razor-sharp edge on the material.

Many metal shops or industrial sites cut sheet steel to your specifications at a small added cost over the price of the material, but they do expect to sell you the basic material if they are asked to cut it.

Deburring Tool

A deburring scraper is an important and inexpensive tool for working with sheet metal. When you use shears or a nibbler on sheet metal, you leave behind a sharp and somewhat jagged edge—perfectly made to slash open your hand. You don't want to cut yourself while working or leave that edge on the finished product, and running the deburring tool along the sharp edge helps avoid that. The tool works like a potato peeler; it's simple and easy.

Bead Roller

A bead roller is an important tool if you want to achieve a finished, professional-looking result with sheet metal. This tool uses replaceable roller dies, and can roll and fold the sharp edges of cut sheet metal, leaving a smooth edge. You can also use a bead roller with different spools to create raised or depressed sections for cross-sectional rigidity. Bead rollers are available in a variety of styles, and you can purchase a bench-mounted roller at a discount tool store for less than $100. High-quality motorized units cost more than $500, but a manual roller is sufficient for most hobbyists.

English Wheel

An English Wheel is a large tool used to form long, smooth curves in sheet metal by running the metal between two rounded rollers. However, using an English Wheel requires patience. Historic and vintage race cars with sheet-aluminum bodies and fenders were often handmade with an English Wheel. You can buy a kit for about $500. The kit includes the rollers, but you need to weld it together. Sometimes discount tool stores carry English Wheels, but these are often flimsy when assembled. You can, however, reinforce these kits as a practical welding project.

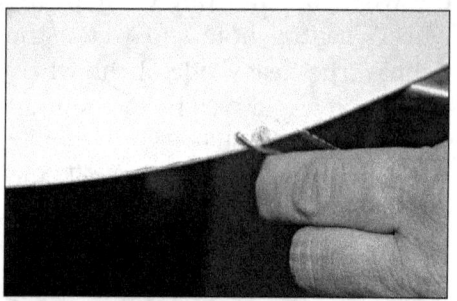

A deburring tool can save you from nasty cuts that happen after you've installed sheet-metal parts and forgotten about their razor edge.

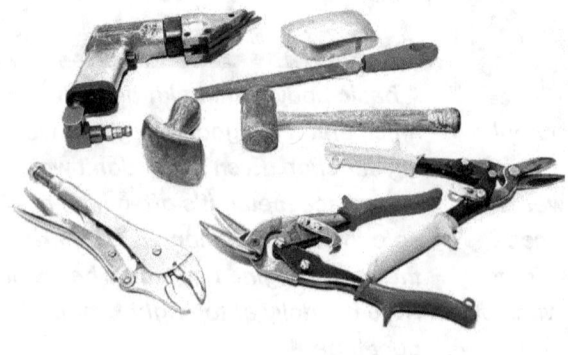

Here's a selection of metalworking tools, including a rawhide hammer, air-powered shears, hand shears, a file, some dollies, and Vise Grips.

A bead roller is used to make those nifty 3-D shapes that give structural strength to sheet metal. A manual roller doesn't cost much and gives your work a professional touch.

A related tool is a slip roller, which is used to make smooth, even-radius curves in sheet metal. These tools start at about $650 for a small unit. However, to make compound curves, you need an English Wheel.

Body Grinder

The body grinder (also known as an angle grinder) is probably the most basic power tool to have in an automotive body shop. This is simply a tool with a replaceable rotating disc and an extra handle that you can grab for support. You can install a disc that grinds on its face, one that grinds on its edge, a disc of overlapping pieces of sandpaper, or any of several kinds of wire wheel or cup-shaped wire brushes. With this variety of abrasives, you can easily grind away metal, rust, or grunge; clean off paint; or rough up a surface. These tools are also handy for cleaning up the slag and crust left over from stick welding, but be sure to wear your eye protection. These tools come in a variety of sizes. Larger units are good for getting a lot of work done fast; smaller tools allow you to get into tight spaces.

Wire wheels and brush cups that attach to a body grinder, power drill, and bench grinder are critical for removing rust, paint, and grunge before you weld. You can also use a wire wheel to clean up the slag left over from stick welding. A wire cup or wheel on a body grinder makes short work of anything standing between you and clean metal. Unfortunately, it can also make short work of paint, chrome, and skin that you didn't intend to remove, so use these tools with care and wear your safety glasses.

Dual-Action Sander

A dual-action sander uses two randomly rotating motions to mix up its action while it sands. This is important because it eliminates the tendency to make swirl marks or cut too long in one location and damage the metal. When you're doing fine bodywork such as paint prep, you should not use any power sander except a dual-action version. These are also known as orbital or random-orbit sanders.

Engine Tools

There's an entire range of automotive specialty tools used exclusively in engine building. If you plan on diving into an engine and doing your own assembly work, you want to have most, if not all, of these tools in your shop.

Compression Tester

The first engine tool to own, even if you don't plan to assemble your own engines, is a compression tester. For the automotive hobbyist, this is an indispensible tool in the buying process, as well as for troubleshooting your car's engine.

You can buy compression testers that thread into the spark plug hole or testers with a rubber tip that you hold against the spark plug hole. Of the two, the thread-in variety gives better results, but the press-in style is much quicker and easier to use. Both designs do the same thing—they tell you how much compression a piston is giving you.

When using a compression tester, follow these simple rules for best results: Make sure the ignition is not on and that all spark plugs have been removed from the engine. Then have someone step all the way on the gas to open up the intake air passage and crank the engine. You need three or four compression cycles to get a good reading.

An English Wheel is a big tool to keep in your shop, but there's nothing like it for custom-curved sheet-metal work.

The basic body grinder is a must-have tool for the automotive hobbyist. You'll end up using it much more frequently than you expected.

Every automotive hobbyist needs a compression tester. It's one of the basic tools for diagnosing engine trouble. If you get a good one that includes an air pressure fitting and a threaded end for the spark plug hole, you can also perform basic leakdown testing.

CHAPTER 7

Leakdown Tester

If your engine failed the compression test in any way, the next step in engine troubleshooting is to use a leakdown tester. This tool pressurizes a cylinder and allows you to determine where the compression is leaking. If your compression tester threads into a cylinder, you can often use the same pieces to perform a leakdown test.

There are expensive leakdown testers on the market that measure how much air is being lost and at what rate, but in most cases you just want to know where the leak is. You can make a leakdown tester out of a hollow threaded fitting that screws into the spark plug hole and keeps a seal. Simply attach an air fitting to the plug and turn the engine until the cylinder under test is at top dead center on its compression stroke. In this position, all the valves should be closed and the cylinder should hold pressure. Now send compressed air through the plug fitting and check for leakage.

If you can hear leakage coming from the carburetor or intake, it's a leaky intake valve. If you can hear it through the exhaust, it's a leaky exhaust valve. If you can hear the leakage through the oil filler hole or dipstick tube, it's leaky rings or a head gasket problem. Finally, if you can hear leakage or bubbling through the radiator cap hole, it's a head gasket problem.

Color Tune Kit

If you have an engine that's difficult to tune, you might consider purchasing a Gunson's Color Tune kit. This is an amazing device that uses a see-through spark plug to allow you to watch the combustion in the cylinder. As you rev the engine through its range, you can watch the color of the combustion and determine if the cylinder is running rich, lean, or some combination of the two at various points.

Synchrometer/Uni-Syn

If you have more than one carburetor on an older car, a synchrometer (such as the Edelbrock Uni-Syn) can help you balance the throttle plates. These devices measure the amount of air passing into the carburetor's mouth. Get the two (or more) carburetors sucking at the same rate and the intakes should be balanced thereafter.

Ring Compressor

If you assemble your own engines, you need a ring compressor. This tool is an adjustable sleeve that fits around a piston to squeeze the rings into their grooves as they are when the piston is working in the engine. Without a ring compressor, it's just about impossible to get the rings into the cylinders without breaking them. In a pinch you can sometimes get a hose clamp to work, but it's risky and a ring compressor doesn't cost much.

Valvespring Tool

Another challenge for engine builders is to depress valvesprings far enough to install or remove valve keepers. A valvespring tool uses a long lever in a C-clamp to hold the valve firmly against its seat while a fork forces down the spring around the valve shaft. You can then manipulate the valve keeper and cap as needed.

Stethoscope

A mechanic's stethoscope is a cheap and valuable engine diagnostic tool. Unlike a doctor's stethoscope, a mechanic's version has a long metal rod on it. When you place the rod against the engine, you can clearly hear rattles, ticks, knocks, and clunks. The noise is loudest near its source, and an experienced mechanic can usually guess the source of the noise.

Automotive Electrical Tools

If you work on any car more modern than a Model T, you'll have to do some wiring work eventually. Get yourself a good set of electrical tools, and then take care of them. Most importantly, store them in a sealed tote to keep them dry.

Code Reader

If your car was made after 1995, it uses an automated system called On Board Diagnostics II (OBD-II) to record critical information from a variety of sensors and computers. If anything gets out of its normal range, the car turns on the dashboard check engine light. You can plug a standard OBD-II code reader into your car's access port and download the codes. The codes are standardized somewhat across manufacturers, and a code reader comes with a book that lists all the standard codes.

Using this tool, you can determine what sensor or component is reporting a malfunction, which is a great first step toward troubleshooting a modern car. A simple code reader costs about $50, and you can also use it to reset trouble codes when you have fixed the problem.

Listen Up

If you don't have a mechanic's stethoscope, simply use a long screwdriver and place the end of the handle against your ear while you place the tip against the engine. ∎

Battery Charger

Sooner or later, every automotive hobbyist ends up with a flat battery. You have a range of choices when it comes to battery chargers, and some are much better than others. The most basic tool is a standard 120-volt charger, which charges a battery at about 10 amps—it fully recharges a battery overnight. If you need more power right now, you can get a starting cart, which is bigger and boosts a dead battery at up to 200 amps. These are handy if you just need to get a dead car started—you can't really charge a battery at 200 amps, because that just boils the electrolyte right out of it.

At the other end of the spectrum are float chargers and trickle chargers. A Float chargers are also known as battery tenders and these are designed to be plugged into dormant cars to keep the batteries gently charged. A trickle charger flows electricity into a battery at less than 2 amps to slowly charge it without any danger of boiling the electrolyte.

If you want a battery tender that works, you have to spend a lot of money for a computerized "intelligent" charger. The cheap ones that cost $5 to $10 do not work.

Battery/Alternator Tester

If you have to use a battery charger frequently, you should invest in a battery and alternator tester. This is a device that you can safely buy at the discount tool store, because it's just a heated-wire resistance meter that creates a load on the current source, with a voltage gauge to let you know how the battery or alternator is performing under load.

In either case, you simply connect the positive lead of the tester to the positive pole of the battery or alternator, the negative lead to the negative pole, and then pull the spring-loaded switch. The gauge tells you how many volts are coming through. If the battery or alternator is good, it should read about 13 to 14 volts and the voltage should stay steady or drop just a bit. If the needle drops below 12 volts after 10 to 15 seconds, the battery or alternator is weak.

Volt Meter/Continuity Tester

If you have to work on your car's wiring (and everyone does), you need a volt/ohm meter. This is a simple device that detects the presence of electrical current in volt-meter mode and sends its own current through its leads to measure resistance in ohm-meter mode. With this you can test ground faults, hot wires, and virtually everything electric in your car that isn't a computer.

For a simpler testing function, you can use a continuity tester. This is nothing more than a 12-volt light bulb in a small device that looks like a screwdriver with a wire coming out of the handle. Connect the clamp at the end of the wire to any suspected source of 12-volt electricity and touch the point of the screwdriver to ground—if the light comes on, you have power. You can make your own continuity tester with a 12-volt light bulb and a couple wires, but these cost just a couple bucks each, so why bother?

Timing Light

An inductive timing light is a must-have tool for the automotive workshop. This device has positive and negative leads that connect to the battery and an induction clamp that goes around your number-1 spark plug wire. Point the gun at the pulley and the light in the nose of the gun strobes in time with the firing of the number-1 piston. Most cars are timed by the number-1 cylinder, so you usually see a timing mark on the pulley coinciding (or not) with a timing mark on the engine body. Twist the distributor to adjust the timing according to your car's specifications.

You can get a basic or a fancy timing light. Fancy ones allow you to dial in a certain number of degrees of advance so you can preset the distributor exactly where you want it. In practice, this more often leads to misadjusted distributors because users forget that advance is dialed into the gun. A basic timing light costs less and works just as well.

Spark Tester

One of the most useful tools for less than $10 is a spark tester. These are simple tools that plug into a spark plug wire and visibly show you the vehicle's spark. Since lack of spark is

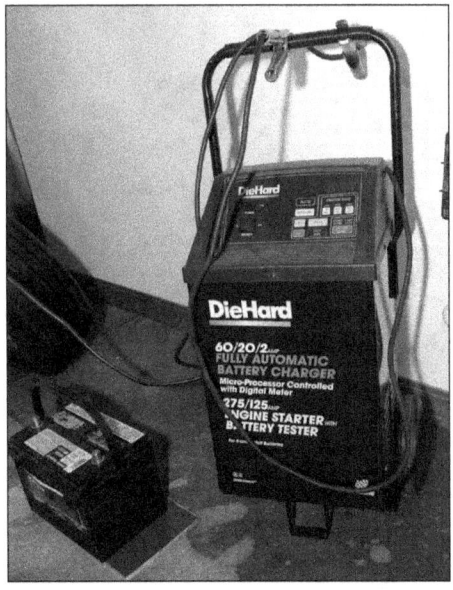

A good battery-starting cart is a big step up from an overnight charger or a battery tender. These tools are worth the price if you have a dead battery, and better ones can also test batteries and a car's charging system.

CHAPTER 7

one of the most common reasons cars don't run, it's good to just run a quick test to be sure you have spark before you dive into other diagnostics.

You can get testers that run in-line to the spark plug, or others that resemble spark plugs with a clamp on the side (just clamp the tester to any ground on the engine and plug it in). Still others resemble a pair of calipers and allow you to test the strength of the spark by increasing or decreasing the distance the spark has to jump.

In a pinch, you can test for spark without any of these tools by using a spare spark plug. Just plug a spark plug wire into the spare plug and put the threads in contact with the engine block. Turn the engine over and it should spark. Just be sure you don't touch the plug or the wire while the ignition is hot.

Miscellaneous Automotive Tools

The rest of these tools don't really fall into any neat categories—they are just good tools that an automotive shop is likely to need from time to time.

Porta-Power

A Porta-Power is another application of hydraulic jack technology—in this case designed to push metal around. Porta-Power kits come with a variety of extenders and pressure feet that allow you to get in and spread metal parts that have been wedged together, or you can use the extenders to put some pressure on frame parts to move them back into alignment. Serious bodyworkers keep a Porta-power around the workbench.

Spring Compressor

One of the most dangerous things you can do is work with automotive coil springs. There's a tremendous amount of energy bound up in the compression of a spring. If it gets out of control, you can be seriously injured. And it's effectively impossible to install some coil springs without a spring compressor. Some spring compressors work from inside the coil, but most are threaded rods with hooks at the top and bottom that grab spring coils. Spring compressors generally come in pairs so you can compress a coil from opposite sides to prevent binding.

There are different styles of compressor for standard suspension coil springs and those used on MacPherson strut suspensions. You can buy a wall-mounted strut compressor, which is the best solution for struts.

Brake Bleeder

There are a variety of tools on the market that claim to help you bleed hydraulic systems, or to allow you to do the job by yourself. It is possible to bleed a brake or clutch system yourself, but the specialty tools generally do not work as well as the old-fashioned method with a bottle and a length of rubber hose. If you have a friend to help you through the process, that's worth more than any specialty tool.

The one tool that improves brake bleeding more than any other is a set of Speed Bleeder valves. These replace the existing bleed valves (in standard and metric sizes) and they incorporate a one-way valve that prevents air and old fluid from being sucked back into the system.

Caliper Press

The other indispensible tool for brake work is a caliper press. This is a

Back Pocket

If you're working around ignition wires on a running engine, put one of your hands in your back pocket, that way you can't easily complete a circuit with your body. ■

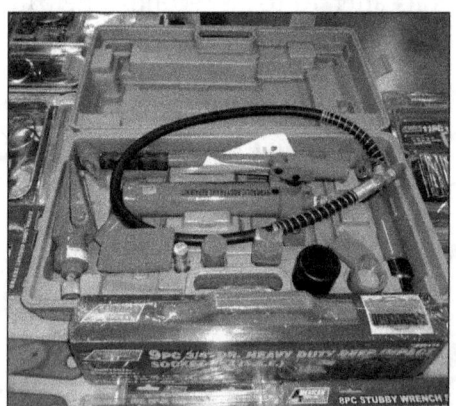

If you need to straighten a bent frame or align big pieces of metal, a Porta-Power is a good tool to have. These can usually be rented if you just need them once.

A wall-mounted strut compressor is handy if you do a lot of strut work. You can get by with a set of spring compressors; be very careful any time you work with springs.

simple screw mechanism that pushes a brake caliper piston back into the caliper body steadily and evenly. The tool costs just a few dollars and makes disc brake pad replacement a snap.

Toe Plate

If you plan to set your own alignment, you can save a lot of money by making a set of toe plates. You can use plywood or sheet metal if you have a brake to put some structural shape in the metal. Regardless of the material, you need a pair of panels about 12 inches high and about as wide as the diameter of the tire—usually 24 to 30 inches. Center each panel against the outside of a front tire with a long side touching the ground and cut a small notch about 2 inches off the ground in the front and back edges of the plate. Make sure both plates are identical in their size and location of cuts.

Next take two measuring tapes and hook them into the notches in one plate, front and rear. Pass the tapes under the car and put them through the notches in the other plate. Take a reading and compare the results. If the front tape reads shorter than the rear tape, you have toe-in. If the rear tape reads shorter, you have toe-out.

Fastener Sorter

This is a simple tool you can make in a few minutes. In any auto shop, nuts and bolts tend to accumulate in coffee cans and cardboard boxes, and occasionally you either have to throw them away or sort them to use them. Sorting nuts and bolts is a boring job, but you can make it go quicker with a sorting rack. This is nothing more than a piece of wood with a series of holes drilled in it and bolts of known size and thread pitch stuck through the holes. Just note the size and thread of each bolt, in order, along the board and you can quickly test each nut and washer to determine its correct classification. For bolts, turn them upside down and hold the threads up to your known threads for verification.

Bathroom Scale

You don't need a bathroom scale in your workshop to gauge your beer consumption, but rather to weigh the many parts of your car that you may put on or take off. For race cars and hot rods, this is a critical performance issue. If you have items that aren't easy to weigh, just hold them in your arms and stand on the scale. Then put down the items and weigh yourself again. Do the arithmetic and find out how much the items weigh—easy! You can do this in the house, but you really want a dedicated scale for your shop to avoid interpersonal conflict.

Here's a handy item that you can make. Unless you're extra conscientious about keeping your fasteners in order, you'll occasionally need to sort a box of hardware, and this makes it easy.

You can make toe plates and save some money on alignment. Any time you change ride height, you need to reset your car's toe-in, so this tool is very useful for hot rodders and racers.

CHAPTER 8

Hoists, Cranes and Lifts

One of the most common problems faced in the automotive hobby is how to get something that is very heavy from one place to another. Most often, the heavy item is an engine, and the place the heavy item is going into or coming out of is a car. You really don't want to drop an engine on your immaculately painted and perfectly formed fender, so you need a reliable lifting device. You are likely to be working on the project alone or with a few friends, and no one wants to get hurt in the process, so a good lifting device is even more important.

There are several good options for heavy lifting, and you may want to have more than one of these in your shop.

Ceiling-Mounted Hoists

The least expensive lift system is to mount a chain hoist to a ceiling truss or trusses. A chain hoist is simply a modern version of the old block-and-tackle system, which multiplies lifting power by reducing the distance lifted versus the distance pulled. A chain hoist uses the principle of leverage implemented in the form of gear reduction. You pull the chain about 3 feet for every 1 foot the load is lifted. Alternately, you can get more expensive chain hoists or cable winches that are electrically powered.

A chain hoist is great for lifting heavy weights, but you need to be sure that you've checked that the trusses or the ceiling joist can bear the weight you're planning to lift. Another potential downside of using a chain hoist is that you can lift something up, but you might not be able to move it around much once it's in the air.

Many builders have mounted chain hoists to a trolley system—usually the trolley runs from the front door to a workbench area. Creating a trolley usually involves mounting an I-beam or some other support to the ceiling, usually by bolting through the top lip of the beam into joists or trusses, and then putting a rolling trolley and a chain hoist on the lower lip of the beam. Again, check to be sure that the joists and trusses are strong enough to support this kind of load. This setup allows you to lift a heavy object at the door and move it along the track to a bench. Obviously, the track goes only to one place, but if you do a lot of engine rebuilding, this may work well for you. You need only trolley the load far enough inside your shop to drop it onto a rolling engine stand or table.

A classic old-school trolley has a chain hanging down to hook on the heavy load. The trolley runs back and forth on a steel I-beam bolted to the ceiling.

HOISTS, CRANES AND LIFTS

This is a heavy-duty cherry picker. Note the side bracing and the long legs for support. This kind of shop crane can pick up just about anything.

Portable Cranes

Portable shop cranes, also known as engine hoists or "cherry pickers," are much more common in amateur garages than trolleys and chain hoists. A cherry picker is a small wheeled crane with a long-throw hydraulic jack and broad support legs sticking out under the load.

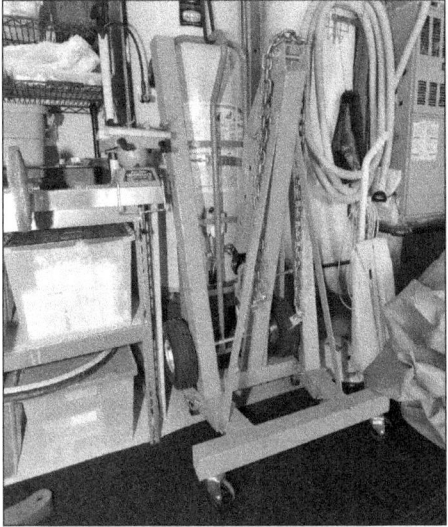

This is a popular style of cherry picker for hobbyists. It folds up easily and still rolls around and fits in a corner.

With a cherry picker, you can pull an engine from a chassis, or just pick an engine up out of a truck bed or off the floor. Virtually all cherry pickers have wheels so you can roll the entire assembly around the shop to deposit the engine (or other heavy object) anywhere you like.

There are several different designs of shop crane, and you can choose the one that meets your needs. At the heavy-duty end of the spectrum are cranes that are well-supported and can lift up to 8 tons. These take time to assemble and break down, but if you don't need that kind of lifting capacity, you can get a lighter-weight collapsible crane. These devices fold right up and stow in a small space. The foldable versions are capable of lifting a small-block V-8 engine, so they're a popular choice among hot rodders, racers, and restorers.

Another variant of the shop crane is a fixed-mount crane. These are often used to lift heavy items into an attic, or sometimes they are mounted in trucks. With these devices, the distance you can move

Keep Your Engine on the Level

Another item for your shopping list is a load leveler. A shop crane or chain hoist hangs its entire load on a single hook. It is frequently difficult to grab an engine at its precise balance point, and it is often handy to change the engine's orientation while it's in the air or being inserted into a car's engine bay. So the load leveler was invented. This is a simple device that uses a threaded rod to change the relative location of the hook to the weight being lifted. You can attach the load leveler to an engine at either end, place the hook in the center, and the engine lifts level. You can then use the crank and threaded rod to move the hook forward or backward and the engine tips accordingly.

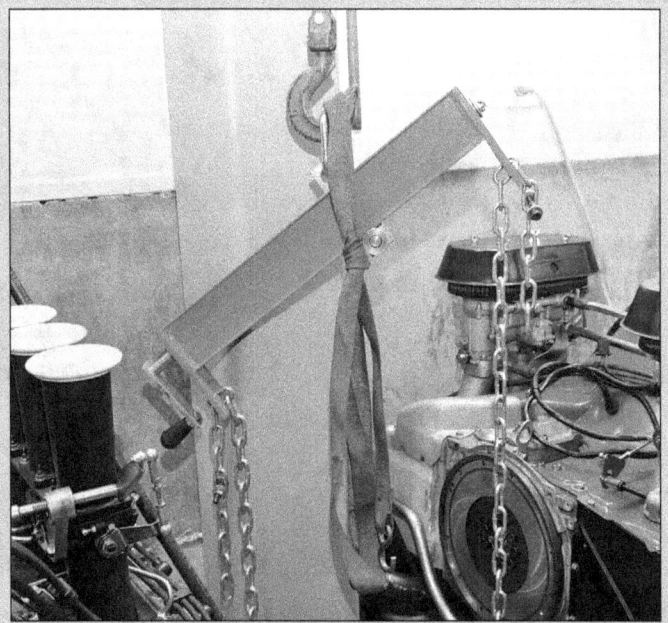

A load leveler is a good investment. These are handy when you're inserting an engine and you need to tilt the load momentarily and then level it out again.

HOW TO DESIGN, BUILD & EQUIP YOUR AUTOMOTIVE WORKSHOP ON A BUDGET

CHAPTER 8

A crane like this one is meant to be mounted in a truck bed, or to a fixed location. It works just like a cherry picker.

This crane is mounted in a pickup truck bed, but a crane like this one (with a cable winch on it) is often used in lofts and attics because it can drop its hook farther than a hydraulic crane. Follow all the usual rules about lifting—don't stand under one of these with weight hanging.

last a lifetime, and you can buy them on www.craigslist.org for next to nothing.

Closely related are taller "underhoist" jacks that support parts like transmissions while you get them installed. These are also handy because they generally allow you more working room than a big floor jack when holding up a transmission or rear axle.

When it comes to supporting heavy parts, you really do need to have the right tools for the job. It saves you time and trouble, and it can potentially save you expense and injury by supporting your work properly.

an item is limited to the swing of the crane arm, but you can get by with a simple cable winch for the lifting mechanism, and that keeps costs down.

Portable Lifts

Aside from the venerable cherry picker, there is a variety of useful lifting and moving devices you can purchase for your shop. Each has its uses, and the one you need depends on the work you plan to do.

Floor Jack

If you plan to do any kind of work on a car in a garage, you need a full-size roll-around floor jack. In fact, you need at least two floor jacks and maybe more. Those little compact trolley jacks sold at auto parts stores are worse than useless in a garage. They don't lift the car high enough to get a wheel off the ground, so you have to use a block of wood on them, and that's not a safe practice. Bottle jacks have their place in a shop, but that place is not lifting a whole car off the ground. A full-size floor jack gets one whole side of a car up in the air in just seconds, allowing you to get on with the work at hand.

Jack Stand and Support

One of the few universal needs is a good set of jack stands. Safety is always a priority, and there's no way to adequately replace a good set of heavy jack stands. Pieces of wood, cinder blocks, and other adapted items just aren't reliable enough if you plan to crawl around under a car. A good set of large, tall jack stands

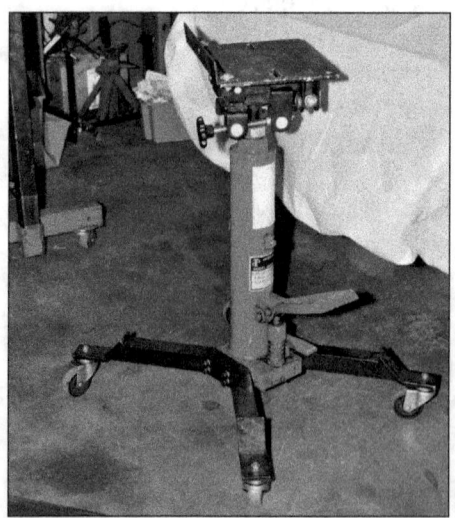

Specialty jacks like this transmission jack have a high reach to work under a lift. Note that you can operate this jack with a foot pedal.

Car Dolly

If you plan to have your car out of commission for any length of time, or if your garage is configured so that you need to move cars sideways to fit everything into the space, a set of car dollies makes life much easier. These tools slide under the tires of a car and cradle the wheels. Spinning casters on the underside of the dollies allow you to push the car in any direction. The fact that the undersides of the dollies are usually curved also helps

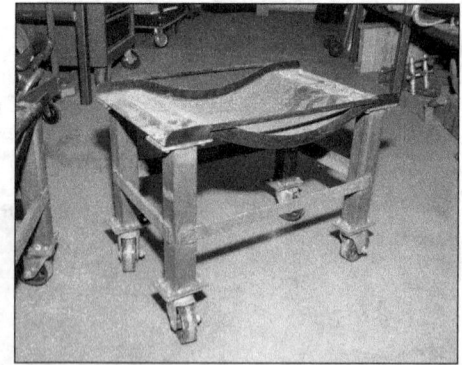

These dollies have been extended so that the cars on the rollers are up in the air. That's a nice modification if you need to get under your stored cars from time to time.

the car avoid developing flat spots on the tires if it sits for a long time.

Some of the better (and more expensive) car dollies do not require you to jack up the car to insert the dollies—they have their own jacks. These cost more than twice as much as the cheaper kind, but they are certainly a nice upgrade.

Dolly Wheels

Get car dollies with the largest diameter wheels that you can find, or adapt the dollies to use larger wheels. Small-diameter caster wheels can hang up on absurdly small obstacles (for example, a 5/16-inch nut on the floor) when you're trying to push a heavy weight on them. Metal wheels are the worst—look for high-density solid rubber wheels with smooth bearings. ■

These GoJak dollies are a lot more expensive than the basic kind, but the ease of using them and the big casters make them worth the investment if you need to push cars around a lot.

If you don't have a set of car dollies, you can still move a car sideways by lifting the front with a big floor jack and balancing it while pushing, and then move the rear in the same way—another reason to have a big floor jack!

Motorcycle Lift

Motorcycles are a special case when it comes to lifting. Most bikes are not that heavy (about 500 pounds) so you don't need a full-scale lift. Most motorcycle lifts are simply ramps with a clamp to hold the bike's front wheel, but you may want to lift bikes by their frames, and special motorcycle frame lifts are available. Most motorcycle lifts use a hydraulic ram and mechanical

A Steep Driveway Solution

Sooner or later, many automotive hobbyists find themselves with a dilemma. They're at the bottom of a sloped driveway with a dead car, and they need to get it up the hill and into the garage. Jeremy Wilson created a low-cost option to solve this problem and save his back—he installed mount points for a removable winch into the floor of his garage.

Using a rented concrete drill, Jeremy used expansion bolts to mount a piece of heavy angle iron to the concrete floor of his working restoration bay in a normal three-car garage. When he needs it, a 120-volt winch bolts to the angle iron and easily drags one of Jeremy's project Packards up his steep driveway.

As with all winches, be sure you have a long cable attached to the winch trigger—you don't want to be near that winch or behind the car if the cable breaks while under strain.

This ingenious mounting point is designed to bolt to a 120-volt electric winch that is powerful enough to pull a car up a steep driveway and into the garage.

Here you can see the expansion bolts sunk into the concrete for the winch bracket. This is a great creative solution to the steep driveway and dead car problem.

CHAPTER 8

scissor action to lift the bike, and often the lift is wheeled so you can move the bike around. A motorcycle lift generally folds up for easy storage when it's not in use. Special motorcycle dollies are also available.

Lift Cart

One of the most useful roll-around items you can buy for your shop is a lift cart. This is a flat cart with a push handle and a foot-operated jack. When you extend the jack, the whole top of the cart rises. A lift cart is easier to use than a cherry picker, and it's much handier for moving heavy boxes and other items that don't have a convenient lift point. It's also safer, since you don't have heavy items dangling in the air by a chain. The lift table rises to the level of an average pickup truck bed, and you can lock the wheels while you work. Simply slide the heavy boxes onto the cart and lower the jack. Then move the cart to your bench or storage shelves, jack it up to the desired height, and slide the boxes into place. You can get one of these tools for less than $100 at most discount tool centers such as Harbor Freight, and it's well worth the price.

Scissor Lift

The largest of the portable lifts is a scissor lift. This is a powered hydraulic lift that slides under a car and raises the vehicle up to 5 feet high. The lift is flat when inserted under the car and raises itself into an X-shape. Some scissor lifts are made with wheels on one leg that roll as the lift rises, while the other leg remains steady on the ground. Others are designed to fit in a small depression in the concrete to reduce the lift's shop footprint.

If parking space is tight in your shop, or you like the idea of being able to move your lift outside, a scissor lift could seem like the right answer for you, but there are substantial problems to consider. The foremost problem is safety—a scissor lift must be exactly positioned under the car and level in order to work safely. If you buy the cheap kind, the pressure exerted on the roller bushings is tremendous, and these can wear out quickly. You should also be aware that the center underside of the car is often obscured, making a scissor lift problematic for work such as clutch, transmission, or driveline repair. Finally, scissor lifts do not cost much less than a fixed lift, so most hobbyists who have an appropriate space opt for a fixed lift.

Rotisserie

If you plan to do serious restoration work, you're going to want a device called a rotisserie. Like its kitchen counterpart, a rotisserie is designed to hold a car's body and chassis off the ground and allow you

If there's one inexpensive lifting device that stands above the rest, it's this kind of lift cart. The table rises to the level of a workbench or pickup tailgate and then drops down for safe transport of heavy items.

This is a high-quality scissor lift that's designed to be unobtrusive when not in use. As with all lifts, you get what you pay for and there are tradeoffs with every design.

If you're going to restore classic cars, there's nothing like a rotisserie. This unit from Whirly Jig is a high-quality product with extensive testing and design behind it. They're not at all expensive compared to dropping your classic project off a cheap body stand! (Photo courtesy of Whirly Jig)

to spin it to provide easy access to any part of the car. Rotating the car's body makes rust repair on the underside of the car far easier than working with the metal overhead.

A rotisserie allows you to work on a car's body without using much more than a single parking space, because it attaches to the frame rails or the bumper attachment points. If you plan to paint the entire car, you can usually do so without removing the body from the rotisserie. Serious restoration professionals swear by these devices and often highlight their work as a "rotisserie restoration."

Quality rotisseries are available from a number of manufacturers, but if you know how to weld, you can make your own using plans and instructions you can find free (or at low cost) on the Internet.

Fixed Lifts

The ultimate in heavy lifting gear is a professional-grade automobile lift, and these require a lot of infrastructure and extra planning. You can always break down the cherry picker or chain hoist and stash it in the corner, but a fixed lift takes up a lot of space permanently.

Lifts are one part of your workshop where budget and quality are likely to come into conflict. A high-quality two-post lift costs a lot of money—$4,000 or more. You can find low-cost lifts made in China for less than $2,000, but these units have serious quality problems. Getting installation help is tough, and getting warranty support and parts can be a challenge down the road. One way to economize is to look into used and reconditioned lifts. For the hobbyist who isn't lifting 20 cars a day in a production environment, a used lift manufactured by a quality supplier and installed and supported by a local lift service can be a smart way to save some money.

The main decision you have to make about a full-size lift is whether to invest in a two- or four-post lift.

Two-Post Type

As the name implies, a two-post lift has two lifting posts, placed on either side of the vehicle. Arms reach out beneath the vehicle to lift it by its frame or jacking points. Within the realm of two-post lifts, you can also choose between symmetric or asymmetric lifts.

With a symmetric lift, the lifting arms are the same length, placing the two posts about at the center of the vehicle. This design is preferred for pickup trucks, SUVs, and vans because their center of gravity is farther back on the vehicle and they benefit from being lifted with the lift posts at the center of the vehicle's length.

An asymmetric lift uses different-length lifting arms, and all the arms are designed to point toward the rear of the vehicle as you drive into the lifting space. Then all the arms swing forward to their lifting points.

The classic two-post lift is the toy that every hobbyist would like to have in a workshop. However, there are substantial differences in design and quality among two-post lifts.

This classic car is lifted on a symmetric lift. Note that the arms are all about the same length and the car is centered on them.

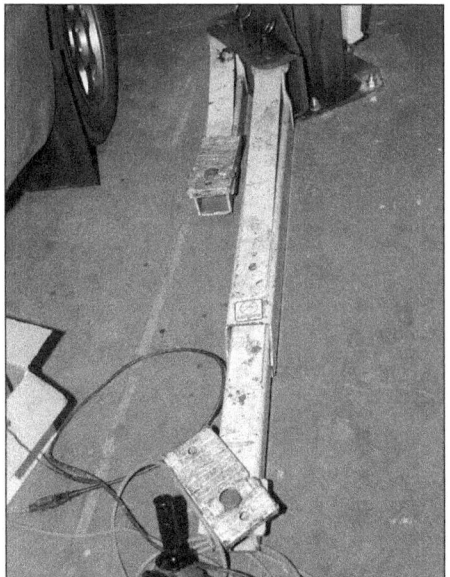

These arms are part of a rotated tower asymmetric lift. Note that the forward arms are much shorter than the rear pickup arms. This design works best with smaller front-wheel-drive cars.

On a symmetric lift, the forward arms point to the forward end of the vehicle and must be swung rearward to come under the frame. Similarly, the rear arms must swing forward. This may not seem like much of a difference, but it means that fitting a small car on a symmetric lift can be problematic because the lift arms may hit the tires.

On an asymmetric lift, you can have the shorter arms toward the front of the vehicle, but pointing backward, and then have the longer arms reaching back toward the rear tires. This allows you to place the lift farther forward in relation to the center of the vehicle, so you can open the vehicle doors. This design is preferred for passenger cars, where the center of gravity is farther forward on the vehicle.

The general rule is that symmetric lifts are preferred for pickups and can be easily used to lift vehicles with a wheelbase more than 100 inches, and asymmetric lifts are preferred for smaller passenger cars. Some asymmetric lifts use a rotated column design, where the columns are each turned about 30 degrees to face the vehicle as it drives into the lifting area. This has some advantages of convenience for opening vehicle doors, but shops use all kinds of lifts effectively every day.

With a two-post lift, you also need to make sure you have the right kind of pads to hold the vehicle and that the pads are well-positioned under the vehicle's strong points, or there's a danger of dropping a car off the lift. To increase versatility, lift manufacturers are now moving toward three-stage extendible arms for more flexibility with different-size cars. All lifts shake a bit when raising a vehicle, so the pads have to be positioned to stay put. Cars can and do fall off two-post lifts with disastrous consequences.

Four-Post Type

A four-post lift places four lifting posts at the four corners of the vehicle, and the device has two large ramps. You drive the car onto the ramps and lift the entire vehicle while it's sitting on its wheels. Some four-post lifts are technically portable, in that they have ingenious little arms that you can pin to the posts. When you let down the lift all the way, the little arms use the lift's own weight to lever itself up onto the wheels. You can then move the lift around a little bit. This is handy if you have space concerns and you're not using the lift every day.

Two-Post Lift

If you install a two-post lift, put the power pack on the passenger side. That way, you can drive into the lift space, get out of the driver's seat and place the driver-side arms, then walk around the car and place the passenger-side arms; the lift controls are right there for you to use. ∎

Four-Post Lift

If you're making custom exhaust systems, never use a two-post lift because the car's suspension hangs free, and the exhaust may not fit when the car is sitting on its wheels. Use a four-post lift for exhaust work. ∎

If you're doing exhaust work, a four-post lift is best because the car is sitting in its operating position.

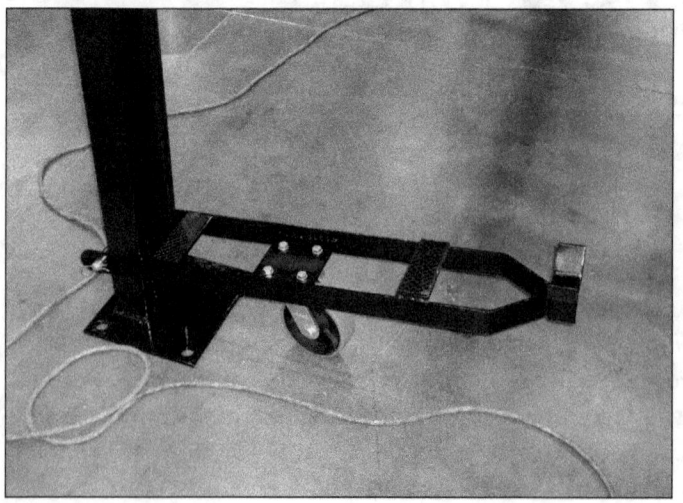

Many four-post lifts include these jacks. Simply attach them to the legs, drop the lift onto the jacks, and the weight of the lift levers itself onto the casters.

A four-post lift is a good solution for a hobbyist because you can put it on just about any concrete slab and perform most hobbyist work on it with ease.

Pro and Cons

There are advantages to each lift design. Two-post lifts are better suited to working on wheels, brakes, steering, and suspension because the wheels are left hanging in the air. However, you can buy specialized jacks that fit between the ramps of a four-post lift to lift the car off the ramps enough to work on wheel-area parts.

Four-post lifts are less expensive than a quality two-post design. And because they spread the weight out more, four-post lifts can be used on floors that cannot support the weight of a two-post lift.

Infrastructure Requirements

To put a lift in your shop or garage, you need to have a few pieces of critical infrastructure in place. Most importantly, to install a two-post lift you need at least a 4½-inch thick slab of high-strength concrete. Most household garages and outbuildings have only a 3-inch slab, which crack

This practice is not recommended, but a lot of four-post lift users put their cars on a set of good jack stands to perform wheel, brake, and suspension work. There are special jacks that fit in many four-post lifts for this purpose, and you should use one of those if you want to lift the car off its wheels.

Most two-post lifts incorporate a top bar that holds the towers in position. This limits the total lifting height and it means you must have enough headroom to clear the top of the lift.

CHAPTER 8

Can You Make a Pit Instead?

If your shop floor can't support a lift (perhaps because it's an older building without a concrete slab), you might consider digging a pit instead. Many old-time shops made great use of the "grease pit" underneath the working floor.

The best design for a pit is to dig a trench about 5 feet deep and 3 feet wide under the spot where you can park a car. For safety's sake, find some boards to cover the pit when it's not in use so you don't accidentally fall in. Of course, it's better if you can line the pit with bricks or concrete. You can use a ladder to climb in and out, or make a set of stairs.

Before you go digging, be sure to check the general level of the water table in your area. You probably don't want to create a swimming pool in your shop.

---

under the strain. In that case, you're limited to a four-post design.

You also need a dedicated 240-volt circuit of at least 30 amps for a two-post lift. Some four-post lifts run on 120 volts.

Look at your parking space—most lifts are designed to take up a space about 12 feet wide, including the lift's power pack, plus you want a couple of feet on either side of the lift to be able to open the car doors and walk around. A standard two-car garage is only 18 feet wide, so if you need to park two cars side by side, you have space problems. You also need to make sure the garage is deep enough to properly position any car you plan to lift. If your car just barely fits in the garage, a two-post lift may be out of the question.

Finally, you need to check the vertical space to make sure that the ceiling is tall enough to accommodate the lift posts. Most lifts require a 12-foot ceiling, or even a little taller

Vertical Clearance

Vertical clearance means everything that's overhead—check for lights, garage door openers, joists and rafters, and anything else that your car might hit. ■

When you're considering a lift, the first thing to do is look up. It's not the distance to the peak of the roof that governs your lift, but rather the distance to the bottom of the roof truss!

This device is a basic heavy-duty jack stand that is tall enough to put under a car on a two-post lift. Get a few of these and put them snugly under strong points to keep the car from rocking off the pads while you work.

HOISTS, CRANES AND LIFTS

if the lift has a crosspiece support at the top.

But even with a shorter lift, unless you have at least 10 feet to the rafters, you won't be able to lift a car high enough to walk under it. For example, most pole buildings place trusses every 10 to 12 feet along their length, and most cars are at least 12 feet long. So unless the trusses are parallel to the parking direction, the available height is really measured to the bottom of the trusses, rather than to the ceiling height between them. You don't want to lift your car into the trusses—that has no good effect on your vehicle or your building.

If you can position the lift so that the car's cabin is between the trusses, then subtract 3 feet from the height to the trusses to figure how far you can lift a car. Leave some safety margin—your Miata may need only 30 inches of clearance, but if you try to lift your friend's Jeep Cherokee to the same height, you could be in for a surprise. And remember that with a four-post design, you have to measure the full height of the vehicle from the bottom of the tires, whereas with a two-post design, you can measure from the chassis lifting points to the top of the car.

When it comes to installing a lift, you can do it yourself with a rented masonry hammer drill and expanding bolts. That works fine for a four-post design, but if you want a two-post lift, it's better to buy from an experienced vendor and have them install it. The main thing is that the lift package weighs much more than a ton. When it arrives, just getting it off the truck can be a challenge. Then you have to move it into place and get it attached to the ground. If any part of the installation is not done right, you can create a major safety hazard, so it's smart money to hire a professional.

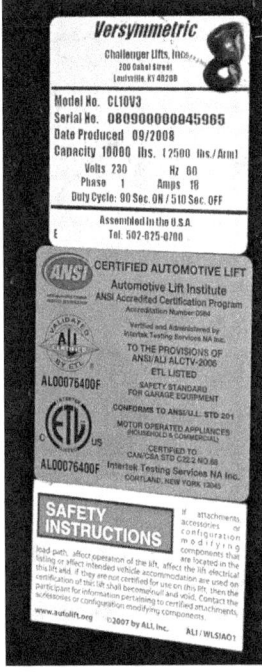

Always look for this ALI-ETL sticker on your lift purchases. It means the lift has undergone strenuous testing and it lifts the weight it says it can lift.

A generic pad like this lifts most older cars, but you may need specialized lift pads for newer cars.

Here are just a few of the specialty pads used to lift modern cars safely.

This is what the package looks like that arrives on your door when you order a lift. It weighs a couple tons, so don't think you can muscle it around with a buddy. You really need a professional installer to do it right.

CHAPTER 9

HUMAN AMENITIES

Your garage or shop is probably designed to be functional—this whole book is about making your working space functional—but it's also important for it to be comfortable and fun. It is a place where you're likely to spend a lot of time, or you wouldn't be putting this kind of effort into it. And it is also a place where you will likely want to invite your friends to join you. With a nice space, your garage or shop can become a center of activity for other hobbyists. And as the owner, designer, and builder of that space, you're an instant rock star.

With that goal in mind, it's time to turn your car's house into a home. The following sections detail some considerations for human amenities that make your garage or shop a fun and pleasant place to hang out.

Do You Need a Bathroom?

Probably the first human amenity that most automobile hobbyists would mention to have in a shop would be a source of beer. But shortly after that, the subject of a bathroom would come up. Depending on your location, it may be enough to simply step out the back door to enjoy the wonders of nature, but for most of us a bathroom immediately adjacent to the workshop is a blessing. If your garage is not located conveniently near to your house or another available bathroom, plumbing may be an issue.

It's challenging to install a bathroom after a building is built. If the concrete floor was not cast with a toilet pipe already installed, you might have to cut or chisel out a section of

Don't underestimate the need for a bathroom if your shop is not connected to your house. If you don't think women will visit your shop often, you might consider putting in a wall-mounted unit like this one.

the floor and then re-pour to retrofit the necessary plumbing, or you have to use a back-outlet toilet fixture. You also have to connect the plumbing to the sewer line. For my project, I was unlucky enough to strike the sewer line during construction, but I was also lucky that the sewer line was conveniently located to allow a connection into the shop. You must have both water coming in and a proper sewer line going out to put in any kind of toilet fixture.

If you can connect to the sewer line but you don't have a toilet flange in the floor, you might consider installing a back-outlet toilet, or placing a urinal on the wall. This gets you around the problem of a concrete floor, and a urinal on the wall saves precious floor space, but it is obviously not usable by everyone.

Keeping Mice Away

Mice (and rats) are a horrendous problem in workshops and garages. Your shop offers a multitude of great places to make a nest because it's generally warmer than outside, it's protected from weather, there's frequently something to eat, and there's an ample supply of cloth to shred. No wonder the mice like it as much as you do.

The first and most important thing to do is to remove temptation. No matter how well you think you sealed the doors and the foundation of your garage, mice can get in. A mouse can squeeze through a space just a fraction of an inch tall, and they'll bring the whole family with them. The best thing you can do is remove the reward they're looking for. That means you have to be relentless in making sure that there's no food accessible to them anywhere in the shop—including in the trash can.

Food in the refrigerator is generally safe, but the smell is still there to attract visitors. Food in the garbage can is fair game. So if you have pizza delivered, or bring a sandwich and an apple into the shop, make sure that your garbage (including wrappers) ends up elsewhere.

You can buy sonic repellers that emit a high-frequency squeal inaudible to human ears, and some people report success in reducing a mouse problem with those devices. But pest-control professionals generally agree that ultrasonic devices have only small effects at best, and the devices that claim to change the frequency of the electric wiring have no effect at all on mice and other pests.

To poison or not to poison—that is a critical question. Poisoning mice and rats works, but it's risky on a number of levels. First, the rodents have to go somewhere to die—and if that place is in your shop, you're in for a stinky problem and a truly unpleasant task of locating and cleaning up the bodies. Second, you run the risk of your pet or someone else's dog or cat either eating the sick or dead rodent, or getting into the poison directly.

If you do decide to use poison pellets, many rodents ignore the bait. In that case, you can mix the pellets with some irresistible food like baked beans but, in general, poison is the worst choice for pest control.

As unpleasant as they are, traps are generally the best choice for controlling mice. Pieces of apple or peanut butter are good baits (cheese just doesn't work). When you choose traps, you really have to choose traps that kill the mouse. If you try to capture them alive and move them away they just come back, plus you run the risk of getting bitten.

If you're a cat person and you spend a lot of time in your shop, you can consider getting a shop cat to live in the garage. Of course, then you have a litter box to deal with, the cat often decides that your nice canvas convertible top is a great place to sleep, and there's no guarantee the cat will even chase mice. But if you want a natural (although not particularly humane) solution to your mouse problems, a cat is not a bad choice.

If you move into a shop or garage that has had a bad rodent infestation, or even if you have to go into such a place to move items out, wear a respirator and rubber gloves, shoe covers, and, in the best case, disposable coveralls. On the Centers for Disease Control website (www.cdc.gov), there is a whole section devoted to dealing with rodents.

Shop Furniture

Human amenities start with furniture. Whether it's a place to sit and socialize or a place to get some paperwork or reading done, the important thing is to have a place to plant your backside and a place to rest your elbows.

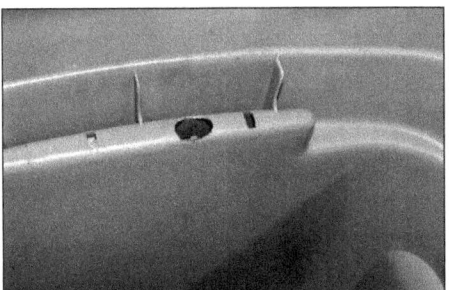

This hole is about the size of my index finger—plenty of room for a mouse to get in and ravage your stuff. Mice chewed through this tote to get at sheepskin seat covers inside.

Here's a sign that mice have invaded your shop. This shop rag is covered in droppings and soaked with mouse urine. Beware: This potentially carries hantavirus.

TECH TIP: Darn Rodents

One thing to remember is that rodent droppings can carry diseases such as hantavirus. Keep a spray bottle with a mixture of one part bleach to nine parts water handy to disinfect rodent droppings before you clean them up. Wear latex gloves and let the bleach solution soak for five minutes before cleaning up, and be careful not to create dust.

CHAPTER 9

Chairs

Step one of making your garage a fun place to hang out is to have some chairs—people like to have a place to sit down. Folding camp chairs are a fine budget-wise choice for this purpose. They also have the advantages of being easily stored when you're not using them and easily tossed in the trunk of your car when you're headed to the beach or the car show.

Shop stools are a great idea for a number of reasons. First, they give you a convenient place to sit when you're doing delicate work at your bench. They're the right height for your bench (or at least they should be, depending on the height of your bench) and they look great. You can find shop stools with any kind of logo you want on the seat, and that's a great dress-up item for any enthusiast. Whether it's a blue oval, a bow-tie, or any other brand, you want at least a couple shop stools at your bench.

For more lavish seating accommodations, you might find some used office chairs or conference room chairs at the used office furniture store or on www.craigslist.org. And if you have the space, you can't beat a comfortable sofa. Just be sure that all the furniture is covered in vinyl or leather for easy cleaning. Also be aware that household furniture can quickly become a comfortable home for mice, if you have that problem in your shop.

Desk

If you plan to do any drawing or other paperwork in your shop, it's a good idea to work a desk space into the plans. An old office desk from www.craigslist.org is perfect and inexpensive—check the free section and you can usually find one for the expense of picking it up. As an extra benefit, desk drawers tend to be fairly secure from mice and they tend to stay dry, so they're a good place to keep delicate items like micrometers, electronics, and cigars. Of course, cigars require a humidor or a cedar box of their own—use your best judgment.

Alternately, you can dedicate a part of the workbench where you can pull up a shop stool or tall chair. If you have a smooth piece of 3/4-inch plywood for the benchtop and a good hinge or two, you can hinge that piece of plywood at the front of the bench and build a support in back (or use hooks from above) to allow you to raise the back side of the work surface to become a comfortable drafting table. Be sure to put a light overhead for best effect, and make the hooks strong enough to hold some weight.

Worktable

One of the most useful pieces of furniture you can have in your shop is a worktable. This should be about the same height as a workbench, but the difference is that the table can be in the middle of the shop, providing access to your work from all angles. This enables you to have several people working on a project at once. For example, assembling a lightweight open-wheel race car or working on a go-kart is much easier on a sturdy table than on the floor—just remember to move it back on the ground before it gets too heavy to lift. A chain hoist or shop crane is helpful in that instance, and you can get the legs of a portable crane under a table far easier than under a workbench.

Building a shop table is easy. You can start with a full sheet of 3/4-inch plywood, put a ladder framework of 2x4 lumber underneath it to stiffen the surface, and then cut 4x4 legs and screw them to the underside. You can brace the legs further, but unless you plan to move the table frequently, it's not really necessary.

At a minimum, keep some folding chairs in your shop so you can take a load off your feet from time to time. They don't cost much, they store easily, and they're plenty comfortable.

Whether you use a cheap wooden stool or a padded, fancy shop stool with your favorite automaker's logo on the seat, a stool is a nice feature to go with your worktable or workbench.

A desk is a good idea in any workshop—you get drawers, writing and reading surface, and a place that naturally tends to stay a bit cleaner than the rest of the shop.

HUMAN AMENITIES

A free-standing shop table is tremendously useful. Size the table to fit your space and your needs. This one was available for free from a local business, but you can build one in an hour with some old plywood and lumber left over from other projects.

This homemade table was found at a garage sale. It's on casters and it's strong enough to carry a V-8 engine. The legs of a cherry picker go right around the table for easy pick-up and drop-off of engines.

A kitchen cabinet from a used building materials store makes a great bookshelf and helps keep dust and moisture out of your books, but any old plywood shelf works in a pinch.

As an upgrade option, consider a set of lockable casters. But if you put the table on wheels, you need to add additional bracing to the legs.

A useful variation on the full-size shop table is the small wheeled table. These are handy for holding things like engines and other heavy items and moving them around the shop. You can push them into the corner when you're not actively working on them, and these little tables are inexpensive and easy to build.

Bookshelves

Garages attract books—the one you're holding now is proof of that. So a bookshelf is a handy thing to have around your desk or workbench. Auto repair books tend to get greasy fingerprints on them—that can't be helped and it's a sign that the book has been well used. But you can keep books dry and straight, and the best way to do that is to store them vertically and tightly packed. A cabinet with doors is the very best, but any good shelf that's off the ground and away from damp areas is good enough.

Fun Stuff

Furniture, tools, wiring, and plumbing is all necessary and good to have, but the real fun starts with the things that are not strictly necessary for a workshop, but which make you happy and make your shop a nice place to be.

A Killer Stereo

The first step toward having the fun workshop you want is to get a great stereo. Like everything else, it doesn't have to be expensive, but it

Your stereo doesn't have to be fancy—these components came from Craigslist and they work well together. The CD player holds five CDs, which is great when your hands are greasy.

Speakers can also be homemade. You can get everything you need from sites like www.parts-express.com, or just pick up some used speakers, put in new cones, and save even more cash.

 **Tune Time**

If you choose a CD player for your shop, get one that accepts five or six CDs at a time, so you don't have to break off work every 45 minutes to change the music with greasy hands. An even better solution is just to get an iPod dock for your stereo. ■

HOW TO DESIGN, BUILD & EQUIP YOUR AUTOMOTIVE WORKSHOP ON A BUDGET

You can hang small speakers from hooks on the ceiling, but if you have big cabinets, you may need to build shelves to hold them. It's always good to get speakers up in the air for sound quality and protection from accidents.

If you want to spend a lot of money and get really crazy, consider restoring an old jukebox. Expensive—yes—but how cool is this?

Whether your TV is just an old set from your living room or a brand-new flat-panel unit, make sure it plays tapes and DVDs so you can put on your favorite programming.

should sound good and have a supply of your favorite tunes and a good radio receiver. Used components and homebuilt speakers are a great solution.

One easy thing you can do to save space and get great sound is to hang speakers from the ceiling or put them up on high shelves. That way they're not taking up valuable bench space and you get the best possible sound throughout the whole shop.

When you're installing a stereo, take extra care to protect the components. Even the cleanest shops generate more dust and crud than the inside of a house, and you want the stereo components to stay clean. A cabinet with doors is the best solution, but a low-cost alternative is simply to cover the top of the stereo with a light cloth. But be careful about heat—you don't want to cook the stereo or, worse, have that cloth catch fire. In general, analog amplifiers and receivers get hot, but tape decks and CD players do not. Give all components enough room to ventilate.

TV and Video

After a stereo, a TV is really nice to have. You can use any old TV, but the best solution is one of the newer models with a DVD or VHS tape player (or both) built into it. They're so inexpensive these days that it hardly makes sense to buy a used one. Get a collection of your favorite car movies or whatever entertainment you like. If you have access to

If you have wireless Internet service at your house, there's a good reason to extend it to your shop and put an old computer out there. You'll be surprised how often you end up looking things up online while you work.

cable or a source of broadcast reception—that's even better.

Mount the TV up high to keep it clean and visible throughout the entire shop. Find a convenient and obvious place for the remote control; they tend to get swallowed up in the clutter of a working shop.

Internet and Computer

Another low-cost luxury feature of a modern shop is Internet access. If you have broadband Internet service with a wireless connection in your home, it's a simple matter to put a wireless signal booster in your workshop—assuming the distances aren't too great. There is a tremendous amount of how-to information for cars on the Internet, and an older laptop or desktop computer makes a great garage research tool. You can even buy keyboards that are coated entirely in vinyl for easy cleaning.

Telephone

With the near-universality of cellular phones, one feature that you may not need in your shop is a phone line, or extension of your home phone. But if you do decide to string a phone line out to the garage

HUMAN AMENITIES

Do You Need a Burglar Alarm?

If you have a great deal of valuable stuff in your shop, you might want to consider an alarm system. Valuable stuff includes not only your car collection, but also your tools and equipment, which are easy for a thief to take and then sell for cash.

Alarm companies tell you that a very high percentage of burglars bypass a home that displays evidence of a working alarm system. If you have warning stickers from a prominent alarm company on your shop door, you might dissuade a burglar on that basis alone.

A full alarm system costs about $50 per month, plus the cost of landline telephone service. That system can include a fire alarm, a carbon monoxide detector, and anti-theft alarms for when you're not in the shop. If you already have an alarm system in your home and the garage is attached or close by, you may be able to extend the coverage of the existing system for far less.

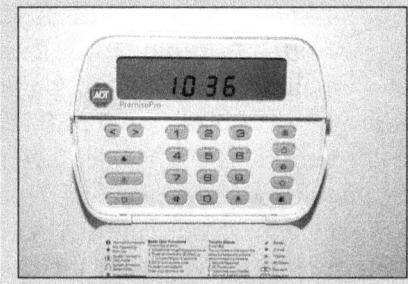

A burglar alarm makes a lot of sense for automotive shops. The value and anonymity of your tools is an even greater draw for thieves than your cars.

or workshop, you'll be able to answer home phone calls easily. If you choose to install a burglar alarm, you may not have a choice because most alarm companies use the phone lines. A phone is also a great safety device if you work alone—put 911 and some nearby support on speed dial.

Fridge

A shop refrigerator is an important feature for several reasons. Besides keeping your beverage of choice at your preferred drinking temperature, a fridge is generally safe from mice, so it's a good place to store anything you're concerned about. It's also good for any parts that need to be cold when you work on them. For example, if you need to heat half of an interference-fit assembly to fit it around the other half, chilling the inside half helps the process along. The most common example is putting valve guides in a cylinder head. The head is heated to slightly increase its size, and the bronze guides can be chilled to slightly reduce their size.

Unlike many appliances in your shop, the main thing to remember about a fridge is not to get a bigger unit than you really need. It's a false economy to run a big fridge for years just because it was cheaper than a smaller one on the day you bought it. However, one advantage of a bigger fridge is that they often include icemakers, so you get a supply of ice for the shop and an extra supply for your home at the same time.

A telephone is another good addition to your shop, especially if you have a burglar alarm wired in place.

A small dormitory fridge is generally plenty for a one-person workshop with occasional guests. You don't want to spend money to keep a lot of air cold.

 **Cold Drinks**

If you expect freezing weather, put a supply of beer, soda, and drinking water into the fridge. The refrigerator is well-insulated and designed to keep things at about 40 degrees Fahrenheit—if the overnight temperature drops below freezing, the fridge can save your drinks from freezing. ■

HOW TO DESIGN, BUILD & EQUIP YOUR AUTOMOTIVE WORKSHOP ON A BUDGET

CHAPTER 9

Keg and Kegerator

One good use for a cheap full-size refrigerator is to turn the bulk of the space inside into a "kegerator" to keep a keg of beer (or soda) cold and ready to dispense. You can get kegs in a variety of sizes, so the question of your consumption rate is not necessarily based on a 30-gallon keg. You can also buy kegs in 15-, 7.5-, and 5-gallon sizes. Soft-drink mix often comes in a "Corny" (or Cornelius) keg, with a separate supply of carbonated water. All kegs need to be pumped, or kept at pressure with a separate bottle of carbon dioxide.

If you really want your shop to be a center of automotive enthusiast activity, there is no better feature than a ready supply of cold draft beverages, served from a creatively decorated refrigerator adapted to the purpose.

Stove/Toaster Oven/Microwave

Another great feature for your workspace is to have a place to heat things up. You can reheat your lunch or pull a snack out of the freezer, but you can also heat up interference-fit parts, perform your own powder coating with a convenient kit, test engine thermostats, and perform a host of other useful functions with an old stove. Remember that a full-size electric range requires a dedicated 30- or 50-amp 240-volt circuit, so a toaster oven and a single-coil hot plate may be enough to meet your needs. A retired microwave oven from the house works wonders for reheating your lunch. If you do choose a full-size range, be mindful of its ventilation requirements as well as its power rating. When you bake powder coating or heat up engine parts, the smoke and fumes can be intense.

Coffeemaker

No shop is really complete without a coffeemaker. Whether it's to help you warm up in the cold months or just because you like coffee, you really need a coffeemaker. As with most shop appliances, the coffeemaker you retired from the kitchen is generally good enough. Be sure to always keep coffee supplies in the refrigerator to keep the mice away.

Self Service

Shelf-stable, single-serving cups of coffee creamer or half and half are generally available at the large-scale food stores that serve restaurants and at some office supply stores. These products are fine at room temperature, but keep them in the fridge to protect them from mice. ∎

This full-size fridge is wasting power to keep those PBRs frosty. A better solution is to drill a hole in the door and put a whole keg inside. Saving money can be fun!

Here's a good workshop kitchen setup: a microwave, a toaster oven, and a simple electric hot plate. Whether it's soup, pizza, or leftovers, you're all set for hot and tasty goodness.

A coffee pot is an absolute necessity. You can get a brand-new 2- or 3-cup unit for well under $20.

HUMAN AMENITIES

Project: Outfit Your Workshop

For the final touch to your workshop, it's time to outfit your human amenities. This includes anything you've read about in this chapter, plus art and visual amenities for the walls and ceiling.

Tools needed:
- Spirit level
- Hammer and nails
- Cups

Supplies needed:
- Stereo
- TV
- Refrigerator
- Chairs
- Wall art
- Refreshments

Follow these steps:

1. Set up the refrigerator and turn it on. Use the spirit level to make sure the fridge is level. Stock the fridge with beverages and test it over several hours to ensure that it's working properly.
2. Consider the placement of amenities for ease of use and best effect.
3. Set up the stereo and get it working with your favorite music.
4. Hang art and decorations on the available wall space in aesthetically pleasing locations.
5. Check that the music and art are just right.
6. Get the TV up and working with your favorite automotive-related programming.
7. Install any other amenities you have chosen.
8. Position the chairs for comfortable socializing.
9. Make sure everything is just as it should be.
10. Enjoy the results of your work.

If you're an ardent gamer, anything from a TV game system to a favorite classic arcade game can make a fun addition to your space.

It's important to make a shop your own. Whether you include a trophy wall, posters, memorabilia, or an expensive neon sign collection—put something up that reflects your passions and your history with the hobby.

Carpeting the areas of your shop where people stand is a nice touch. You can pick up easily replaceable carpet squares from salvaged commercial installations for bargain prices at a used building-materials store.

HOW TO DESIGN, BUILD & EQUIP YOUR AUTOMOTIVE WORKSHOP ON A BUDGET

Resources

Chapter 1

Incompetech
www.incompetech.com/graphpaper
Free online graph and grid paper

Sweet Home 3D
www.sweethome3d.eu
Free 3D design application

The Online Garage
www.portlandhomesforcars.com
Gallery of garages and ideas

Chapter 2

The Concrete Network
www.concretenetwork.com
Concrete and pavement information

Griot's Garage, Inc.
www.griotsgarage.com
Automotive and shop tools and accessories

Eastwood Company
www.eastwood.com
Automotive and shop tools and accessories

Chapter 3

Wiring a House 4th Edition, by Rex Cauldwell
Taunton Press, 2010
ISBN 978-1-60085-261-9.

Northern Illumination Company, Inc.
www.northernillumination.com
Lighting and lighting controls

Philips Day-Brite
www.daybritelighting.com/day-britehid/hidfixture.cfm?ID=3095
Fluorescent high-bay lighting

Ugly's Electrical References, by George V. Hart and Sammie Hart
Burleson Distributing Co, 1999
ISBN 978-0-96232-296-9

Chapter 4

PEX Information
www.pexinfo.com
Everything you need to know about plumbing with PEX

Chapter 5

PVC Distributors
www.flexpvc.com
PVC pipe and plastic pipe fittings

RapidAir
www.rapidairproducts.com
Compressed air piping systems
Duratec air line systems

Miller Electric Manufacturing Co.
www.millerwelds.com/interests/projects
Popular welding projects

Chapter 6

Collected Spaces
www.collectedspaces.com
Organizing and maximizing your available space

DIY Porting
www.diyporting.com/flowbench.html
Information on building your own flow bench

Performance Trends, Inc.
http://performancetrends.com/ez_flow_system.htm
EZ Flow System flow bench

Pull Down Attic Stairs
www.pulldownatticstairs.net
Pull-down attic stairs for storage in unused spaces

Attic Trusses by Behm Design
http://attictruss-garages.com
Attic truss garage plans

Chapter 7

ReadyKor
www.readykor.com/first-response-kit/fr-kits.html
First-aid kits

Riv Nut Tool
www.rivetnuttool.com
Riveting tools

Chapter 8

Shop Equipment Co., Inc.
www.shopequipmentcoinc.com
Automotive service equipment

Automotive Lift Institute
www.autolift.org
www.autolift.org/faq.htm
Automotive lifts information

Whirly Jig
www.whirlyjig.com
Auto body rotisseries

Reen Machine, Inc.
www.reenmachine.com/misc/Automotive_Rotisserie_Plan_Set.pdf
Automotive rotisserie plans

Chapter 9

Living Direct, Inc.
www.kegerator.com
Home and commercial keg refrigerators, draft beer dispensers, and accessories

Pest Control Canada
http://pestcontrolcanada.com/Questions/electronic_pest_devices.htm
Electronic pest devices and information

Centers for Disease Control
www.cdc.gov/ncidod/diseases/hanta/hps_stc/stc_clean.htm
Information on hantavirus

Parts Express
www.parts-express.com
Sound systems and speakers

www.ingramcontent.com/pod-product-compliance
Lightning Source LLC
Chambersburg PA
CBHW051413070526
44584CB00023B/3416